"Interpreters with experience of working in numerous conflicts and their aftermaths have repeatedly called for better training to prepare future language intermediaries for these challenging roles. For the first time, this volume draws together perspectives on interpreter training from a wide spectrum of organisations and conflicts into a collection that anyone who trains, recruits or prepares interpreters to operate in conflict and post-conflict settings should read."

Catherine Baker, University of Hull, UK

INTERPRETER TRAINING IN CONFLICT AND POST-CONFLICT SCENARIOS

The role of interpreters in conflict situations is of increasing real world importance. There are ethical, cultural, and professional issues that have yet to be explored, and there is a need for specialised training that addresses the specific contexts in which interpreters perform their duties, considering the situated nature of interpreting in these contexts.

This volume is structured around interpreter training in different contexts of conflict and post-conflict, from military operations and international tribunals to asylum-seeking and refugee, humanitarian, and human rights missions. Themes covered include risk management and communication, ethics and professional demeanour, language technology and its use, intercultural mediation, training in specific contexts, such as conflict resolution and negotiation, and working with trauma. Chapters are authored by experts from around the world with a range of different profiles: military personnel, scholars, the staff of international organisations, and representatives from refugee and asylum-seeker-assisting institutions.

Interpreter Training in Conflict and Post-Conflict Scenarios is key reading both for students and scholars researching interpreting in conflict zones and conflict-related scenarios and for practising and trainee interpreters and mediators working for international organisations and the military.

Lucía Ruiz Rosendo is an associate professor at the University of Geneva's Interpreting Department. She has co-edited *Interpreting Conflict* (Palgrave 2021). Her research has appeared in *Linguistica Antverpiensia*, *Target*, *War & Society* and *Armed Forces & Society*, among others. She is the coordinator of the project AXS.

Marija Todorova is a research assistant professor at the Department of Translation, Interpreting, and Intercultural Studies at Hong Kong Baptist University. She has authored *Translation of Violence in Children's Literature* (Routledge 2022) and co-edited *Interpreting Conflict* (Palgrave 2021). She is editor of *New Voices in Translation Studies*.

INTERPRETER TRAINING IN CONFLICT AND POST-CONFLICT SCENARIOS

*Edited by Lucía Ruiz Rosendo
and Marija Todorova*

Routledge
Taylor & Francis Group

LONDON AND NEW YORK

Cover image: Getty Images | fotojog.

First published 2023
by Routledge
4 Park Square, Milton Park, Abingdon, Oxon OX14 4RN

and by Routledge
605 Third Avenue, New York, NY 10158

Routledge is an imprint of the Taylor & Francis Group, an informa business

British Library Cataloguing-in-Publication Data
A catalogue record for this book is available from the British Library

Library of Congress Cataloging-in-Publication Data
Names: Ruiz Rosendo, Lucía, editor. | Todorova, Marija, editor.
Title: Interpreter training in conflict and post-conflict scenarios / edited by Lucía Ruiz Rosendo, Marija Todorova.
Description: Abingdon, Oxon ; New York, NY : Routledge, 2023. | Includes bibliographical references and index.
Identifiers: LCCN 2022025981 | ISBN 9781032136592 (hardback) | ISBN 9781032136615 (paperback) | ISBN 9781003230359 (ebook)
Subjects: LCSH: Translators—Training of. | Translating and interpreting—Study and teaching. | Social conflict—Study and teaching. | Conflict management—Study and teaching. | LCGFT: Essays.
Classification: LCC P306.5 .I624 2023 | DDC 418/.02071—dc23/eng/20220822
LC record available at https://lccn.loc.gov/2022025981

ISBN: 978-1-032-13659-2 (hbk)
ISBN: 978-1-032-13661-5 (pbk)
ISBN: 978-1-003-23035-9 (ebk)

DOI: 10.4324/9781003230359

Typeset in Bembo
by Apex CoVantage, LLC

CONTENTS

CONTRIBUTORS

Michele Arcella is a UNHCR protection associate in Italy. Since 2011 he has been focusing on training case owners and interpreters involved in the personal interviews to assess the international protection needs of asylum seekers and in the quality monitoring of decision-making-related procedures.

Alma Barghout is a senior interpreter at UNOG. She holds a MAS in interpreter training from the University of Geneva's Faculty of Translation and Interpreting (FTI). She teaches interpreting at the MA in Conference Interpreting and at the CAS in Interpreter Training of FTI. She is currently working on her PhD thesis, which addresses interpreter training in UN field missions.

Eleonora Bernardi is an AIIC conference interpreter and former medical interpreter in Italian, English, French, and Croatian. After having worked as an adjunct professor at the University of Bologna and Macerata, she enrolled in a PhD project at Bologna's Department of Interpreting and Translation in 2019.

Nathalie Collart has over 15 years' experience within the interpretation team of the Office of the Prosecutor of the International Criminal Court. She currently works as an Associate Interpretation Coordinator in the sourcing, recruitment, training, and deployment of field interpreters, mostly for languages of lesser diffusion.

Magnus Dahnberg is a senior lecturer and deputy director of the Institute for Interpreting and Translation Studies (TÖI), Stockholm University. He defended his thesis in 2015 on interpreter-mediated conversations as role play. He is also the former head of the Swedish Armed Forces Interpreter School, a Swedish–Russian interpreter, and a translator of Russian literature into Swedish.

Dimitri Elman has been in charge of sourcing, recruiting, training, and coordinating the deployment on assignment of field interpreters for the Office of the Prosecutor of the International Criminal Court, mostly for languages of lesser diffusion, since 2015. He graduated with concentrations in law, political science and history, European studies, and psychology.

Fabrizio Gallai is a research fellow and lecturer at UNINT in Rome. Prior to joining the university, he worked at the Universities of Salford, Manchester, and Bath in the UK and the Universities of Bologna (Forlì) and Macerata in Italy. He has extensive experience as a freelance translator and interpreter.

Tian Luo is a professor of translation studies in College of International Studies, Southwest University, China. He holds a PhD from the University of Macau. His main research interests include military translation history, discourse analysis, and multimodal translation. He is the corresponding author of Chapter 4 in this volume.

Simo K. Määttä is an associate professor of translation studies at the University of Helsinki. His research topics include language ideologies and the politics of language in translation and interpreting, verbal aggression and hate speech, legal and community interpreting, and the theory of discourse and ideology.

Anjad A. Mahasneh holds a PhD in translation studies from the State University of New York at Binghamton, NY, USA. She is currently an associate professor at Yarmouk University, Jordan. Her research interests include, among others, Arabic–English translation, interpretation in conflict zones, and interpretation and memory.

Nada Melhem works as an Associate Interpretation Coordinator with the Office of the Prosecutor of the International Criminal Court, assisting in the sourcing, recruitment, training, and deployment of field interpreters, mostly for languages of lesser diffusion. Her credentials include a BA in translation and an MA in interpretation.

Sonja Pöllabauer is a professor for interpreting studies (community interpreting) at the Centre for Translation Studies at the University of Vienna. She has been involved in projects on interpreting in asylum procedures, healthcare interpreting, and interpreter-mediated communication in institutional settings, as well as the organisation of training courses for lay interpreters.

Lucía Ruiz Rosendo is an associate professor at the University of Geneva's Interpreting Department. She has co-edited *Interpreting Conflict* (Palgrave 2021). Her research has appeared in *Linguistica Antverpiencia*, *Target*, *War & Society*, and *Armed Forces & Society*, among others. She is the coordinator of the project AXS. She is an active member of AIIC.

Mariachiara Russo is a professor of Spanish language and interpreting at the Department of Interpreting and Translation of the University of Bologna at Forlì. She coordinated the *European Parliament Interpreting Corpus* (EPIC) project and co-coordinated the project *SHIFT in Orality: Shaping the Interpreters of the Future and of Today*.

Pekka Snellman is a general staff officer and Master of Arts in multilingual communication and translation studies, currently serving in the Finnish Defence Forces. His research focuses on military interpreters, interpreter tactics, linguistic support for military operations, and the language policies of armed forces.

Nicoletta Spinolo is an assistant professor at the Department of Interpreting and Translation of the University of Bologna and a member of the Laboratory for Multilectal Mediated Communication and Cognition (MC2Lab). She focuses on interpreting between Italian and Spanish, figurative language in interpreting, and technologies and methods for remote interpreting.

Indira Sultanić is an assistant professor of Spanish translation and interpreting studies at Virginia Commonwealth University. She has authored articles and book chapters on medical interpreter education and training, interpreting for vulnerable populations and unaccompanied refugee children in the United States, and remote interpreting in pediatric therapy settings.

Ebenezer Tedjouong holds a PhD from the University of the Free State in South Africa. He has been training interpreters in various African settings for close to 20 years, advocating a training methodology that is grounded in theory, inspired by practice, and tailored to the needs of diverse settings.

Marija Todorova is a research assistant professor at the Department of Translation, Interpreting, and Intercultural Studies at Hong Kong Baptist University. She has authored *Translation of Violence in Children's Literature* (Routledge 2022) and co-edited *Interpreting Conflict* (Palgrave 2021). She is the editor of *New Voices in Translation Studies*.

Zerong Wei is an associate professor at the Army Engineering University of PLA, China. He is interested in military translation practice and research. From August 2017 to August 2018, he worked as a liaison officer for Chinese UN peace-keeping forces deployed in Sudan.

1

INTRODUCTION

Lucía Ruiz Rosendo and Marija Todorova

This introductory chapter will provide a literature review of interpreter training in conflict and post-conflict scenarios throughout history by analysing different geographical contexts. It will also provide an overview of current thought on interpreter training in conflict-related scenarios. The innovative nature of this book comes from the analysis of a range of case studies based on different settings through which the themes will be addressed. While some training aspects are common to the different contexts, many others are specific to one setting, in line with the view of interpreting as a situated practice. The introduction will provide an overview of the subsequent chapters by individual contributors and will specify how each chapter connects to the general theme.

1.1 Background

This volume is conceived as the natural continuation of our recent publication entitled *Interpreting conflict: A comparative framework* (Todorova and Ruiz Rosendo 2021) in the series *Palgrave Studies in Languages at War*. In fact, in the concluding chapter to said volume, we identify training needs as an emerging topic that requires further exploration. Despite increasing awareness of the role of interpreters in conflicts and expanding scholarly literature on the topic, there is still a dearth of studies addressing the specific nature of how interpreting skills are acquired in these settings. This hinders the comprehension of how interpreters develop their skills in the field. Indeed, one of the issues highlighted in the literature is the need for specialised training that addresses the specific contexts in which interpreters perform their duties, considering the situated nature of interpreting (Radicioni and Ruiz Rosendo 2022; Ruiz Rosendo 2022).

Defining the context is the first step in any thorough process of reflection about training needs. According to Ruiz Rosendo (2020a), *interpreting in conflict zones*

DOI: 10.4324/9781003230359-1

refers to working in a place where there is a conflict, usually an armed conflict; whilst this definition might read as a truism, it is, however, important to explain, and an example would be interpreting for the armed forces in the recent conflicts in Afghanistan or Iraq. A *conflict-related scenario* refers to a situation that is related to the conflict, one that often comes about as a consequence of it, but one that may take place in a zone that is not itself in conflict – for example, interpreting in Italy or Greece in the context of the refugee crisis. In their study on interpreting for international NGOs, Tesseur and Footitt (2019) use yet another term, *post-conflict settings*, to refer to settings that had been in conflict but which are now character-ised by the cessation of violent conflict and of immediate danger. In such settings, the emphasis is rather placed on collaboration and participation. The present vol-ume includes contributions pertaining to all of these different settings.

As some authors have stated, even though the presence of interpreters in con-flict situations has been clearly observed throughout history (see Ruiz Rosendo and Persaud 2016) the provision of training for those specific contexts is rarely referenced in the literature (Roland 1999; Baigorri Jalón 2015). One may wonder whether this scarcity of studies is due to an actual lack of sources chronicling this training or, plainly and simply, to the lack of interpreter training in the first place. Indeed, the absence of trained interpreters has been reported by many scholars, particularly those who have analysed the role of the interpreter in contemporary conflicts (e.g., Baker 2010b; Inghilleri 2010; Ruiz Rosendo 2020a, 2020b, 2021, 2022). As Ruiz Rosendo and Persaud (2016, 3) argue:

> Not all interpreters working in conflicts are professionals, however . . .; nor does the fact that an interpreter is working in a conflict setting necessarily mean that he or she has professional experience as an interpreter or a lin-guistic mediator.

Despite the many differences between the categories of interpreters that we can find in a conflict or post-conflict situation, the lack of training can be applied to all. This is the case of interpreters locally recruited by the military (Baker 2010a, 2010b; Footitt and Kelly 2012; Kujamäki 2016; Gómez Amich 2017, 2021; Tesseur and Footitt 2019; Ruiz Rosendo 2020b), interpreters recruited by humanitarian organisations (Delgado and Kherbiche 2018), and military interpreters – that is, military personnel who act as interpreters (Snellman 2014, 2016; Méndez Sánchez 2021). Whilst the latter have received specific military training, they have seldom received specific training in interpreting. Similarly, volunteers listed on the emer-gency response teams of some humanitarian organisations, such as the United Nations High Commissioner for Refugees (UNHCR), have been trained to work in an emergency situation, but these interpreters, who are (usually) locally recruited, have not received specific training in interpreting (Todorova 2017). The only exceptions to this endemic lack of trained interpreters are UN conference interpreters deployed on field missions. However, the training they received in interpreting skills does not necessarily equip them to face the multiple challenges that can be encountered in the field (Ruiz Rosendo et al. 2021). This means that interpreters are usually recruited or deployed to conflict zones not because they have received contextualised interpreter training as such but because they speak the relevant languages.

A historical approach allows us to compare the training of interpreters who have worked in different geographical and temporal spaces. Indeed, they have seldom received specific training, with some noteworthy exceptions such as: the training schemes put in place by Pharaoh Psamtik II in Ancient Egypt (Baigorri Jalón 2015); Alexander the Great in Ancient Greece; Quintus Sertorius in the Roman Empire (Roland 1999); Samuel de Champlain, coloniser of New France and founder of Quebec City (Delisle and Woodsworth 2012); the dragomans in the Ottoman court (see Rothman 2012 and 2021 for a detailed account of the role of dragomans); or the Military Institute of Foreign Languages (MIFL) in the first half of the 20th century (Probirskaja 2016). Training interpreters to work in conflict zones has not been devoid of difficulties due to the imminence of military deployment and the myriad languages needed; therefore, despite these exceptional training schemes, interpreters "were usually not individuals who had previously self-identified as interpreters; rather, they were most often individuals who, through life experience, had gained a command of languages" (Ruiz Rosendo and Persaud 2016, 17).

Moreover, designing training programmes that correspond to the roles that interpreters are expected to perform in a specific context is not an easy task (Todorova 2021). This is due, first and foremost, to the interpreter's complex positionality. Tesseur and Footitt (2019, 274) very eloquently reflect this complexity and its implications for the interpreting profession when they say that "the conflicts in Iraq and Afghanistan delivered a profound challenge to the profession of interpreting, particularly in terms of interpreter ethics and neutrality. To begin with, interpreters in these conflicts were dying." Therefore, there are many implications that have to be considered when designing the training, including aspects that go beyond interpreting skills to encompass psychological (Barea Muñoz 2021), legal, security, and ethical implications (see Delgado Luchner and Kherbiche (2019) and Snellman (2016) for an analysis of ethics for humanitarian interpreters and military interpreters, respectively). Moreover, it is worth noting that interpreters sometimes belong to the community in conflict – which is the case of local interpreters recruited by the military – or share the same status as the beneficiaries in humanitarian contexts – that of the refugee, for example.

Making decisions can pose challenges in non-routine situations. Such settings are rarely foreseen in interpreters' codes of ethics, and there is sometimes a mismatch between the expected ethical behaviour stipulated in these codes and the roles that interpreters in conflict and post-conflict settings actually perform. Delgado Luchner and Kherbiche (2019, 254) posit that current codes of ethics for interpreters who work in conflict zones are based on deontological codes that were developed for times of peace and that do not account "for the specific constraints of a given context." A critical reasoning that takes into account the particularities of the context and the outcomes of one's decisions – a teleological approach to ethics – is increasingly considered to be more effective in guiding ethical interpreting practice (see Dean and Pollard, 2011, for an in-depth analysis of a teleological approach to ethical reasoning). Ethical reasoning in decision-making is as important as interpreting skills when training interpreters who work in conflict zones.

Moreover, interpreters working in such settings often have to juggle overlapping roles and dual identities. Sometimes these are dual professional roles, such as being a soldier and an interpreter (see Snellman's chapter in this volume). At other times, these roles involve belonging to and/or identifying with different countries and communities (an issue raised by several of the contributors to this volume). Another additional challenge encountered when designing training programmes is the need to train interpreters who speak languages of lesser diffusion (see Melhem, Collard and Elman, and Tedjouong and Todorova in this volume) in which resources are not always available. This is particularly true in the case of very specific terminologies in which the concepts, and hence the terms, do not exist or require a laborious explanation in said languages.

In conclusion, there has been a lack of definition in the roles and tasks attributed to interpreters in conflict zones throughout history, and this still holds true today in that training programmes continue to be rare, both in the military and in the humanitarian field (see Delgado Luchner and Kherbiche's 2018 study of the positionality of interpreters working for the International Committee of the Red Cross – ICRC – and for the UNHCR). Therefore, in most instances, interpreting in conflict and post-conflict situations is still an unregulated activity performed by untrained interpreters. This being said, in the 21st century, there has been an increasing recognition of the roles that interpreters play in conflict zones, and some studies have been undertaken to understand the nature of learning in these contexts (Tipton 2011; Radicioni and Ruiz Rosendo 2022; Ruiz Rosendo 2022) or to develop pedagogical tools (Bergunde and Pöllabauer 2019; Delgado Luchner and Kherbiche 2019) and professionalise their roles. The objective of this volume is precisely to take stock of these training initiatives in different settings.

This volume is structured around interpreter training in different conflict and post-conflict contexts, such as military operations, international tribunals, asylum-seeking and refugees, humanitarian missions, and human rights missions. The idea is to compile a volume that follows the general topic of interpreter training in conflict and post-conflict scenarios and that is based on the notion of interpreting as a situated practice. Themes included in the different chapters are interpreting skills, risk management and communication, ethics and professional demeanour, language technology and its use, intercultural mediation, training in context-specific topics (social issues, working with children and vulnerable individuals, conflict resolution, negotiation), empathy and working with trauma, and psychological implications and self-care.

In this volume, we subscribe to the point made by Tesseur and Footitt (2019, 281) that "the professionalism of interpreters depends on other professions surrounding the interpreter." Consequently, it is our view that we should not limit our research to traditional understandings of interpreting, given that, in so doing, we risk excluding many of the practices that are vital to the relationships that develop in conflict and post-conflict scenarios. Therefore, the main strengths of the volume are that it analyses the practice of interpreting in very different contexts, some of them far removed from the traditional settings usually analysed in interpreter training, and that it brings together contributors with different profiles: military personnel, scholars, the staffs of international organisations, and representatives from refugee- and asylum-seeker-assisting institutions; in other words, those professions surrounding the interpreter. These contributors come from different geographical contexts and their contributions focus on different regions – Australia, Asia, Europe, Africa, the Middle East, and the United States – in order to go beyond the largely Eurocentric approach that has defined most of the analysis of interpreter training to date.

1.2 Structure and content

This volume is divided into four parts, the first three parts each dealing with a different context: military interpreting (Chapters 2 to 4), interpreting in international organisations and tribunals (Chapters 5 to 7), and asylum response (Chapters 8 to 12). The last part (Chapters 13 to 15) addresses crosscutting implications of interpreter training in conflict and post-conflict scenarios.

Part I of the volume, dealing with military interpreting, starts with Pekka Snellman's "Ethics in military interpreter training." The author engages in the training of military interpreters, defined as "a uniformed and armed soldier, serving in a military organisation, with the primary task of interpreting." Snellman describes the particularities of this category of interpreter as compared with other categories, such as civilian interpreters locally recruited by the armed forces, although both categories face similar ethical issues. Drawing on interviews with trainers of military interpreters in Finland, Denmark, and Sweden, the chapter argues that military interpreters "occupy larger spaces for ethical deliberation and decision-making than typically attributed to the interpreter profession" and that, therefore, they have to be trained in both military and interpreting aspects. Role plays are considered important pedagogical tools in this context. The chapter posits that, for military interpreters, the ethos of the military profession, in many ways, prevails over that of the interpreter profession and that some ethical principles that are central to interpreting codes of ethics, such as impartiality and confidentiality, may be disapproved of by the military.

Subsequently, Magnus Dahnberg's "Military interpreter training for context specific situations" examines the challenges encountered by military interpreters in conflict zones and how these challenges, as well as the required interpreting skills, are acquired in contemporary military interpreter training. The chapter focuses on a case study on the training provided at the Swedish Armed Forces Language School in Uppsala (Sweden). It offers a description of the requirements for admission to the programme and of the skills taught to military interpreters, as well as the sequencing and progression followed in skill acquisition. The author concludes that interpreters deployed in conflict zones face myriad situations that call into question traditional notions of what constitutes the profession of interpreting.

The next chapter also addresses the training provided to interpreters who are deployed in conflict zones but focuses on China's peacekeeping forces that are deployed under the UN's mandate. Zerong Wei and Tian Luo's "Training liaison officers interpreting for China's peacekeeping missions" draws on the analysis of a training programme organised in Beijing and Darfur to train Chinese interpreters, also called liaison officers, and on the findings of an interview with a liaison officer who is a trainer on said course and who has worked for Chinese UN peacekeeping units in Sudan. The findings of this study reveal that interpreters play indispensable roles in communication among the members of peacekeeping units and that training is necessary to equip interpreters with the necessary knowledge and tools to face the challenges of interpreting in the field. However, even if the training was considered effective, judging from the subsequent performance of liaison officers, the authors posit that more thought has to be given to the challenges that interpreters encounter in the field, particularly regarding notions of identity and to ethical implications, as well as the implementation of more tailored pedagogical tools.

Part II addresses interpreting and the role of interpreters in international organisations and tribunals. Alma Barghout and Lucía Ruiz Rosendo's chapter, "Developing interpreter competence: Training interpreters servicing UNOG field missions," examines a different category of interpreters that has not been the focus of sustained inquiry: conference interpreters who are deployed on missions to the field and who are characterised by their roles as fully fledged interpreters who have received prior training in interpreting skills but who are not necessarily equipped to face the difficulties inherent in field missions. Drawing on the analyses of the different initiatives organised by UNOG and on data stemming from an ongoing mixed-methods research project, the authors discuss the particularities of UNOG field missions and the contents of the different activities launched to train interpreters. The analysis shows that there has been an increasing awareness on the part of the organisation as to the specific needs of interpreters who work in the field. The findings also highlight the need to organise tailored training programmes focusing on the specific (and complex) needs of this group of interpreters.

In "Resourcefulness when resources are lacking: A case study of field interpreters at the Office of the Prosecutor at the International Criminal Court [ICC]," Nada Melhem, Nathalie Collart, and Dimitri Elman provide their invaluable insight as members of the interpretation team and describe the training programme put in place for interpreters of languages of lesser diffusion (LLDs). As they explain, the main challenge they face is the lack of resources in these languages regarding legal and procedural international criminal law terminology. Drawing not only on their own experience but also on the feedback provided by field interpreters, the chapter examines the extent to which the conventional interpreter training resources apply to interpreters of LLDs working in the field for the Office of the Prosecutor at the ICC. The authors also explore other, somewhat unconventional, resources for interpreters of LLDs as well as the techniques that can be deployed when resources are found wanting. This arises most notably in the case of international criminal law and its specific terminology, where the concepts themselves often do not exist in the LLDs. The challenges presented by work at the ICC seem to largely coincide with some of the challenges seen in other ad-hoc tribunals, such as the International Criminal Tribunal for Rwanda (ICTR). However, work at the ICC also presents additional recurrent challenges, owing to its permanent status and extensive territorial jurisdiction, such as the greater range of languages it needs to support, the fact that resources are even scarcer for many of these languages, and the fact that many of the languages have strong non-standardised oral traditions. This chapter opens the door to future studies about the interpreter's agency and knowledge production as well as about the problem of dissonance between international criminal justice and non-Western languages and cultures.

The last chapter of this part moves to the setting of refugee status determination procedures (RSD) conducted by UNHCR. One of the key aspects of interpreting in the asylum context, including those of impartiality and confidentiality, has been the focus of research over the past decades (Inghilleri 2005, Jacquemet 2005) acknowledging the visibility and agency of interpreters in these contexts. In his chapter, entitled "Main challenges of interpreting in the context of the international protection determination procedures," Michele Arcella examines the challenges faced by interpreters in RSD interviews and highlights that, in many asylum systems, interpreters lack sufficient professionalisation due to the absence of an institutional recognition of the interpreters' role, the wide range of languages involved, and their frequent turnover. The chapter addresses the measures taken by the Italian asylum authorities together with the UNHCR to address these challenges by training interpreters in the asylum context. Drawing on a qualitative study carried out with interpreters that have undergone such training programmes, the chapter analyses relevant issues of trust, empathy, and ethics that illustrate the difficulties faced by interpreters. These difficulties can manifest when setting boundaries in their roles as well as when making decisions that are compliant with the principles taught in the programme in real situations, which are challenging and non-routine by nature. This chapter further confirms the tendency for developing institutionally codified guidelines in order to standardise the interpreter mediated asylum interview procedure (Tipton 2008; Jacquemet 2013). Moreover, the chapter gives prominence to the need for the interpreters in the RSD environment to point out difficulties encountered during the interview, especially when working with vulnerable asylum seekers. However, the neutral role of the interpreter is still seen as the preferred norm within the institution codes besides the attempts in academic research to give interpreters more leeway in basing decisions on personal ethical standards (Inghilleri 2012). This mismatch between the ethical behavior expected in interpreters' professional ethics and the roles that interpreters actually perform is further explored in other chapters (see Gallai, Snellman and Sultanić in this volume).

The other distinct context that requires specifically trained interpreters is that of humanitarian responses to conflict. Part III of this volume focuses on training interpreters in national and regional contexts to work with asylum seekers, refugees, and other vulnerable populations affected by the trauma of war.

Bearing in mind the specific tasks they perform, interpreters working in conflict-related humanitarian emergency situations should be provided with appropriate training. Such programmes should draw on the most recent developments not only in interpreting studies but also in conflict resolution and peace-building studies. Training in dealing with high levels of stress, effective decision-making, and specialised training in working with children and other vulnerable groups can prove highly effective to interpreters working in humanitarian contexts (Todorova 2021). Additionally, special attention should be given to training on how to respond to interpreting trauma and vicarious trauma resulting from re-voicing the stories of the war victims. The five articles in this part present the specific training needs and provide examples of training activities to address these needs.

Cameroon is one of the many countries in Africa affected by several conflicts, both within and across national borders. As a result, Cameroon is the scene of three unfolding humanitarian crises and is home to about five refugee camps. The biggest among them is Lolo, home to more than 12,000 refugees, mainly from the Central African Republic. In "Training needs of interpreters in the refugee crisis in Africa," Ebenezer Tedjouong and Marija Todorova compare the training needs for interpreters working in refugee camps from two perspectives: the perspective of the service users from humanitarian NGOs providing support in refugee camps and the perspective of the interpreters working in refugee camps. By narrating six different stories, this chapter underlines the need for better language and interpreting training for community volunteer interpreters who are familiar with the cultures of and enjoy the trust of the respective refugee communities.

Still on the topic of interpreting for vulnerable populations, Indira Sultanić, in her chapter "Interpreting for vulnerable populations: Training and education of interpreters working with refugee children in the United States," examines the education, training, and skills required in interpreting for refugee children seeking asylum in the United States. Interpreting for refugee children requires a high level of skill and knowledge; however, an online survey carried out by the author revealed a significant shortage of existing interpreter training programmes for vulnerable populations and yielded no tangible results with regard to the existence of programmes training interpreters to work for refugee children in the United States. The chapter examines the challenges in training interpreters in this context due to the varied nature of the interactions and settings, each with its own set of rules. These place different demands on the interpreters' abilities to ensure effective communication between the different interlocutors. The chapter concludes with the insightful statement that tailored programmes, as well as the standardisation on asylum training content, are needed to guarantee due process.

Another context that calls for specific training is the provision of interpreting in asylum procedures in host countries. In this context, asylum seekers fleeing violent conflict use interpreters to narrate and re-narrate their oral stories of trauma. In "Interpreting in an asylum context: Interpreter training as the linchpin for improving procedural quality," Sonja Pöllabauer provides a comparative analysis of a dozen of training programmes that offer specialised training – be it face-to-face, blended, or online – for interpreters working alongside asylum authorities. By evaluating the course details and materials available on the respective websites, Pöllabauer concludes that these programmes "mostly seem to focus on bilinguals with no specific interpreter training, though some are also expressly open to additional target groups (trained interpreters, interpreter trainers, users of interpreters)". Specific training for users of interpreters (e.g., institutional representatives or legal advisors), which is also frequently mentioned as another element for improving interpreting quality, does not yet seem to be comprehensively available.

Staying within the context of asylum procedures in legal settings, Fabrizio Gallai, in his chapter "Ethics and training of interpreters in the asylum context," provides an in-depth analysis of the ethical issues and principles highlighted in theoretical works on interpreting in asylum settings. In the second part, the chapter presents empirical research on interpreting in asylum settings. Finally, Gallai identifies the "mismatch between deontology (normative norms and expectations) and professional practice." This disparity between the expected ethical behaviour, often laid out in professional codes of ethics, and the performed roles of interpreters in asylum settings needs to be reflected in training programmes. In this context, Gallai provides a few ideas of useful activities that can be used in the classroom, including debates, critical essays, and role plays.

The recent European refugee crises have particularly affected Italy, as one of the entry points of asylum seekers and migrants taking the Mediterranean route on their way to Europe. However, Italy and Italian educational institutions have not offered a course in humanitarian interpreting. In "Technology affordances in training interpreters for asylum seekers and refugees," Mariachiara Russo and Nicoletta Spinolo examine the design of a training course for interpreters working with asylum seekers in the Italian context. They specifically focus on the technology tools in training interpreters to work for asylum seekers and refugees based on the use of innovative educational approaches and digital technologies for synchronous and asynchronous teaching and learning. This solution can prove to be applicable to all language pairs to meet humanitarian interpreters' challenges and needs.

Regardless of whether they work with the military or providing support to civilian victims of war and trauma, interpreters in conflict zones encounter some common challenges. The final part of the volume, Part IV, includes three articles that present some crosscutting implications of interpreter training in conflict and post-conflict scenarios.

The psychological issues and emotional effects of an interpreting assignment on the interpreter in conflict zones have been identified as recurrent factors taking a toll on the work and personal well-being of interpreters in conflict zones (Barea Muñoz 2021). With this in mind, in "Interpreting trauma: Service providers' and interpreters' perspectives," Simo K. Määttä examines the topic of interpreting for victims of trauma from two perspectives: that of the councillor for trauma victims and that of the interpreter working with victims of trauma. In both cases, the analysis is conducted by looking at diaries. Although the cases presented in the diaries are set in different times and locations, and the councillors are not specifically instructed to reflect on interpretation, they still offer a very meaningful insight into the work of the interpreter, especially the need for trust in such an encounter. Additionally, the chapter suggests journaling as a tool to relieve stress and help healing from trauma and vicarious traumatisation.

The psychological implications of interpreting in conflict zones are also the main concern of the next chapter. In "The psychological implications of interpreting in conflict zones, elements for potential mental-health and self-care training for interpreters," Eleonora Bernardi sets out to identify factors relating to their emotional response to the conflict and the coping strategies they adopt. She proposes three sets of factors that attribute to interpreters' trauma in conflict zones: context-related, job-related, and content-related factors. Furthermore, the chapter outlines a "trauma curriculum" built on "a triangular structure based on prevention, self-care and support", designed by consulting training programmes and guidelines for therapists, mental health workers in conflict zones, and community interpreters.

Interpreters in conflict zones are undoubtfully performing their duties under considerable stress, which can influence their performance. Additionally, research (Baker 2010b; Todorova 2019) has shown many times that these interpreters working in conflict zones are often volunteers or non-professional interpreters with ad hoc or informal employment relationships. They are engaged because of their bilingual or multilingual skills but rarely have any interpreting training. Therefore, in the last chapter of this volume, Anjad A. Mahasneh considers training activities that can help interpreters enhance their short-term memory. "Enhancing short-term memory for conflict zone interpreters" identifies short-term memory as one of the most important interpreting-related skills for conflict zones since it helps produce "faster and more accurate interpretation" and improves effective decision-making. Based on previous research, Mahasneh outlines various exercises and techniques to be included in training workshops for interpreters in conflict zones.

Finally, training is not only needed for current and future interpreters in conflict, but there also is an absence, among service users and beneficiaries, of a clear idea of the interpreter's role and professional ethics. Clarification of some of these issues could avoid misunderstandings regarding crucial elements, such as trust and confidentiality. Some of the articles in this volume consider the needs and views of the service users when suggesting topics that should be covered in training. However, future research should consider special training programmes for users of interpreting services who are keen to learn how to work with interpreters more effectively. Future studies will also have to consider two additional spheres of international response and language contact in conflict and post-conflict settings: journalism and diplomacy. In journalism, studies could focus on what training, upskilling, and aftercare foreign media organisations do or should provide towards their locally recruited "fixers," who combine interpreting with other essential roles and tasks. In diplomacy, research studies could potentially consider the interpreter training needs of states that become directly involved in conflict.

This volume advances the literature on interpreting in conflict and post-conflict settings – characterised by urgency, unpredictability and insecurity – in that it directly addresses training as one of the greatest challenges for practitioners and managers of interpreters.

References

Baigorri Jalón, Jesús. 2015. "The History of the Interpreting Profession." In *The Routledge Handbook of Interpreting*, edited by Holly Mikkelson, and Renée Jourdenais, 11–28. London: Routledge.

Baker, Catherine. 2010a. "It's Not Their Job to Soldier: Distinguishing Civilian and Military in Soldiers' and Interpreters' Accounts of Peacekeeping in 1990s Bosnia-Herzegovina." *Journal of War and Culture Studies* 3: 137–150.

Baker, Catherine. 2010b. "The Care and Feeding of Linguists: The Working Environment of Interpreters, Translators, and Linguists during Peacekeeping in Bosnia-Herzegovina." *War & Society* 29 (2): 154–175.

Barea Muñoz, Manuel. 2021. "Psychological Aspects of Interpreting Violence: A Narrative from the Israeli-Palestinian Conflict." In *Interpreting Conflict. A Comparative Framework*, edited by Marija Todorova, and Lucía Ruiz Rosendo, 1082–1208. London: Palgrave Macmillan.

Bergunde, Annika, and Sonia Pöllabauer. 2019. "Curricular Design and Implementation of a Training Course for Interpreters in an Asylum Context." *Translation & Interpreting* 11 (1): 1–21.

Dean, Robyn K., and Robert Q. Pollard, Jr. 2011. "Context-Based Ethical Reasoning in Interpreting." *The Interpreter and Translator Trainer* 5 (1): 155–182.

Delgado Luchner, Carmen, and Leila Kherbiche. 2018. "Without Fear or Favour? The Positionality of ICRC and UNHCR Interpreters in the Humanitarian Field." *Target* 30 (3): 408–429.

Delgado Luchner, Carmen, and Leïla Kherbiche. 2019. "Ethics Training for Humanitarian Interpreters Working in Conflict and Post-Conflict Settings." *Journal of War & Culture Studies* 12 (3): 251–267.

Delisle, Jean, and Judith Woodsworth. 2012. *Translators through History*. Amsterdam: John Benjamins.

Footitt, Hilary, and Michael Kelly. eds. 2012. *Languages at War*. Basingstoke: Palgrave Macmillan.

Gómez Amich, María. 2017. *Estudio descriptivo de la autopercepción de los intérpretes en zonas de conflicto: estudio de caso en Afganistán*. PhD diss., University of Granada.

Gómez Amich, María. 2021. "Local Interpreters versus Military Personnel: Perceptions and Expectations Regarding the Local Interpreter's Role and Agency within the Afghan Conflict." In *Interpreting Conflict. A Comparative Framework*, edited by Marija Todorova, and Lucía Ruiz Rosendo, 85–112. Cham: Palgrave Macmillan.

Inghilleri, Moira. 2005. "Mediating Zones of Uncertainty: Interpreter Agency, the Interpreting Habitus and Political Asylum Adjudication." *The Translator* 11 (1): 69–85.

Inghilleri, Moira. 2010. "You Don't Make War without Knowing Why: The Decision to Interpret in Iraq." *The Translator* 16 (2): 175–196.

Inghilleri, Moira. 2012. *Interpreting Justice. Ethics, Politics and Language*. New York: Routledge.

Jacquemet, Marco. 2005. "The Registration Interview: Restricting Refugees' Narrative Performances." In *Dislocations/Relocations: Narratives of Displacement*, edited by Mike Baynham, and Anna De Fina, 197–220. Manchester: St Jerome.

Jacquemet, Marco. 2013. "Transidioma and Asylum: Grumperz's Legacy in Intercultural Institutional Talk." *Journal of Linguistic Anthropology* 23 (3): 199–212.

Kujamäki, Pekka. 2016. "And then the Germans Came to Town. The Lived Experiences of an Interpreter in Finland during the Second World War." *Linguistica Antverpiensia, New Series: Themes in Translation Studies* 15: 106–120.

Méndez Sánchez, Verónica. 2021. "The Spanish 'Military Interpreter': A Practical Application in International Operations Arising from Armed Conflicts." In *Interpreting Conflict. A Comparative Framework*, edited by Marija Todorova, and Lucía Ruiz Rosendo, 135–154. Hobokem, NJ: Palgrave Macmillan.

Probirskaja, Svetlana. 2016. "How Do Interpreters Become Heroes? Narratives on Soviet/Russian Military Interpreters." *Linguistica Antverpiensia, New Series: Themes in Translation Studies* 15: 205–226.

Radicioni, Maura, and Lucía Ruiz Rosendo. 2022. "Learning Dynamics between Cultural Mediators in Humanitarian Healthcare: A case study." *JoSTrans* 37: 139–159.

Roland, Ruth A. 1999. *Interpreters as Diplomats: A Diplomatic History of the Role of Interpreters in World Politics*. Ottawa: University of Ottawa Press.

Rothman, Natalie. 2012. *Brokering Empire: Trans-Imperial Subjects between Venice and Istanbul*. Ithaca, NY: Cornell University Press.

Rothman, Natalie. 2021. *The Dragoman Renaissance: Diplomatic Interpreters and the Routes of Orientalism*. Ithaca/London: Cornell University Press.

Ruiz Rosendo, Lucía. 2020a. "Translating and Interpreting in Conflict." In *The Oxford Handbook of Translation and Social Practices*, edited by Meng Ji, and Sara Laviosa, 45–65. Oxford: Oxford University Press.

Ruiz Rosendo, Lucía. 2020b. "Interpreting for the Afghanistan Spanish Force." *War & Society* 39 (1): 42–57.

Ruiz Rosendo, Lucía. 2022. "Interpreting for the Military: Creating Communities of Practice." *JoSTrans* 37: 16–34.

Ruiz Rosendo, Lucía, Alma Barghout, and Conor H. Martin. 2021. "Interpreting on UN Field Missions: A Training Programme." *The Interpreter and Translator Trainer* 15 (4): 450–467.

Ruiz Rosendo, Lucía, and Clementina Persaud. 2016. "Interpreters and Interpreting in Conflict Zones and Scenarios: A Historical Perspective." *Linguistica Antverpiensia, New Series: Themes in Translation Studies* 15: 1–35.

Snellman, Pekka. 2014. *The Agency of Military Interpreters in Finnish Crisis Management Operations*. Master's thesis, University of Tampere. https://urn.fi/URN:NBN:fi:uta-201403061187

Snellman, Pekka. 2016. "Constraints on and Dimensions of Military Interpreter Neutrality." *Linguistica Antverpiensia, New Series: Themes in Translation Studies* 15: 260–281.

Tesseur, Wine, and Hilary Footitt. 2019. "Professionalisms at War? Interpreting in Conflict and Post-Conflict Situations." *Journal of War & Cultural Studies* 12 (3): 268–284.

Tipton, Rebecca 2008. "Reflexivity and the Social Construction of Identity in Interpreter-Mediated Asylum Interviews." *The Translator* 14 (1): 1–19.

Tipton, Rebecca. 2011. "Relationships of Learning between Military Personnel and Interpreters in Situations of Violent Conflict." *The Interpreter and Translator Trainer* 5 (1): 15–40.

Todorova, Marija. 2017. "Interpreting at the Border: "Shuttle Interpreting" for the UNHCR." *Clina* 3 (2): 115–129.

Todorova, Marija. 2019. "Interpreting for Refugees: Empathy and Activism." In *Intercultural Crisis Communication: Translation, Interpreting, and Languages in Local Crises*, edited by Federico Federici, and Christophe Declercq, 153–173. London: Bloomsbury Academics.

Todorova, Marija. 2021. "Pressing Issues and Future Directions for Interpreting in Conflict Zones." In *Interpreting Conflict: A Comparative Framework*, edited by Marija Todorova, and Lucía Ruiz Rosendo, 305–316. London: Palgrave MacMillan.

Todorova, Marija, and Lucía Ruiz Rosendo. eds. 2021. *Interpreting Conflict. A Comparative Framework*. Cham: Palgrave Macmillan.

PART I

Training interpreters for the military

2

ETHICS IN MILITARY INTERPRETER TRAINING

Pekka Snellman

The two very different professions of an interpreter and a soldier are combined in a specialised military occupation: a military interpreter. This chapter analyses how the military's interests are reflected in the ethics training of military interpreters, focusing on the values and norms that form the professional ethics of each profession. The ethical requirements for military interpreters are evaluated in terms of the two theoretical orientations of the ethical dimension of military action competence as well as interpreter ethics. Drawing on interviews conducted with trainers of military interpreters in Finland, Denmark, and Sweden, the chapter outlines the expectations of military personnel and articulates the different positionalities and ethical dilemmas that are specific to military interpreters. The results propose topics and methods for the ethics training of military interpreters, support all interpreters working with the military, and contribute to the discussion on the ethics and the accountability of interpreters in conflict zones.

2.1 Introduction

Military operations invariably require linguistic support,[1] as conflicts that involve military intervention routinely occur across language borders. Military organisations fulfil their requirements for linguistic support primarily by recruiting civilian interpreters and translators either locally from the conflict area or domestically, or by enlisting and training their own personnel, referred to as military linguists (NATO 2011). The concept of a *military interpreter* refers to a uniformed and armed soldier serving in a military organisation, with the primary task of interpreting (Snellman 2014, 9–10).

Armed forces recruit and train military interpreters primarily for their immediate availability, existing high-level security clearance, and better military skills[2] (NATO 2011, 3-5, 4-1-4-2). However, research suggests that armed forces also

DOI: 10.4324/9781003230359-3

prefer working with military linguists over civilian linguists due to more profound reasons that have ethical implications (see Snellman 2016; Tesseur and Footitt 2019; Ruiz Rosendo 2020). This chapter presents an analysis of how the distinct interests of military organisations regarding linguistic support are reflected in the ethical aspects of military interpreter training. I argue that the professional ethics and positionalities[3] of military and civilian interpreters exhibit fundamental differences and that these differences should be considered in the training of military interpreters.

My personal experiences from serving in Afghanistan (see Snellman 2014, 3) impressed upon me the importance of ethical considerations regarding linguistic support and motivated me to further examine the subject matter. However, ethical questions are by definition ambiguous, and I had difficulties in approaching the topic. For example, one possibility was to acquire research data through military interpreters' responses to case examples of ethical dilemmas that occur in military crisis management operations, but this would have been beyond the resources available to me. The current volume with its perspective on interpreter training provided me the opportunity to interview personnel from the organisations responsible for the training of military interpreters in the Armed Forces of Finland, Denmark, and Sweden (Interview A, Interview B and Interview C, respectively).

2.2 The ethical dimension of military action competence

Ethics has traditionally been considered as a branch of philosophy, which examines concepts such as good and bad, right, or wrong, as well as morality and virtues. Ethics can also be more generally regarded as constituting practical solutions and choices between alternatives, in which case it is usually referred to as ethicality. Ethicality generally relates to an individual's actions and choices, but the actions and principles of organisations may also be considered from the perspective of ethicality. Actions may be ethically conscious and deliberate, or they may be unconscious when they are not based on a justified argument. Actions are ethically founded upon arguments that are typically referred to as norms and values. Norms are usually legal, administrative, or moral, while values may be individual, customary, or general understandings that are socially respected. Norms and values can be contradictory, which presents the individual or organisation with ethical dilemmas (Pääesikunta 2021).

The Finnish Defence Forces (FDF) adopt the concept of *military action competence* in military pedagogy. This refers to an individual soldier's potential to act consciously and responsibly in complex and unforeseen situations. Military action competence comprises four interrelated dimensions – the psychical, physical, social, and ethical dimensions of action competence – which together form a holistic system. Action competent soldiers are able to act as required by the mission, to adapt, recover and maintain their ability to act in changing conditions on the battlefield (Pääesikunta 2020).

The psychical dimension of action competence entails an individual's perceptiveness, confidence, decision-making, and motivation. The social dimension focuses on group cohesion, which is something decisive for combat effectiveness, and involves empathy, co-operation and communication skills, peer support, and leadership. The physical dimension of action competence consists of an individual's physical endurance, strength, speed, and skills. This dimension supports the other three dimensions by enabling resilience[4] and recovery from stress.

Finally, the ethical dimension of action competence necessitates self-awareness, the ability to justify one's actions to oneself and to others, as well as the consciousness of one's values and of right and wrong. By developing these abilities and by aligning them with the values of the FDF and the mission, ethical action competence can be improved. Soldiers who are ethically action competent are committed to their duties, understand different values and points of view, and are prepared to deliberate independently. Ethical action competence thus supports a soldier's self-confidence, determination, morale, and resilience (Pääesikunta 2020).

Toiskallio (2005, 136) argues that the ethical dimension of military action competence constitutes the core of the military profession: "An individual cannot be action competent without being ethically competent." Ethical action competence therefore underscores the individual's capability to cope with whatever environments, conditions, and tasks that the soldier encounters during the mission. This competence requires a high level of personal independence, which is not an excuse for individualism. For moral reasoning to occur, an individual must first become aware of the ethical matters at hand, which calls for moral situational attentiveness (see also Johnson 2015).

The concept of *ethos* is closely linked to ethics. Ethos refers to the fundamental character of a group and reflects its socially shared values, rules, habits, and behaviour. The ethical action competence of an individual as well as a group is supported by habituation into the ethos of a social group. Soldiers need a strong moral identity and a sense of duty, supported by critical thinking in terms of social and ethical deliberation. Ethical action competence therefore plays an integrative and executive role in a soldier's decision-making, self-development, and self-regulation (Toiskallio 2005).

2.3 Interpreter ethics for military interpreters

Both the soldier and the interpreter are considered established professions, with their associated training, standards, norms – and ethics. During recent interactions between the interpreting and military professions, practices that are linked to military professionalism have dominated the tenets of the interpreting profession. The work and status of interpreters have been conditioned by their close co-operation with the military profession, and this has even challenged the traditional notions of what precisely constitutes the interpreting profession (Tesseur and Footitt 2019, 4–9).[5] A military interpreter fuses the professions and professional ethics of a soldier and an interpreter. Merging both professions has a series of implications.

Chesterman (2001, 152) analyses professional translation ethics based on values and the virtues that derive from them.[6] Chesterman implies that a translator's primary professional value is understanding, closely followed by the values of truth, clarity, loyalty, and trust. He then lists the resultant virtues of a professional translator, such as the will to be or become a good translator, fairness, truthfulness, trustworthiness, empathy, courage, and determination (145–147). Chesterman underlines that the professional translation ethics that he illustrates are separate from the translator's personal ethics and subservient to universal ethics. On a different note, Delgado Luchner and Kherbiche (2019, 255–256) argue that in conflict situations, interpreter ethics should adopt a consequential approach that focuses on the outcome of ethical choices, each occurring in their unique circumstances (see also Baker and Maier 2011, 3).

The role and position of the military interpreter may not be compatible with the established ethics of professional interpreters in all situations. Military organisations tend to hold those values in high regard that are characteristic of military professionalism (see Johnson 2015, 266–269). At the same time, the military may disapprove of the values that are central to the established ethics of the interpreter profession, such as impartiality and confidentiality (cf. Tesseur and Footitt 2019; Snellman 2016). The possibilities of interpreters to remain impartial in conflict situations have been questioned in broad terms (see Tesseur and Footitt 2019), but the position of military interpreters in this regard is clear: military interpreters are not impartial or neutral, and according to international humanitarian law, they can unquestionably be considered combatants (Interview C; see Tesseur and Footitt 2019, 13). Understandably, this stance by military organisations has also caused resentment in civilian linguists participating in linguistic support (Tesseur and Footitt 2019, 5–7; Ruiz Rosendo 2020, 56–57).

A fundamental interest at the core of military culture and professionalism is security, and military organisations consistently prioritise it. Testimony to this orientation in linguistic support can also be found in doctrines on linguistic support (MoD 2013),[7] as well as in military organisations' guidelines and reports on the use of interpreters (Snellman 2018, 123–124). Security and trust are key factors for military organisations in the recruitment, training, and deployment of military interpreters (Interview A; B; C; cf. Stocklauser 2018, 82–86). Tesseur and Footitt (2019, 6) note that security clearances are symbolic of the loyalty that linguists have to their employers. Ruiz Rosendo (2020, 57) goes further in stating that interpreters' reliability, loyalty, allegiance, and effectiveness surpasses their language or interpreting skills as priorities.[8] The interviewees in the present study believed that military organisations typically consider military interpreters more trustworthy than civilian interpreters (Interview A; B; C; cf. Snellman 2014, 57–58; Ruiz Rosendo 2021).

Military organisations typically adopt a pragmatic approach to interpreting: it is paramount to accomplish the assigned task and the result matters (Interview A). Military interpreters generally want to "get the job done" instead of considering the subtleties of interpreting such as fidelity or equivalence and strive to achieve an equilibrium in a tense and unstable environment. From the perspective of interpreter ethics, the role of military interpreters is to "participate in the pursuit of security by means of managing instability" (Monacelli and Punzo 2001, 265–266).

Translation scholars may find the preferences of military organisations to be somewhat unorthodox. For example, Méndez Sánchez (2021, 136) notes that the field of professional interpreting remains "unlinked" to the armed forces, and Delgado Luchner and Kherbiche (2019, 265) claim that military norms are "inherently . . . incommensurable" with the professional norms of interpreting. Nonetheless, most military professionals have clear-cut views on the role and position of military interpreters: they are soldiers with the consequent duties and responsibilities (Interview A; B; C). The interviewees' position corresponds with military interpreters' personal perceptions of their professional ethos, in which the identity of a soldier usually prevails over that of an interpreter (Snellman 2014, 56–57; Méndez Sánchez 2021, 141, 150–151).

This means that even if most of the ethical issues that military interpreters face appear similar to those encountered by civilian linguists working for the military (Delgado Luchner and Kherbiche 2019), military interpreters are immersed in military culture, which must be considered in their ethical training.

2.4 Methodology

The research data for this chapter was acquired by interviewing three men, who were either military officers experienced in international military crisis management, working with military interpreters, and/or instructors of military interpreters. One of the interviews was conducted in person, one as an on-line video conference and one in writing using a questionnaire. The interviews were semi-structured and allowed free deliberation. The interview questions were designed to approach ethical questions indirectly by addressing military interpreters' professionality,[9] identity, positionality, and training methods. A review of the transcribed interviews revealed four distinct areas in the answers, which formed the basis for a thematical categorisation:

- military professional ethics,
- interpreter professional ethics,
- personal ethics, and
- training methods.

After determining these themes, I highlighted and rearranged the interviews into segments pertaining to them. In the final phase of the analysis, I examined the thematically organised interviews against the theoretical backdrop of the ethical dimension of military action competence as well as interpreter ethics. Let us now examine the issues that arose from the interviews, which are organised into the four thematic categories.

2.5 Military professional ethics

All interviewees emphasised the soldiership of military interpreters. A military interpreter holds an official military position with the inherent roles and responsibilities of that function. Soldiership also involves the moral code and ethos of the Armed Forces to which the military interpreter belongs. As soldiers, military interpreters are expected to follow the orders of their commanding officers, which in turn are based on tasks assigned by the national government (Interview A; B; C). Military organisations articulate explicitly the non-neutrality of soldiers, and the ethical instructions for FDF personnel are certainly clear in this regard:

> Anyone working for the Defence Forces must . . . see to that he always acts according to his position and duties, so that the interests of the Defence Forces will not be compromised. He must not pursue his personal interests over those of the Defence Forces.
>
> *(Pääesikunta 2021)*

Military interpreters receive the same military training as all other soldiers, including instruction in military ethics. Their language and cultural skillsets are considered military specialisations; this is a bonus added to their military competences, and military interpreters can perform other soldiers' tasks (Interview A; B; C; cf. Méndez Sánchez 2021). Should military interpreters demonstrate their unsuitability for interpreting tasks or show that they are better suited for another role, they may be reassigned. Conversely, any soldier with the right competencies and language skills can be assigned to interpret and is thus considered a military interpreter. The military training and subsequent use of military interpreters can be adapted so that an equal or acceptable level of military competence is achieved (Interview A). Military interpreters must not be a liability to their unit in combat. Yet training expert interpreters while maintaining physical fitness and tactical skills can be difficult (Interview B).

Military interpreters have a limited mandate to act independently. For example, they may participate in the planning and preparation of operations, as well as in analysing their results. For some missions, they have a more inclusive mandate as cultural advisors, than, for example, in training missions (Interview B). Owing to their cultural expertise, military interpreters can act as sources of information, such as by following local media. Furthermore, they should be able to assess local clients' reliability by analysing their behaviour and non-verbal communication with the intention of posing more specific questions and retrieving the needed information independently of their primary user.[10] These responsibilities increase the military interpreter's trust as well as unit cohesion (Interview A; B; C).

To be able to relate to and integrate into their units, military interpreters must have sufficient knowledge regarding the structure of the armed forces and the role of their unit within that structure, as well as military virtues and traditions. To this effect, military interpreters are familiarised with concepts such as service, honour, citizenship and state, as well as serving society. The aim is to increase their understanding of the role of the military in a democratic society because, as military interpreters, they are in direct contact with persons who question these values and are exposed to views that challenge them.[11] Thus, interpreters should also be able to represent the values that are expected of them when speaking in a different language. To mitigate the risk of the vagueness of these fundamental values when interpreting, it is important that military interpreters possess a clear understanding of who they are and what they stand for. This could be further emphasised in military interpreter training (Interview B; C).

2.6 Interpreter professional ethics

While we have determined that military interpreters are actors who have a limited mandate from the Armed Forces to act independently, at the same time, they also are mediators who convey messages whilst remaining neutral. Here, the primary user leading the interaction has full responsibility, and the interpreter is the primary user's tool to accomplish the task. Military interpreters are responsible for language issues, but their role does not extend to deciding which pieces of information are important. Thus, they need to convey the messages of their primary user but not their opinion of them (Interview B). This distribution of responsibility is addressed in training as all military interpreters, while further developing their skills and confidence, are susceptible to acting too freely. When this occurs, they are reminded of their role and responsibilities (Interview A).

Military interpreters are trained not to take direct ownership in the conversations they mediate. For example, in an argument between their clients, the military interpreter should ideally remain calm and detached. Nevertheless, in training simulations, military interpreters repeatedly become deeply involved emotionally. This is only natural due to their empathy for and affiliation with their primary user. To counter this, military interpreters are instructed to view themselves as mediums or instruments through which others can communicate and taught that the escalating of tensions and emotions is not their concern (Interview B).

The ethics of civilian interpreters in a civilian environment do not necessarily apply to military interpreters (Interview C). Should their primary users unwittingly place themselves at a disadvantage or make a mistake, military interpreters are trained to support them actively by offering advice when they possess the required resources and overview.[12] For instance, if interpreters know the client from an earlier meeting, they might assist their primary user in adopting a suitable approach, or they might fill gaps in the interpreting and explicate the topic during a debriefing after the meeting (Interview B). Luo and Zhu (2021, 41–43) emphasise the importance of loyalty in military cultures and the decisive role of personal ethics when professional ethics and military interest might conflict.

2.7 Personal ethics

Military interpreters are usually highly motivated and proud of their status as soldiers. They had to apply for their positions and wanted to join a crisis management operation and to become parts of units (Interview A; C). Military interpreters often exhibit sociable, extrovert, and inquisitive traits, a hunger for information and an eagerness to learn, and these qualities are encouraged in their training to develop their communication skills (Interview B). Military interpreters must also adopt their intended positions and roles in the unit, which experienced military interpreters usually process more consciously and quickly (Interview A). Broadly speaking, military interpreters have established their own group identity within the military (Interview B).

Military interpreters are typically highly valued by the other members of their unit. Sometimes they are initially held in lower regard, but their competence and absolute necessity is soon acknowledged, and their status grows as a result (Interview A; C). Having a military interpreter assigned to a unit supports its effectiveness as well as its morale and cohesion. For example, a junior officer may be more confident with a military interpreter in the patrol. The status of military interpreters is also supported by the fact that they often accompany commanding officers[13] in their duties, regardless of their own rank. This practice is likewise applied during the pre-deployment training to underscore their important role (Interview A).

The integration of military interpreters into the unit to which they will be attached as well as building cohesion and trust are considered to be important, albeit implicit, parts of the training (Interview A; B; C). The ethical action competence of military interpreters hinges on the willingness and ability of the other soldiers to use a language intermediary (Delgado Luchner and Kherbiche 2019, 264). Monacelli and Punzo (2001, 276–277) note that the clients of military interpreters often have a different rank than their interpreters and affirm that their rank indicates their status as participants in hierarchical military structures and that this invariably affects communication. The interviewees, however, rejected the idea that military rank is a factor in the generally good personal relations of military interpreters with everyone in their unit (Interview A; B; see also Ruiz Rosendo 2021).

Military interpreters may be threatened or pressured by hostile actors. These interpreters become potential targets for opponents owing to their official military position and the obligations associated with it, as well as their close interaction with commanding officers. Due to their military training, military interpreters usually understand these dangers well and can avoid being provoked or influenced. A few military interpreters have immigrant backgrounds[14] with some connections to the operation areas. There have been isolated cases of a military interpreter who has sympathised or had affiliations to one party in the conflict, which has impeded the ethical action competence of the military interpreter (Interview A; cf. Snellman 2014, 80–81).

It is important that military interpreters be prepared in their training to face a range of stressful situations (Interview C). A military interpreter's superior understanding of languages and cultures may entail higher stress than for the other soldiers. On the other hand, the same competencies may also lead to a better grasp of the situation (Interview A; B). The greatest source of stress for military interpreters, nonetheless, derives not from the circumstances but from their responsibility for assuring the quality of the interaction. The interpreter is the only person who understands both sides and thus possesses a complete picture of what is being said, including any faults that arise in the communication (Interview B). Military interpreters are encouraged to openly report their stress levels and excessive workloads to their superiors and debriefings after stressful situations, which are common practices on all levels. Their superior officers also need to sufficiently know their military interpreters to notice signs of stress and fatigue (Interview A).

2.8 Training methods

Perhaps the most effective method of training military interpreters involves exercises that incorporate role-playing scenarios.[15] These exercises are included in both the basic training of military interpreters as well as during the pre-deployment training before missions. These scenarios involve the trainees interpreting between unfamiliar external personnel, which the trainees have not met before, and a familiar primary user. The backgrounds of the external actors in the scenarios may differ. For example, the FDF has hired university students in translation studies for these exercises. The trainees are allowed to prepare for the scenario, occasionally in co-operation with the primary user. After each scenario, the trainees are given a debrief and feedback, sometimes by reviewing a video recording of the interaction, which has proven highly useful.[16] The number and detailed structure of the role-playing exercises varies between the represented Armed Forces but also depends on the type of preparation necessitated by the approaching mission. For example, a training mission would require fewer simulations of key-leader engagement meetings. Moreover, the training is adjusted to fit the competence level and experiences of the trainees (Interview A; B; C).

Ethical dilemmas are purposely incorporated into role-playing exercises. The training scenarios typically simulate realistic settings such as meetings with the local stakeholders and key leaders as well as foot patrols and potential conflict situations. The simulations are able to replicate many aspects of the real circumstances of the operation area because the instructors have themselves served in the crisis management operation for which they are training new personnel. The instructors understand the situation in the operation area and are pedagogically competent to re-create demanding scenarios. The role-players, typically acting in the role of a local stakeholder, may have pre-scripted disagreements, which result in events unfolding dynamically. For example, the situation may involve a direct threat or attempted bribery towards the primary user, preserving the honour of the local actor, and so forth. However, the depth and accuracy of the role-players' cultural knowledge cannot be verified, as personnel with backgrounds from the region in question are seldom available. Ethical issues also often arise through mishaps in the communication and interpretation. Should the trainee make an error or fail to notice a misunderstanding, the scenario can escalate so that the errors, and their consequences become obvious to all parties. The progressively more difficult role-playing exercises provide a safe environment to make mistakes and learn by trial and error. The instructors prepare the external personnel in advance but usually remain out of sight of the trainees during the scenario, taking notes for the sub-sequent debrief (Interview A; B; see also Delgado Luchner and Kherbiche 2019, 257–258, 262).

The ethical training for military interpreters also includes many activities for building team spirit and unit cohesion, such as field exercises and physical train-ing. The fundamental idea, values, and routines of a military unit are maintained throughout the training (Interview B; C; see Ruiz Rosendo 2021, 15). During their pre-deployment training, the crisis management force lives under similar con-ditions to those in the operation area. This provides an opportunity to acclimate to field conditions and military culture.[17] In practice, however, military interpreters learn most of their duties hands-on during the Hand-Over-Take-Over[18] phase in the operation area, which is arguably the most critical phase of military interpreter training (Interview A).

The Armed Forces that the interviewees represent have not formulated specific ethical guidelines for military interpreters. Moreover, none of the Armed Forces apply the ethical guidelines of the NATO publication[19] on linguistic support in their military interpreter training (Interview A; B; C). Instead, ethics training is interwoven implicitly into other elements of the training. For example, matters regarding confidentiality, neutrality, loyalty, and the duty to report[20] are repeatedly confronted in the role-playing scenarios. These issues frequently also appear in the debriefings of the training scenarios and highlight the role of an interpreter and the duties and responsibilities that accompany it (Interview B). Training for ethical action competence means developing the intellectual capacity, responsibility, and motivation to identify problems and find solutions for them (Toiskallio 2005, 138). In conclusion, the ethics training of military interpreters focuses on reflexivity and adaptability, as ethical action competence is not simply the knowledge or skill to address a specific problem but an individual's personal capacity, both moral and intellectual (138).

2.9 Training professional ethics to military interpreters

A trained military interpreter is habituated to two professional ethe: the ethos of the soldier as well as the ethos of the interpreter. Both ethe are constructed dur-ing social interaction within each professional group and reflect the established ethics of each profession. Hence, interpreting training needs more than merely ethics instruction in military ethics – which is included in the training plans of all soldiers – or only in interpreter ethics. The interviewees repeatedly referred to the "role"[21] of a military interpreter within the military structure. For example, an interviewee observed that "one of the most important but at the same time most challenging issues in military interpreter training is to get the interpreter to understand his role" (Interview A). The aim of the interviewees appears to have been to instil in the trainees an understanding of the shared values, rules, habits, and behaviour of all military interpreters – in other words, a military interpreter's ethos. The results indicate that for military interpreters immersed in military culture, the ethos of the military profession prevails in many ways over that of the interpreter profession.

The interviews propose that ethics is not taught to military interpreters explicitly and intentionally. Instead, their ethics instruction is implicit in their language, cultural,[22] and military training. In terms of ethics, it is possible to draw parallels between military interpreters and scientists serving in armed forces at large. Military interpreters have acquired a specialised knowledge and bear a responsibility for how this capability is used, especially if they themselves are instrumental in its application and can foresee the consequences (Pichevin 2015, 242–244). It seems clear that, from a military perspective, the existing ethical guidelines for interpreters involved in linguistic support, such as the Conflict Zone Field Guide[23] (AIIC 2012), or the NATO document on linguistic support (NATO 2011, Annex C), provide inadequate grounds for the ethics instruction of military interpreters (cf. Delgado Luchner and Kherbiche 2019, 254). Thus, a conceptual tool is needed to support their ethics training, such as a hybrid set of ethical guidelines or instructions drawing on both military and interpreting ethics (cf. Delgado Luchner and Kherbiche 2019, 255–256), which is formulated specifically for military interpreters (Kähärä 2019, 33–35, 59; Snellman 2016, 227; see Baker and Maier 2011, 4–5).

The results suggest that military interpreters occupy larger spaces for ethical deliberation and decision-making than typically attributed to the interpreter profession (cf. Snellman 2014, 95–97). Military interpreters are encouraged to act independently and proactively in the interests of both their primary user and of the military mission at hand. The tasks of military interpreters may vary and occur within very different ethical frameworks. For example, tasks such as collecting and analysing information (e.g., following local media), training language and culture to the other members of the unit, and interpreting for a primary user all require different ethical approaches.[24] Some tasks emphasise military ethics, others interpreter ethics, and all involve the military interpreter's personal ethics. In short, ethics training for military interpreters should be inclusive and strengthen their ethical action competence as well as resilience. The training should aim at enhancing military interpreters' capabilities for independent reflection on ethical issues as well as their abilities to act fluently and accountably within their assigned role (see Delgado Luchner and Kherbiche 2019, 262; Baker and Maier 2011, 4, 7). The preferred method of achieving this is by using realistic role-playing exercise scenarios that pose ethical questions for consideration, supported by critical analysis and feedback.

Notes

1 *Linguistic support* is the military term for the provision of language services, such as translation and interpretation, to support military operations (NATO 2011, Annex A).
2 The NATO document uses the expressions "familiar with the military environment" and "may . . . be expected to have a combat role" to implicitly describe these military skills (NATO 2011, 4–1–4–2).
3 The concept of *positionality* is used broadly in this chapter and refers to the interpreters' perspective, shaped by factors such as their identity, affiliations, and status (see Ruiz Rosendo 2020, 45–46).
4 The concept of *resilience* and its correlation to ethics in this chapter draws on Southwick and Charney (2012).
5 Tesseur and Footitt (2019) analyse civilian interpreters, but their conclusions can also be applied to military interpreters.
6 Chesterman's analysis draws not only on virtue ethics, but also on the deontological and consequential approaches to translation ethics (cf. Delgado Luchner and Kherbiche (2019, 255–256).
7 The document was withdrawn from being current government policy on 23 July 2019, but it continues to serve as an example of the military's cultural stance on linguistic support, as cultures change slowly.
8 The competencies prioritised by the military could be understood collectively as an overall understanding of the military environment, which allow military interpreters to better evaluate the context of the messages being interpreted (cf. Méndez Sánchez 2021).
9 The concepts professionality and professionalisation in the framework of linguistic support draw on Snellman (2018, 117–123).
10 The term *primary user* refers to a military interpreter's military client, typically a superior officer.
11 The military ethos of the three Nordic countries represented is deeply rooted in the protection of a democratic society, in which the role of the military and the use of armed force are clearly defined. The armed forces are generally trusted, and military interpreters' ethics can be developed on this firm foundation.
12 Military interpreters are provided with the security clearances needed to perform their duties. However, their capability of requesting information in advance varies depending on their experience (Interview A).
13 Commanding officers refers here to military leaders on many levels, typically platoon leaders, company commanders, staff officers, or the commander of the crisis management force.
14 The number of military interpreters with immigrant backgrounds varies between countries and missions.
15 In Chapter 3 of the current volume, Dahnberg highlights that military interpreters must be well informed about the overall situation to be able to communicate the position of their primary users in a conflict, and that this is best achieved in simulating realistic, ethically demanding situations in role-playing scenarios.
16 Feedback supported by video was mentioned by one interviewee (Interview B), while one interviewee mentioned *RETEX* (Retour d'Expérience) as a feedback method (Interview C).
17 Snellman (2014) reports on how Finnish military interpreters experienced and adapted to the field conditions and military culture of crisis management operations.
18 Hand-Over-Take-Over (HOTO) designates a period of a few days or weeks when the new rotation of forces is briefed and familiarised with their tasks before they relieve the previous forces.
19 The NATO publication's Annex C provides ethical guidelines, but does not differentiate between civilian and military linguists in this regard (NATO 2011, Annex C).

20 *Duty to report* refers to the military obligation of conveying vital information to a superior officer.

21 The terms *role* and *position* were often used close together and sometimes interchangeably.

22 It is important to note that the cultural training of military interpreters also includes military culture with all its particularities.

23 The Field Guide is aimed at civilian translators/interpreters, as its full name indicates (AIIC 2012).

24 This classification of military interpreter activities is inspired by the three categories of anthropology *of* and *for* the military suggested by Lucas' (2009, 85–87).

References

AIIC (International Association of Conference Interpreters). 2012. *Conflict Zone Field Guide for Civilian Translators/Interpreters and Users of Their Services.* https://aiic.org/document/8804/T-I_Field_Guide_2012_ENG.pdf

Baker, Mona, and Carol Maier. 2011. "Ethics in Interpreter & Translator Training." *The Interpreter and Translator Trainer* 5 (1) 2011: 1–14. https://doi.org/10.1080/13556509.2011.10798809

Chesterman, Andrew. 2001. "Proposal for a Hieronymic Oath." *The Translator* 7 (2): 139–154. https://doi.org/10.1080/13556509.2001.10799097

Delgado Luchner, Carmen, and Leila Kherbiche. 2019. "Ethics Training for Humanitarian Interpreters Working in Conflict and Post-Conflict Settings." *Journal of War & Culture Studies* 12 (3): 251–267. https://doi.org/10.1080/17526272.2019.1644412

Interview A. Interview with Personnel at the Crisis Management Centre of Pori Brigade, Finland. 18 June 2021. Material in Possession of the Author.

Interview B. Online interview with Personnel from the Royal Danish Defence Language Academy, Denmark. 21 September 2021. Material in Possession of the Author.

Interview C. Questionnaire to the Swedish Armed Forces Interpreter School, Sweden. 30 November 2021. Material in Possession of the Author.

Johnson, Rebecca J. 2015. "Serving Two Masters." In *Routledge Handbook of Military Ethics*, edited by George Lucas, 265–275. London: Routledge.

Kähärä, Jari. 2019. "Sotilastulkki kriisinhallintatehtävässä." [Military Interpreters in Crisis Management Operations]. Master's thesis, University of Helsinki.

Lucas, George. 2009. *Anthropologists in Arms: The Ethics of Military Anthropology.* Lanham: Altamira Press.

Luo, Tian, and Ruiqi Zhu. 2021. "To Be or Not to Be Loyal: Loyalty of Military Interpreters Serving the Japanese Army in the Second Sino-Japanese War (1931–1945)." In *Interpreting Conflict. A Comparative Framework*, edited by Marija Todorova, and Lucía Ruiz Rosendo, 37–59. London: Palgrave Macmillan.

Méndez Sánchez, Verónica. 2021. "The Spanish 'Military Interpreter': A Practical Application in International Operations Arising from Armed Conflicts." In *Interpreting Conflict. A Comparative Framework*, edited by Marija Todorova, and Lucía Ruiz Rosendo, 135–154. London: Palgrave Macmillan.

MoD (Ministry of Defence). 2013. *Linguistic Support to Operations. Joint Doctrine Note 1/13.* The Development, Concepts and Doctrine Centre, Ministry of Defence, United Kingdom. https://assets.publishing.service.gov.uk/government/uploads/system/uploads/attachment_data/file/819765/archive_doctrine_uk_linguistic_support_to_ops_jdn_1_13.pdf

Monacelli, Claudia, and Roberto Punzo. 2001. "Ethics in the Fuzzy Domain of Interpreting. A "Military" Perspective." *The Translator* 7 (2): 265–282. https://doi.org/10.1080/13556509.2001.10799105

NATO (North Atlantic Treaty Organization). 2011. *Linguistic Support for Operations (AlingP-1)*. 12 September 2011. NATO Standardization Agency. https://nso.nato.int/nso/nsdd/main/standards/ap-details/1316/EN

Pääesikunta. 2020. *Varusmieskoulutuksen yleisjärjestelyt ja yhteisesti koulutettavat asiat* [General Arrangements and Common Subjects for Conscript Training]. Defence Command, Finnish Defence Forces. HQ778, 13 October 2020.

Pääesikunta. 2021. *Ethical Instructions for the Defence Forces Personnel*. Defence Command, Finnish Defence Forces. HR322, 23 June 2021.

Pichevin, Thierry. 2015. "The Military Scientist: Deconflicting Moral Responsibilities." In *Routledge Handbook of Military Ethics*, edited by George Lucas, 235–247. London: Routledge.

Ruiz Rosendo, Lucía. 2020. "Interpreting for the Afghanistan Spanish Force." *War & Society* 39 (1): 42–57. https://doi.org/10.1080/07292473.2019.1701620

Ruiz Rosendo, Lucía. 2021. "The Role of the Affective in Interpreting in Conflict Zones." *Target* 33 (1): 47–72. https://doi.org/10.1075/target.18165.rui

Snellman, Pekka. 2014. *The Agency of Military Interpreters in Finnish Crisis Management Operations*. Master's thesis, University of Tampere. https://urn.fi/URN:NBN:fi:uta-201403061187

Snellman, Pekka. 2016. "Constraints on and Dimensions of Military Interpreter Neutrality." *Linguistica Antverpiensia, New Series: Themes in Translation Studies* 15: 260–281. https://lans-tts.uantwerpen.be/index.php/LANS-TTS/article/view/391/379

Snellman, Pekka. 2018. *Language Policy, Translation Culture, and Interpreter Tactics in the Finnish Defence Forces*. General Staff Officer Course Thesis, National Defence University, Helsinki. https://urn.fi/URN:NBN:fi-fe2018120349618

Southwick, Steven M., and Dennis S. Charney. 2012. *Resilience: The Science of Mastering Life's Greatest Challenges*. Cambridge: Cambridge University Press.

Stocklauser, Stefan. 2018. *Dolmetschen im Militär und DolmetscherInnen in Uniform – das Österreichische Bundesheer als Beispiel* [Interpreting in the Military and Military Interpreters – The Austrian Armed Forces as an Example]. Vienna: Bundesministerium für Landesverteidigung.

Tesseur, Wine, and Hilary Footitt. 2019. "Professionalisms at War? Interpreting in Conflict and Post-Conflict Situations." *Journal of War & Culture Studies* 12 (3): 268–284. https://doi.org/10.1080/17526272.2019.1644415.

Toiskallio, Jarmo. 2005. "Military Ethics and Action Competence." In *Civil-Military Aspects of Military Ethics Vol. 2*, edited by Edwin R. Micewski, and Dietmar Pfarr, 132–143. Publication Series of the National Defence Academy, Vienna. www.bundesheer.at/pdf_pool/publikationen/10_cma_12_mea.pdf

List of Key Terms

Military Interpreter. A soldier who has been assigned to interpretation duties. Military interpreters undergo military training and have a military rank, wear a uniform with military insignia, and carry weapons. (Snellman 2014)

Interpreter Tactics. The skills, knowledge, and resources needed to organise and implement the linguistic support for a military operation. (Snellman 2018)

Linguistic Support. The provision of language services, such as translation and interpretation, to support military operations. (NATO 2011, Annex A)

3

MILITARY INTERPRETER TRAINING FOR CONTEXT SPECIFIC SITUATIONS

Magnus Dahnberg

This chapter addresses how the specific needs for interpreting skills, knowledge and abilities in conflict zones are met in military interpreter training. It outlines the requested interpreting skills identified in literature on interpreting in military operations and then explores to what extent these skills are acquired in contemporary military interpreter training, and how this is done. The description takes Swedish military interpreter education as a starting point but also makes comparisons with other countries, and with Public Service interpreter training. A conclusion is that several of the interpreting skills, knowledge and abilities, requested for military interpreters, are actually met by contemporary military interpreter training. Besides general interpreting skills, in-depth knowledge of the languages and cultures in question and a good grasp of the situation at hand in the conflict zone, military interpreters need physical stability, ability to protect themselves from violent attacks, knowledge of international law and the military code of ethics, and a strong sense of both professional loyalty and professional identity.

3.1 Introduction

Working as an interpreter in a military conflict zone is a demanding, stressful and at times dangerous job. In practice, this work is carried out by several different categories of interpreters, ranging from volunteers and civilian interpreters to officers with military interpreter training. While all of these interpreters' need for knowledge and skills to carry out their work in a conflict zone is relatively similar, their training and qualifications often differ significantly. This study examines the knowledge and skills identified in the literature when it comes to being able to work as an interpreter in a conflict zone, and takes the training of military interpreters in Sweden as an example of how this is implemented in practice.

DOI: 10.4324/9781003230359-4

The study also introduces a relationship between interpretation in conflict zones and Public Sector interpreting (PSI). The latter expression refers to interpretation between, for example, refugees or newly arrived immigrants and representatives of a country's authorities or health care. This correlation can be seen as twofold. Firstly, military conflicts often generate refugee flows to other countries, which in turn generates a need for interpretation between these refugees and the various authorities and institutions of the receiving country. Secondly, as already mentioned, it is not uncommon for civilian interpreters (e.g., from the public sector) to also serve in military conflict zones together with military officers. For these reasons, I find it interesting to make some comparisons between the training of military interpreters and the training of public sector interpreters in Sweden.

Military personnel with tasks related to foreign languages and communication is a staff category with different names and a variety of tasks. They are called, for example, *military linguists* (Mitchell and Shevchenko 2015), *interpreters/translators* (Goarmy.com), *language officers* (Forsvarsakademiet 2022), or *military interpreters* (Snellman 2016). Here I have chosen to use the name of *military interpreter* to include all of these. By this term I mean a soldier or military officer who has undergone a military education that includes both foreign language training and interpreter training, and who is hired by a country's armed forces to fulfil tasks related to interpreting, translation, or communication with military personnel or civilians from other countries, usually in a conflict zone.

Since interpreting between military officers and local representatives in a conflict area is carried out in dangerous or potentially dangerous situations, military interpreters need to be able to physically protect and defend themselves and their colleagues while interpreting or fulfilling other tasks. As a specialist in local languages and cultures, a military interpreter sometimes runs the risk of being perceived as a representative of one or the other local party to a conflict. That is why an ongoing or recently terminated conflict between different population groups may elucidate the need for a military interpreter to clarify their affiliation or loyalty to the armed forces of which they are a part. In order to enable communication between, for example, a Swedish military officer and an Afghan village head, the military interpreter needs to have insights in the professional and country-related culture of both sides, the local military and civilian situation, among other aspects.

The military interpreter training for the Swedish Armed Forces, presently being carried out at the Swedish Armed Forces Language School in Uppsala, part of the Armed Forces Intelligence and Security Centre, was launched in 1957. Today, it offers interpreter training with Swedish and English as working languages, on one hand, and either Arabic, French, or Russian on the other (Forsvarsmakten 2021). Thus, each military interpreter has a language combination of three languages: Swedish-Arabic and English-Arabic, or Swedish-French and English-French, or Swedish-Russian and English-Russian. The training programme includes military leadership, combat training, tactics, language studies, intercultural communication, and interpreting skills. The latter is conducted inter alia with the use of professional role-playing in realistic situations.

Interpreting and translation work in conflict zones is far from always carried out by military personnel. Civilian interpreters and translators, sometimes hired locally, play an important role (see, for example, Tipton 2011). Since military interpreters and their civilian colleagues often work side by side in the same conflict area, it is of interest to make some comparisons between military and civilian interpreter training. Several comparisons are made in the following to public service interpreter (PSI) training, because armed conflicts are often the cause of refugee flows (Hayes et al. 2016; Schon 2019), which in turn generate a need for public sector interpretation in the countries hosting the refugees. One comparison with PSI training in Sweden shows that it does not include language training, while military interpreter training does. The concept of simulating real situations for role-playing exists in both military interpreter training and PSI training, although the situations simulated differ significantly from each other.

3.2 Interpreting skills requested for military interpreters

The role of interpreters in conflict or post-conflict zones, be that military personnel or civilian volunteers, includes a wide range of tasks and is usually not restricted to interpreting (Todorova and Ruiz Rosendo 2021). This is reflected in the literature on the skills and knowledge needed for carrying out such a work. Some of the skills identified are not limited to military interpretation only, but are also needed for other categories of interpreters. Such skills are an in-depth understanding of at least two languages and cultures, message reformulation skills, note-taking, concentration, and endurance (Moser-Mercer et al. 2014). Mahasneh and Obeidat (2018) add to this communication skills, dialect awareness, accuracy, fluency in both source and target languages, and awareness of rules and ethics, such as confidentiality. In the literature on PSI, the same skills are identified (see Hale 2007). Thus, here we deal with such interpreting skills that are not limited to interpreting in conflict zones only.

As is often the case also in PSI, there may be rapid changes of the actual language and culture combinations needed (Ria Novosti 2021). This has partly the same reason for both military interpreting and PSI, namely the emergence of armed conflicts in different parts of the world where the armed forces of different countries can become involved, in need of military interpreters who master the languages in question. The same conflicts may cause refugee flows, which in turn affect the language needs in interpretation in the public sector in the refugee-receiving countries.

Another qualification needed for interpreters in conflict zones is a good grasp of the subject matter at hand (Moser-Mercer et al. 2014). This, too, is a kind of knowledge that could be expected from interpreters in different contexts, not only in conflict and post-conflict zones. Yet the subject matter in itself is, in some respects, different from what interpreters in other contexts need to know. It includes military terminology (Banman et al. 2017) and covers both legal, humanitarian, and diplomatic areas (Moser-Mercer et al. 2014).

When it comes to culture, interpreters in conflict zones are expected to know not only the culture of the people who live in the conflict zone and of the country or countries from where, for example, the military officers who take part in an ongoing peace keeping operation come. The interpreters should also know, more specifically, the professional culture of the hiring body for which they work (Mahasneh and Obeidat 2018). This hiring body could, for example, be an international or a non-governmental organisation, or a joint command of military units from several countries' Armed Forces.

Working within the frames of an ongoing armed conflict, or dealing with the consequences of such a conflict in a post-conflict zone, means that the interpreter has to cope with sensitive cases and at the same time maintain a professional level to effectively handle many situations. This requires a certain psychological stability of the interpreters (Mahasneh and Obeidat 2018). More so: an interpreter in a conflict situation has to show patience and tolerance when faced with hard working conditions in general, and with unexpected reactions by victims of the conflict (ibid.). Since the interpreters are supposed to be acquainted with two or more languages and cultures of different ethnical or professional groups with different or even opposite positions in a conflict, they have to be able to perform tasks which may strain their professional loyalty or even challenge their sense of identity (Baker 2010). An interpreter is often perceived as a boundary spanner (Tipton 2011). For a military interpreter, who belongs to the military personnel of their country's Armed Forces, the professional loyalty to these Armed Forces may override the traditional concept of the interpreter's neutrality (Snellman 2016).

The notion of identity concerns not only how interpreters think of themselves. It can sometimes be of even greater importance how an interpreter is perceived by the parties in an armed conflict: if the interpreter is a friend or a foe, one of "us" or one of "them." The answer to this question may have life-threatening consequences for the interpreter (Baker 2010). Therefore, a military interpreter, as well as any interpreter in a conflict zone, needs to be able to protect themselves in a violent situation (Mahasneh and Obeidat 2018). Banman et al. (2017) go one step further, stating that a military interpreter must be able to work in war conditions. The presence of potential or real violence and threats to one's own security is perhaps the most specific circumstance in the work of an interpreter in a conflict zone compared to many other categories of interpreters.

The work of interpreters in conflict zones is seldom restricted to interpreting only, which also has an impact on the skills required. First of all, the interpreter should know how to translate and have a very good command of at least two written languages and also of Computer-Assisted Translation (CAT) tools (Mahasneh and Obeidat 2018). Interpreters are also supposed to have good administrative and time-management skills. They can be asked to make appointments or write reports (ibid.). They might even get the role of general fixers for their unit or organisation (Palmer 2007).

3.3 Skills acquired by military interpreters from training

Based on the abilities identified in the previous section as desirable for interpreters in conflict zones, this section makes a review of what abilities and knowledge Swedish military interpreters are expected to have after completing training. Then the next section describes in more detail how the training is organised.

A Swedish military interpreter must be a Swedish citizen. He or she must be fluent in both Swedish and English when the training starts (there is no requirement of prior knowledge of any of the other languages). A basic conscription service must also be completed before one can be admitted to the military interpreter training (Forsvarsmakten 2021).

In the following, a comparison is made between the abilities and knowledge identified in the literature as desirable for interpreters in conflict zones and the abilities that Swedish military interpreters are expected to have after completing training, according to available sources (first and foremost, Forsvarsmakten 2021). Some comparison is also made with military interpreters trained in Denmark according to the Danish system (Forsvarsakademiet 2022).

The abilities and knowledge reviewed are as follows: interpreting, local languages and cultures; ethics; subject matter and terminology; culture of the hiring body; mental stability, professional identity, and loyalty; self-defense and work in war zones; translation; administration; and other abilities.

Interpreting, local languages and cultures

Swedish military interpreters who have gone through the training programme are expected to be fluent in three languages: Swedish, English, and one of either Arabic, French, or Russian. They are able to interpret (and translate) from Swedish and English into either Arabic, French, or Russian, and vice versa. They also have good cultural knowledge of the area where their target language is spoken (Forsvarsmakten 2021). Especially in the case of Arabic, this means focusing on one or a few of the many areas and countries where different varieties of Arabic are spoken (Horesh and Cotter 2016). At the moment, focus is at Damascus Arabic and Modern Standard Arabic (Forsvarsmakten 2021).

As for military interpreters in Denmark, trained in a different program than in Sweden, the emphasis on cultural knowledge is even stronger: Danish military interpreters after training have the skills of being cultural advisors for their fellow officers (Forsvarsakademiet 2022).

Ethics

The code of ethics is the same for military interpreters as for all Armed Forces personnel. It includes anti-discrimination and respect for equal rights but does not contain any specific code of ethics for military interpreters. Military interpreters also have some knowledge of international law (Forsvarsmakten 2021). As

Snellman (2016) points out, military interpreters are rarely perceived as strictly neutral actors when interpreting between their colleagues in the armed forces and local representatives in a conflict area. Unlike the ethics of public sector interpreters, where interpreter neutrality is a cornerstone, there is nothing in the military code of conduct that requires military interpreters to see themselves as neutral.

Subject matter and terminology

Military interpreters are trained in international law and in the organisation, structure and working concept of the national armed forces. Their military terminology knowledge includes all of their working languages (Forsvarsmakten 2021). They also have some knowledge of foreign policy terminology, which is connected to the fact that military interpreters often work also for Swedish embassies abroad (ibid.). (Knowledge of humanitarian terminology, also identified as desirable for interpreters in conflict zones by Moser-Mercer et al. [2014] is not mentioned in the descriptions available as part of the military interpreters' professional profile).

Culture of the hiring body

As military officers of the armed forces of their country, military interpreters are likely to be well acquainted with the professional culture of the armed forces in question. However, most peacekeeping missions are carried out by international coalitions of national armed forces, the professional culture of which may in some cases differ significantly from each other. For that reason, military interpreters, as well as other personnel, may from the have start a limited understanding of how the culture of a joint coalition will finally take shape, when deployed in the conflict or post-conflict zone.

Mental stability, professional identity, and loyalty

Before even being admitted to military interpreter training, all applicants are interviewed by a psychologist (Forsvarsmakten 2021). In the selection of applicants, psychological stability is a main criterion (Dahlquist 2004). Regarding professional identity and loyalty, both Swedish and Danish military interpreters form their own unit within the Armed Forces – Interpreter Platoon (Sweden) and the Language Officer Corps (Denmark). In Sweden, there is a voluntary Association of Military Interpreters, open also for those who presently are not serving in the Armed Forces (Militartolkar 2022). As Snellman (2016, 277) points out concerning professional loyalty in conflict zones, "uniform-wearing military interpreters have unquestionably chosen their allegiance."

Still, there is also another part of the military interpreters' professional loyalty that is shown in some cases: the loyalty to their fellow interpreters, locally hired in Afghanistan. Working in a conflict zone as a military interpreter usually means working together with local interpreters from the country in conflict. After finishing the mission in Afghanistan, Sweden received claims from Afghan interpreters that they be provided with asylum in Sweden. Some military interpreters showed a deep engagement in this matter (Candal 2013).

Self-protection and work in war conditions

Military interpreters are trained specialist officers with combat skills and ability to work in zones of armed conflict. They are deployed in Armed Forces units that are sent to international peacekeeping missions for six months at a time (Forsvarsmakten 2021).

Translation

Military interpreters are trained in translating between their working languages. Translating skills are identified as desirable for interpreters in conflict zones by Mahasneh and Obeidat (2018), who also point out the need for acquaintance with Computer-Assisted Translation (CAT) tools. Forsvarsmakten (2021) does not, however, mention whether Swedish military interpreters are familiar with CAT tools or not.

Administration and other skills. Nothing is mentioned by Forsvarsmakten (2021) when it comes to administration skills, but military interpreters can have both pedagogy and leadership skills. Swedish military interpreters offer training for other categories of military officers in how to communicate with the help of an interpreter (Forsvarsmakten 2021). Their Danish military interpreter colleagues offer both lectures on culture and society of the countries where international peace-keeping operations take place, and training of intercultural communication (Forsvarsakademiet 2022). Over the years, military interpreters have also been trained in questioning and interrogation (Wiman 2013). Although this is not part of the training now (Forsvarsmakten 2021), an interpreter is always a crucial member of an interrogation team in a military context (Russano et al. 2014).

3.4 Training of military interpreters

The length of training to become a military interpreter is in some ways depending on the interpreter's previous military background, but is normally two years in Sweden and Denmark (Forsvarsmakten 2021; Forsvarsakademiet 2022), where the training takes place at the Interpreter School at the Armed Forces Intelligence and Security Centre in Uppsala and at the Royal Danish Defence College in Copenhagen, respectively. In Russia, a military interpreter training lasts for five years, offered at the Military University of the Ministry of Defence and National Research Tomsk State University (Orlov 2016). Language training for military linguists in the United States has lasted up to 64 weeks at the Defense Language Institute in Monterey (Lange 2018).

In Sweden, as has already been mentioned, applicants to the military interpreter training must be fluent in Swedish and English in advance, while the third working language of the military interpreters – Arabic, French, or Russian – is studied from scratch during the training. A similar system is used in Denmark. That is, for the language combination Swedish-Arabic and English-Arabic, one starts the training without knowing any Arabic. Similarly, for the combination Swedish-Russian and English-Russian, there is no requirement of knowing Russian in advance. This is a difference compared to training of PSI in Sweden, where one has to be fluent in working languages before the training starts. The PSI training offered at Stockholm university lasts for one academic year. Containing, among other things, professional theory, ethics, and role-play exercises, the PSI training does not include any language classes (Stockholm University 2019, 2022).

The language training for future military interpreters is highly intensive. In the Swedish Armed Forces it consists of three 12-week courses with an average of 22 hours of language classes each week, homework not included. The trainers are professional language teachers, often native speakers of the language they teach. Besides grammar and vocabulary, the syllabus includes culture and literature studies, films, interpreting and translation exercises, scripted and unscripted role-play exercises in the classroom, and unscripted role-play scenarios in the field with native speakers – both Swedish military officers and immigrants from Arab-, French-, or Russian-speaking countries. Study trips are made to a place where the working language is spoken (Forsvarsmakten 2021).

Since interpreting exercises are included almost from the very start of the language training (Forsvarsmakten 2021), they can be said to serve a dual goal: to get the participants used to code-switching and working with equivalents in two or three languages but also to study the new working language in itself. Thus, interpreting exercises are not only interpreting exercises as such, but are also a fundamental part of the language training. At the beginning of the training, such exercises may involve interpreting a simple, bilingual dialogue that the teacher reads aloud in a language lab. Over time, the dialogues become more advanced and contain more special terms or grammatically complicated expressions.

Role-play exercises and scenarios are a central pedagogical tool in the military interpreter training. Since these role plays span a fairly large field of different exercises, there is reason to focus on the different practice arrangements that occur and to describe them based on a systematic toponymy (Dahnberg, forthcoming):

> A *closed* role play is based on a script with written lines, which the participants read out aloud. When the role-playing game represents a conversation to be interpreted, the interpreter usually does not have access to this text but has to interpret based on what they hear.
>
> An *open* role play is based on role cards or other instructions, which tell the participants more generally what to do during the role play, but does not provide them with their exact lines. Thus, the utterances that are to be rendered by the interpreter are more spontaneous than in a closed role play.

The participants of a *non-professional* role play are students only. This means that for carrying out a non-professional role play, there is no need to involve any external actors or teachers as participants. With due instructions or scripts for the students, this type of role play can be carried out on a daily basis.

In a *semi-professional* role play a teacher participates together with their students, and thus has the possibility of managing the dialogue and the role play in a desired direction.

A *professional* role play includes, for example, a military officer playing their professional self together with the students. This gives some opportunity of creating a certain realism in the exercise, at least when it comes to professional language and professional behaviour.

The role plays used in military interpreter training go from closed (scripted), semi-professional (with teacher and students involved) role play in a language lab setting, over closed, non-professional (with student participants only) in a classroom setting, to open (unscripted), professional (with military officers acting their personal self) in more realistic encounters, the latter usually called role play scenarios. Finally, a combination of a tactics and combat exercise which involves several role play scenarios, including the use of all of the military interpreters' working languages, is carried out during several days (Linderfalk 2021). In such a final exercise several external actors take part, as well as the interpreters' language and combat teachers. The knowledge, experience, and contacts of both language and combat teachers are used to make the encounters as realistic as possible.

While language classes are not included in public service interpreter training in Sweden, role play certainly is. It is a fundamental part also in PSI training and includes more or less the same conceptual settings as the military interpreter training does. Both scripted and unscripted role plays are used, and the participants also vary between students only (non-professional), teacher and students (semi-professional), and professional service providers and students (professional). However, the more specific settings and subject matters are quite different. If the majority of the public service interpreter role plays take place – as it were – in a hospital, a police station, or in a social security office, the military interpreters place their role-playing, for example, in simulated military international operations or in an embassy abroad. Both the subject matter and the intended encounters differ significantly from each other in many cases.

The 18-month training programme for military interpreters is an officer education which includes both modules that are related to language and interpreting, and modules that are of a general military combat character. Before entering the programme, the applicants must pass a basic conscript military training. Application for military interpreter training programme can be made before or during the conscript training. Within the 18-month programme, a 7-week combat training course is included, usually in a military training area. A three-week tactics course aims to teach how to plan and complete tactical operations and tasks, including also military terminology, while a three-week leadership course focuses on group dynamics and personal development (Forsvarsmakten 2021).

Public service interpreting courses do not, naturally enough, include any combat or leadership training, but the military tactics course might be compared, at least distantly, to the courses of terminology work that the public service interpreting students complete in the area of social service, medicine, and law. For both categories of future interpreters, these in itself utterly different courses still have in common the aim of making the future interpreters acquainted to their area of work (military operations on one hand, social service, medicine, and law on the other) and of the interprofessional reality of their future.

The professional culture of the Armed Forces is not a part of the syllabus as such, but since all of the training is carried out in military premises, under the direction of military officers, the military interpreters get well acquainted with it during their training programme. After graduating, they are hired by the Armed Forces as Specialist (Non-commissioned) Reserve Officers and serve in that capacity when needed (Forsvarsmakten 2021), which makes it possible for them to keep in touch with the ongoing development of the professional culture. This also helps to build professional loyalty.

The professional identity of the military interpreter is built through an intensive and hard training programme, which has given these interpreters the reputation of belonging to the "elite troops" of the Armed Forces (Holmström 2009). The Language School has its own sign, which is also seen at the uniform badges of military interpreters. After graduation, the interpreters can join the Association of Military interpreters and take part in its voluntary courses and events.

Public service interpreters have a one-year university programme and several professional associations.

Before being sent to a conflict or post-conflict zone to take part in an ongoing peacekeeping mission, all personnel, including military interpreters, complete a *pre-deployment* training. This training lasts from two weeks and up to several months and includes combat and security training. It aims also at providing a clear picture of the conflict zone in question, the political situation in the country, about the UN mandate that forms the basis of the operation and of the concept of peace enforcement and peacekeeping (Forsvarsmakten 2022b).

3.5 Discussion and conclusion

The literature on interpreter work in conflict zones has identified several skills that are said to be necessary for such interpreters, including military interpreters. Some of these skills can be called general interpreter skills which are normally required from all interpreters, regardless of the context: language and culture knowledge, communication skills, message reformulation, fluency, accuracy, working memory capacity. Others are specific for the context of armed conflicts and peacekeeping operations: self-protection and ability to work in war conditions. Subject matter knowledge is usually required from any interpreter. In the case of military interpreters, the subject matter is specifically focused on military terminology and military operations.

Examining the sources mostly on Swedish military interpreters' skills and training, one can see that a majority of the skills identified in literature, but not all, are actually said to be present with these interpreters. A possible area of development could be the use of Computer-Assisted Translation (CAT) tools, which are not mentioned in the sources.

To some extent the training programmes of military interpreters and public service interpreters coincide, especially concerning the use of role play as a training method, but they differ significantly already when it comes to the subject and simulated settings of the role plays, not to mention the natural absence of combat training for public service interpreters. Although these two types of education and training may be seen as connected through the working languages and cultures involved, both the requested skills and the training programme content differ in accordance with the highly different tasks that the interpreters fulfil.

References

Baker, Mona. 2010. "Interpreters and Translators in the War Zone: Narrated and Narrators." *The Translator* 16 (2): 197–222. https://doi.org/10.1080/13556509.2010.10799469

Banman, Polina, A.A. Legler, and T.V. Matvievicha. 2017. *Teoriticheskie osnovy specialnogo perevoda: uchebnoe posobie* [The Theoretical Foundations of Specialized Translation: A Teaching Aid]. Stavropol: Severo-Kavkazskiy federalnyj universitet.

Candal, Tora. 2013. "Den första snön har precis lagt sig över Stockholm." [The First Snow Has Just Come to Stockholm]. *Hugin & Munin* 4. https://slideum.com/doc/4876563/nr-4-2013.pdf – bef%C3%A4lsf%C3%B6reningen-milit%C3%A4rtolkar.

Dahlquist, Harriet. 2004. "Vem klarar tolkskolan? Om urvalsförfarandet i samband med uttagningarna till Försvarets tolkskola." [Who Can Become a Military Interpreter? On the Selection of Applicants to the Armed Forces Language school]. *Pliktverkets rapportserie* 91. www.yumpu.com/sv/document/read/20383266/vem-klarar-tolkskolan-rekryteringsmyndigheten.

Dahnberg, Magnus (forthcoming). "Role Play as a Means of Training and Testing Public Service Interpreting." In *Routledge Handbook on Public Service Interpreting*, edited by Laura Gavioli, and Cecilia Wadensjö. London: Routledge.

Forsvarsakademiet [Royal Danish Defence College]. 2022. www.fak.dk/da/uddannelse/skoler/forsvarets-sprogskole/sprogofficersuddannelsen/.

Forsvarsmakten. [Swedish Armed Forces]. 2021. https://jobb.forsvarsmakten.se/sv/utbildning/befattningsguiden/officers-befattningar/militartolk/.

Forsvarsmakten 2022a. *"Expertis – för operativ effekt: Utbildningskatalog 2022." [Expertise – for operative effect: Course catalogue 2022].* www.forsvarsmakten.se/siteassets/3-organisation-forband/fmundsakc/fmundsakc-utbildningskatalog-2022.pdf

Forsvarsmakten 2022b. https://jobb.forsvarsmakten.se/sv/jobba-i-forsvarsmakten/utlandstjanst/insatsutbildningen/

Hale, Sandra. 2007. *Community Interpreting*. London: Palgrave Macmillan.

Hayes, Sherrill, Brandon D. Lundy, and Maia Carter Hallward. 2016. "Conflict-Induced Migration and the Refugee Crisis: Global and Local Perspectives from Peacebuilding and Development." *Journal of Peacebuilding and Development* 11: 1–7. https://doi.org/10.1080/15423166.2016.1239404

Holmström, Mikael. 2009. "Tolkskolan varnar för frivillighet." [Language School Warns for Voluntary System]. *Svenska Dagbladet*. www.svd.se/tolkskolan-varnar-for-frivillighet.

Horesh, Uri, and Willam M. Cotter. 2016. "Current Research on Linguistic Variation in the Arabic-Speaking World." *Language and Linguistics Compass* 10 (8): 370–381. https://doi.org/10.1111/lnc3.12202

Lange, Katie. 2018. *How Military Linguists Learn their Craft*. www.defense.gov/News/Inside-DOD/Blog/Article/2061759/64-weeks-to-fluency-how-military-linguists-learn-their-craft/.

Linderfalk, Julia. 2021. "Med språng i Spång [Running in Kvarn]." *Hugin & Munin* September: 14–16. www.militartolkar.org.

Mahasneh, Anyad A., and Mohammed M. Obeidat. 2018. "Conflict Zones: A Training Model for Interpreters." *The Interpreters' Newsletter* 23: 63–81. https://doi.org/10.13137/2421–714X/22399.

Militartolkar [Military interpreters]. 2022. www.militartolkar.org/bli-medlem

Mitchell, Peter J., and Mikhail A. Shevchenko. 2015. "Teaching Military Linguists: The Experience of the United States Army." *Vestnik Moskovskogo universiteta* 19 (1): 89–93. https://cyberleninka.ru/article/n/teaching-military-linguists-the-experience-of-the-united-states-army/viewer.

Moser-Mercer, Barbara, Leïla Kherbiche, and Barbara Class. 2014. "Interpreting Conflict: Training Challenges in Humanitarian Field Interpreting." *Journal of Human Rights Practice* 6 (1): 140–158. https://doi.org/10.1093/jhuman/hut025.

Orlov, Stepan. 2016. "Opisanie i sravnenie sistem obucheniya voennykh perevodchikov v Rossii i za rubezhom: razlichiya i obshchie cherty v sistemakh obucheniya [Description and Comparison of Educational Systems of Military Interpreters in the Russian Federation and Abroad. Differences and Similarities in the Educational Systems]." *Psikhologiya, sotsiologiya i pedagogika* 5. https://psychology.snauka.ru/2016/05/6765.

Palmer, Jerry. 2007. "Interpreting and Translation for Western Media in Iraq." In *Translating and Interpreting Conflict*, edited by Myriam Salama-Carr, 13–28. Amsterdam/New York: Rodopi.

Ria Novosti. 2021. *Vladimir Vinokurov: voennyj institut inostrannykh yazykov nuzhno vozrodit* [Vladimir Vinokurov: The Military Institut for Foreign Languages Has to Be Reborn]. https://ria.ru/20210521/vinokurov-1732955816.html.

Russano, Melissa B., Fadia M. Narchet, and Steven M. Kleinman. 2014. "Analysts, Interpreters, and Intelligence Interrogations: Perceptions and Insights." *Applied Cognitive Psychology* 28: 829–846. https://doi.org/10.1002/acp.3070

Schon, Justin. 2019. "Motivation and Opportunity for Conflict-Induced Migration: An Analysis of Syrian Migration Timing." *Journal of Peace Research* 56 (1): 12–27. https://doi.org/10.1177/0022343318806044

Snellman, Pekka. 2016. "Constraints on and Dimensions of Military Interpreter Neutrality." *Linguistica Antverpiensia, New Series – Themes in Translation Studies* 15: 260–281.

Stockholm University. 2019. www.tolk.su.se/english/education.

Stockholm University. 2022. www.su.se/sok-kurser-och-program/htotk-1.412328

Tipton, Rebecca. 2011. "Relationships of Learning between Military Personnel and Interpreters in Situations of Violent Conflict: Dual Pedagogies and Communities of Practice." *The Interpreter and Translator Trainer* 5 (1): 15–40. https://doi.org/10.1080/13556509.2011.10798810.

Todorova, Marija, and Lucía Ruiz Rosendo. eds. 2021. *Interpreting Conflict: A Comparative Framework*. London: Palgrave Macmillan.

Wiman, Edvard. 2013. "Hjältar och pirater i Adenviken." [Heroes and Pirates in the Gulf of Aden]. *Hugin & Munin* 4: 7–10. Nr 4 2013.pdf – Befälsföreningen Militärtolkar | slideum.com.

4

TRAINING LIAISON OFFICERS INTERPRETING FOR CHINA'S PEACEKEEPING MISSIONS

Zerong Wei and Tian Luo

Since 1990, under United Nations (UN) mandate, China's peacekeeping forces have performed their duties and contributed to world peace and common development. However, until now, no study has been conducted to investigate the role of interpreting in China's peacekeeping operations (PKOs) or the impact of training on interpreter performance. Accordingly, this chapter presents a case study of the training programmes provided for liaison officers interpreting for the Chinese Military Utility Helicopter Unit deployed in Sudan from August 2017 to August 2018. The study is mainly based on an interview with a Chinese liaison officer who participated in said training as well as on memoirs of several Chinese liaison officers who were involved in similar missions. The results suggest that the training courses were rich in content, covering aspects of linguistic competence, military and security issues, cross-cultural communication and UN regulations. It is showcased that training is critical for liaison officers interpreting for PKOs, as it equips them with the knowledge and skills required to address challenges in war-torn zones. The study also reveals that interpreting plays an indispensable role in mediating communication for Chinese UN peacekeepers.

4.1 Introduction

Translation and interpreting play a critical role in global United Nations (UN) peacekeeping operations (PKOs), that should never be underestimated. In recent years, academic interest has grown in this field (e.g., Baker 2012; Footitt and Kelly 2012; Kelly and Baker 2013; Ruiz Rosendo and Persaud 2019). For instance, the monograph *Interpreting the Peace, Peace Operations, Conflict and Language in Bosnia–Herzegovina* (Kelly and Baker 2013) delves into the complex language issues confronting the international forces that sought to bring peace to Bosnia–Herzegovina in the 1990s; it examines how language differences were integral to

DOI: 10.4324/9781003230359-5

conflicts in the country and how the multinational UN and NATO forces addressed their own problems of communication and linguistic support. These studies have expanded this research area, providing significant findings and insights.

The People's Republic of China, since being founded in 1949, has contributed significantly to world peace and development due to its active participation in UN PKOs. China is the second largest contributor to both peacekeeping assessment and UN membership fees, and it is the largest troop-contributing country among the permanent members of the UN Security Council. Since 1990, China has sent more than 40,000 peacekeepers to 25 UN PKOs across an expanding range of deployments, who have faithfully performed their duties (State Council Information Office of China 2020). Chinese peacekeepers have engaged in UN PKOs in a variety of areas and positions – engineer, medical, transport, helicopter, force protection, infantry units, staff officers, military observers and seconded officers – in over 20 countries and regions, including Cambodia, the Democratic Republic of the Congo, Liberia, Sudan, Lebanon, Cyprus, Mali and South Sudan. They have facilitated the peaceful settlement of disputes, safeguarded regional security and stability and promoted economic and social development in host nations.

Among Chinese peacekeepers are a group of experts with special tasks (i.e., liaison officers), whose main duty is to provide interpreting and translating services to help other Chinese peacekeepers overcome linguistic barriers. For instance, in November 2020, roughly 60 liaison officers were working to help Chinese peacekeeping personnel (including 13 units) deployed in six African countries (Sudan, the Democratic Republic of the Congo, the Central African Republic, Western Sahara, Mali and South Sudan) to accomplish their missions (Wei 2021). In this instance, typically, for a unit of roughly 150 personnel, there were six liaison officers in service, whereas, for a medical unit of roughly 60 personnel, there was only one liaison officer in service.

Wei Zerong was one of the Chinese liaison officers deployed in Sudan. Wei was an instructor from the Army Engineering University of the People's Liberation Army of China. In the winter of 2015, Wei and five other men were recruited from different affiliations as a liaison team for the first Chinese peacekeeping helicopter unit under UN mandate, officially referred to as the Chinese Military Utility Helicopter Unit (CMUHU). In March 2016, the liaison team gathered in Beijing to join an intensive training, which lasted more than a year. From August 2017 to August 2018, they fulfilled their liaison mission for the CMUHU deployed in Darfur, Sudan.

The story of Wei working as a liaison officer for UN PKOs has been reported by Chinese Army Online (Zhang and Li 2018). However, the news report did not present much details about the training of liaison officers and the role of interpreting for peacekeepers in Sudan. In general, little attention has been paid to Chinese interpreters in contemporary UN PKOs (Mu and Wang 2014). This chapter aims to rectify this by examining Wei's case. Specifically, the purpose of this chapter is to find out how Chinese liaison officers (or interpreters) were trained and what roles they played in Chinese PKOs. The case study is mainly based on an interview with Wei conducted in

March 2021 and on the memories of several other liaison officers who participated in similar UN PKOs.

4.2 The need for interpreting services in Chinese peacekeeping units

Since 2003, the armed conflict between two rebel groups from Sudan's western region of Darfur and the Sudanese government has drawn the country into inter-communal clashes to gain control over land, water, livestock and mineral resources and, which led to continuous violence against civilians, banditry and criminal activities exacerbated by the proliferation of arms. It was estimated that 200,000–400,000 people died due to military conflict, disease and famine. To improve the overall human-rights situation in Sudan, the Doha Document for Peace in Darfur was signed in 2006, but progress towards its implementation was limited. In 2007, the UN Security Council passed resolution 1769 and thereby authorised an international peacekeeping force in Darfur.

To implement the resolution, the African Union – the UN Hybrid Operation in Darfur (UNAMID) – was established in July 2007. The core mandate of the UNAMID was the protection of civilians. Over the years, UNAMID has reduced the number of armed clashes, improved access to previously denied areas, provided support to mediation between the Sudanese government and armed movements and contributed to creating and supporting a protective environment; it has also practiced community policing, strengthened traditional community-based mechanisms in internally displaced person (IDP) camps, improved access to provide protection in previously denied areas and provided protection through thousands of short-, medium-, and long-range patrols to remote, isolated and high-risk areas as well as inside IDP camps. Due to constant UNAMID efforts, the situation in Darfur gradually stabilised. UNAMID ended its activities on 31 December 2020, and Sudan embarked on a road of peacebuilding (UN Department of Peace Operations 2021).

It is not difficult to envisage that interpreting and translation played an essential role in UNAMID mission implementation. More than 10 countries – Rwanda, Pakistan, China, Ethiopia, Jordan, Nepal, Egypt, Indonesia, Tanzania, and Kenya – contributed military, police, and civilian personnel to the UNAMID mission, and, as these personnel spoke different languages, the need emerged for interpreters and translators to aid in communication among different units and UN organisations. The total authorised number of uniformed personnel was more than 19,200, which included more than 15,800 military personnel (consisting of contingent troops, mission experts and staff officers), 1,500 policemen, and 13 formed police units (with each unit consisting of up to 140 personnel), which suggested the a need for diversified linguistic help.

In November 2007, a Chinese multipurpose engineer unit of 315 was sent to the UNAMID mission area (The State Council Information Office of China 2020). In August 2017, a CMUHU of 140 personnel was deployed to Darfur together with four medium multi-purpose helicopters to perform the tasks of force delivery, operational support, search and rescue, medical evacuation, and logistic supply. Despite the complexities of challenges in overseas missions, CMUHU fulfilled its multiple tasks, acting as an essential airborne force of the UNAMID and a major pillar of UN PKOs in Darfur.

As Wei (2021, 10) recalls, the demand for linguistic help was prominent among camps that accommodated displaced persons and UN peacekeeping forces: "there are five super camps in Darfur, one of which is the El Fasher super camp where both the headquarters of UNAMID and CMUHU were stationed." Staff officers, military observers, civilian personnel and volunteers in the headquarters had a high level of English. However, some local employees could only communicate orally in English, and their writing abilities were limited, which led to the need of help from translators.

The UN peacekeeping units deployed in the El Fasher super camp were from nine countries (China, Pakistan, Nepal, Indonesia, Egypt, Kenya, Ethiopia, Rwanda, and Gambia). The number of personnel in these units varied from dozens to hundreds. As different languages and dialects were spoken, communication could only be secured through interpreters who could speak worldwide or regional lingua franca, such as English or Arabic. As a result, each peacekeeping unit had their own liaison officers who were mainly responsible for translation and interpreting.

> Since the major language spoke in Sudan is Arabic, some units had liaison officers who could spoke Arabic. Zhang Hanghang, for instance, was an interpreter between Chinese and Arabic language in the 13th batch of Chinese engineering units deployed in Darfur, and he helped to achieve very smooth communication. On the whole, the communication between peacekeepers of various units in the Darfur super camp and other camps was mediated in most cases through English, and the need of English interpreters and translators was the most urgent.
>
> *(Wei 2021, 10)*

Particularly, most CMUHU personnel could speak and write English in ordinary situations; however, they were less capable of handling official documents written in English. This situation echoes what Li (2009) found in a survey on the English proficiency of Chinese peacekeeping forces. Overall, more than 67% of the interviewed peacekeeping officers encountered major language barriers while participating in UN military meetings, and 75% of foreign military officers reported that the English oral communication skills of Chinese military officers were sufficient only on daily life occasions. More than 90% of military officers could read official documents in English, but more than 30% had great difficulties in writing official documents. It is worth mentioning that the level of English proficiency varied among different Chinese peacekeeping units. The medical units were much more competent in English than other units, with 70% of doctors and nurses capable of noting down medical records and diagnose logs in English, probably due to the nature of their work and the better education they received. In comparison, more than 50% of staff officers were weak in writing and speaking English, which prevented them from clearly expressing their viewpoints in multilingual military meetings and composing reports in English. The engineering unit personnel were troubled by an overall low level of English proficiency. Nearly 96% of them were unable to communicate efficiently at UN military meetings, 92% could not prepare official documents in English, and 83% encountered difficulties in reading English documents. They depended on interpreters and translators for communication with foreign troops.

To function properly, the CMUHU also required translation and interpreting services to facilitate communication with UNAMID headquarters, units from other troop-contributing nations and local personnel. Accordingly, a liaison team of six linguists (including Wei Zerong, Mou Shancheng, and Liu Guangcai) was recruited to provide linguistic and other support for the Chinese helicopter unit (Wei 2021). Four members of the team from military universities had rich experience in teaching university students English for military purposes and in training foreign military personnel; the rest two from military forces were skilled in peacekeeping interpreting and translation as well as large-scale joint international military exercises.

A basic qualification for Chinese peacekeeping liaison officers is to pass at least the College English Test Level 6 in China (CET 6), a test that is essentially equivalent to the Test of English as a Foreign Language. For example, Wei was an undergraduate and postgraduate of Sichuan International Studies University and passed the Test for English Majors (Band 8), which is much more difficult than CET 6. Wei's linguistic competence gained him access to CMUHU, the first overseas Chinese helicopter unit that prioritised English-major graduates when selecting liaison officers. Despite this proficiency in English and Chinese, Wei and his liaison team members required further intensive pre-deployment and in-mission training.

4.3 Training programmes for general United Nations peacekeepers

Before we move to the training of liaison officers for CMUHU, it is necessary to overview the training programmes required of UN peacekeepers as a whole. The UN Department of Peace Operations attaches great importance to the training for all civilian, military and police personnel engaging in PKOs. According to their official website, there are three types of training programmes: pre-deployment, in mission and functional.

Pre-deployment training (generic, specialised and, where appropriate, mission specific) is based on UN standards and takes place before being deployed. pre-deployment training is delivered by member-state trainers to all military and police personnel or units in their home countries and by the UN Integrated Training Service (ITS) for civilian personnel up to the director (D-1) level. According to the General Assembly Resolution A/RES/49/37 (1995), member states have the responsibility to deliver pre-deployment training for uniformed personnel deploying to UN operations, whereas ITS is responsible for developing training materials and offering guidance and assistance to member states. ITS prepared the Core Pre-Deployment Training Materials (CPTM), which aim to promote a shared understanding of the fundamental principles, concepts, guidelines and policies of UN peacekeeping that guide personnel as they carry out critical tasks. In other words, CPTM represents the essential knowledge required by all peacekeeping personnel to function effectively in UN PKOs. The materials are a core resource for any UN pre-deployment training course. In 2017, CPTM was updated with a strengthened curriculum that included cross-cutting themes and priorities, such as conduct and discipline, sexual exploitation and abuse, the protection of civilians, human rights, gender mainstreaming, conflict-related sexual violence, child protection, safety and security, stress management, and environmental protection.

In-mission training refers to all training activities and learning initiatives undertaken after deployment by military, police or civilian peacekeeping personnel. It includes mission-specific induction training and ongoing training. The Mission-Specific Induction Training Standards are mandatory for all peacekeeping personnel; they are delivered on arrival to equip incoming personnel with knowledge of important issues and the information required to facilitate both their early integration into the system and the commencement of early support to mission operations. It is worth noting that ITS, in collaboration with subject specialists and mission trainers, has developed self-paced online courses that can be studied by new staff prior to mission entry or as part of the induction training package.

Ongoing training activities are undertaken during duty assignment, subsequent to induction at headquarters or in a peacekeeping mission. They may include "refresher" training to reinforce previous individual or collective training and on-the-job training to address gaps in attributes, skills, and knowledge or enhance skills in different areas and at different stages of deployment. Ongoing training is based on individual, mission or organisational needs. There are a number of listed mandatory courses that all staff members must take, including uniformed personnel.

Functional training is delivered by ITS teams for different peacekeeping-personnel categories in accordance with General Assembly Resolution A/RES/49/37 (1995). It comprises specialised, reinforcement and leadership training. The target audience of this specialised training is military decision-makers, staff officers and tactical-level unit leaders. Specialised training aims to improve the skills required for effective performance in peace operations for specific functions or employment categories. Reinforcement training is targeted at a specific category of deployed personnel or personnel deployed in missions mandated to carry out tasks related to this area. Leadership training is delivered to enhance the knowledge and skills of actual or potential senior peace-operations leaders.

ITS has developed a comprehensive training package that is to be applied in both pre-deployment and in-mission training, which combines conceptual, legal and operational frameworks for specific type units. For instance, the UN Specialised Training Materials cover a number of areas, such as force-headquarters support, military aviation, engineers, logistics, police, riverine, signals, special forces and transport. They are used to design both small exercises and complex scenario-based exercises, which can be run at the end of a course to strengthen participants' understanding of how to better operate in a UN peacekeeping environment. The ITS recommends that personnel receiving this training must be proficient in basic military tasks (individually and collectively) at the tactical and technical levels. It is also recommended that instructors develop and implement an initial written test and final test (post-instruction) to reinforce the learning objectives and evaluate participant training level/knowledge. It shall be noted that, when designing a particular course, trainers must adapt these materials to the needs of their audience. Accordingly, the duration of training courses may vary greatly. Training may vary for different units from different countries based on priorities and resources. However, some fundamental training methods are suggested: training should be interactive and encourage trainee participation; training should be mission specific; mission examples from deployed trainees are welcome; and training methodology should be based on practice.

As an integral part of UN peacekeeping personnel, liaison officers should, at the very least, receive the mandatory training courses requested and planned by the ITS. However, at present, no specific interpreting and translation courses are provided and prepared by the ITS, which leaves significant room for improvement with respect to the training of liaison officers, interpreters, or translators participating in PKOs. Ruiz Rosendo and Persaud (2019) investigated interpreter positionality in PKOs in the Bosnian War and found out that specific training programmes were required to better train interpreters; they also suggested that consideration should be given to the issue of how better to train peacekeeping forces to work with interpreters.

China attaches great importance to the training of its UN peacekeepers. In June 2009, the Peacekeeping Affairs Centre of the Ministry of National Defence of China was established in Beijing, which is responsible for peacekeeping training, research, and international cooperation for China's armed forces. As of 2020, China has provided 20 training programmes to over 1,500 peacekeepers from more than 60 countries, covering civilian protection and courses for senior mission officials, military observers, staff officers, trainers, and female officers (The State Council Information Office of China, 2020). The Chinese Ministry of Public Security has also trained more than 1,000 foreign peacekeeping police officers. These training programmes have laid a solid foundation for the training of liaison officers.

A number of textbooks have been compiled for the training programmes targeted at Chinese peacekeepers as a whole. These textbooks include *Military English for UNPK* (Liu 1997), *Observation Course for UNM* (Liu 1998), *Communication Course for UNPKOS* (Liu, 2003), *English for UN CHINTPT* (Wu 2014), *A Writing Course for Peacekeeping Police* (He 2014), and *English for Peacekeeping Contingents* (Wu 2020). These textbooks cover a wide range of PKO topics. Although none of these textbooks are designed for liaison officers, they are nevertheless valuable resources.

4.4 Training Chinese liaison officers in peacekeeping operations

UNAMID liaison officers must be properly trained before deployment. According to Zhao Chuang (2016), a former Chinese liaison officer who worked for the UN Mission in Liberia, the position of liaison officer is one of the most important in UN peacekeeping forces, as they are responsible for communication between UN peacekeeping forces and its leading organs, friendly neighbouring forces, local government, and citizens. In general, qualified liaison officers create favourable conditions for peacekeeping forces to accomplish their tasks. The qualifications required of a liaison officer fall into four categories: linguistic competence, military skill, UN regulations, and diplomatic capability.

First, a liaison officer will sometimes performs military operations in conflict, or in quasi-war scenarios. Due to the nature of this work, they are often ordered to leave the camp and perform duties independently, and, therefore, they shall be proficient in basic military skills (e.g., light-weapons firing, armed swimming, and weight-bearing cross-country exercise). Moreover, they must be able to drive a variety of vehicles in complex road conditions, and skilfully use UN communication equipment. A liaison officer must have good military literacy and vigorous and enterprising military spirit to unite friendly forces and, in some cases, deter potential enemies. Second, since Chinese peacekeepers usually need linguistic aid in many important situations, liaison officers are often expected to have the competence to undertake interpreting tasks (conference, escort, and whispering interpreting) and translation (of reports and memorandums). This demands high-level bilingual competence, and skills of interpreting and translation. Third, a liaison officer shall abide by UN Standard Operating Procedure (SOP) and the local laws of the country where the peacekeepers are deployed. Consequently, a liaison officer needs to study and master the UN SOP and gain an understanding of the laws of the host country. All UN PKOs must be performed in accordance with SOP regulations, and all tasks related to local people shall be completed while complying with local laws. Fourth, liaison officers need to be upright, respectable and open-minded peace ambassadors or military diplomats. They shall firmly defend UN interests (and the interests of the motherland) and be able to refuse any unlawful, unjust, or unreasonable requests. Moreover, they are expected to be well-versed in international relations and maintain positive or friendly relations with other contributing countries. In essence, they are supposed to help communication or exchange with other UN departments, local governments, and people within their capabilities.

The aforementioned qualifications summarised by Zhao (2016) provide a guide for us to understand the training of Chinese helicopter-unit liaison officers for the UNAMID. The sections below explore the training that CMUHU liaison officers received. After being recruited, Wei and his team members were sent to a Beijing-based brigade to receive training so as to improve their skills in linguistic, military, legal, and regulation. The training was first given from March 2016 to August 2017 in Beijing and again shortly after being deployed at the El Fasher super camp in Darfur.

4.4.1 Training in military skills

Although liaison officers undertake different tasks and duties than other CMUHU members, they should as well have a good command of military skills. In Beijing, liaison officers received one-year military training instructed by the commander of the peacekeeping helicopter unit, including physical training, light-arms shooting, gun disassembly, battlefield rescue, and casualty evacuation. They learnt how to complete routine PKO tasks and how to deal with emergencies. The military training lasted more than a year (from March 2016 to August 2017), as it was the first time that China deployed a helicopter unit overseas. Each week, there were well-designed regular training classes for peacekeeping helicopter units and corresponding tests. Training materials including battlefield rescue manuals were used, and the trainees were required to practice what they had learnt. The training in military skills was consistent with the ITS requirements of pre-deployment training and in-mission training.

4.4.2 Training in flight attendant skills

CMUHU liaison officers were also entrusted with the task of flight attendants. As a result, they needed to learn how to perform attendant duties after becoming acquainted with aviation procedures. In Beijing, they studied materials such as *The United Nations Peacekeeping Missions Military Aviation Unit Manual*, which elaborated on various requirements for helicopter units to perform PKOs as well as on whole-crew capabilities and training standards. Training based on the manual was relatively simple, as information was lacking concerning the abilities and standards of flight attendants.

However, when the CMUHU was deployed in Darfur, the in-mission training for liaison officers directed by UN aviation departments became more specific and rigorous almost in accordance with the requirements of flight attendants in civil aviation. Such training for liaison officers in Darfur was offered by China air stewardesses by means of video conference. As Wei (2021, 4) recalls:

> The stewardess was the wife of a pilot in our unit, who was pregnant at that time. Due to the six-hour time difference between Sudan and China, the teaching and learning process faced many inconveniences and challenges. However, with tremendous efforts by the trainer and trainees, satisfactory results were finally achieved. Six liaison officers passed the flight attendant test in the Aviation Department of UNAMID at one time

4.4.3 Training in linguistic competence

Interpreting and translation skills are vital for liaison officers in UN peacekeeping units. Wei and his CMUHU teammates received only translation training in the form of internships; since they were highly proficient in English and Chinese, they did not need further training in English and Chinese for common purposes.

The training in translation skills was, for the most part, finished during the Beijing session. The liaison team translated peacekeeping documents of 500,000 words in total, which involved translating in both directions – from and into Chinese. Before performing PKOs, a number of English documents were required by the UN: common documents required of all peacekeeping units and specific documents for special tasks of each unit. For example, the CMUHU liaison team translated into English flight manuals and pilot maintenance records required by the helicopter unit to give to UN peacekeeping agencies. To provide the reference for CMUHU personnel, documents in English from UN peacekeeping organisations, such as SOP related to air traffic control, were translated into Chinese within a limited time frame. As Wei (2021, 4) remarks:

> During the intensive training in Beijing, our unit received two inspections by UN officers, to make sure various English signs on peacekeeping equipment meet UN standards and our unit can provide relevant documents and instructions in English as required by UN agencies. These materials essential for the proper functioning of our unit were translated by our liaison team. Such translation practice is very helpful to the improvement of subject-specific English-Chinse interpreting and translation capability.

Similarly, training in interpreting was conducted in the field instead of the classroom. Since the CMUHU was the first Chinese helicopter unit in UN PKOs, earnest long-term preparation was conducted, which attracted intense international attention. When UN officials and foreign guests visited Beijing, they made special inspections to CMUHU training. Such inspections offered liaison officers an internship to improve their interpreting skills. As Wei (2021, 4–5) recalls:

> Our team have interpreted for the inspections by UN undersecretary general for peacekeeping affairs Su He and then Secretary General Ban Ki Moon. We also accompanied and interpreted for guests and ambassadors from Germany, New Zealand and other countries who visited CMUHU and introduced the peacekeeping equipment for them. As an interpreter, I felt very honored to have the opportunity to introduce them China's helicopters and peacekeeping missions that we were going to perform in near future.

In addition to visits by UN officials and foreign guests, the liaison team was responsible for interpreting various meetings held by the UN check team in Beijing. Specialized subject knowledge and the local accent of inspectors posed both challenges and opportunities for liaison officers. Frequently, liaison officers would offer interpreting services for UN personnel in daily life. Wei (2021, 5) pointed out the benefits of providing linguistic aid for the visits, meetings and daily life:

For instance, a UN inspector from Sweden stayed in Beijing for a month and each week he went to the helicopter unit to evaluate and guide our preparation for peacekeeping equipment. We worked together and had meals together, which was very helpful for us in improving communication skills in foreign languages. Further, such experiences have broadened our horizons, added to our knowledge in military equipment, enriched our translation experience, and laid a good foundation for us to participate in overseas PKOs.

4.4.4 Training in United Nations laws and regulations

Before performing tasks, every peacekeeper (including liaison officers) was expected to secure a good understanding of UN PKO-related laws and regulations, including the rules of engagement, traffic rules, civil military relations, zero tolerance of sexual exploitation and abuse, as well as the SPO for peacekeeping units. These regulations were studied by the CMUHU during the Beijing-based training. More detailed training was provided by the training staff from UNAMID headquarters after the CMUHU was deployed in super camps in Darfur. In most cases, the training process was assisted by liaison officers who would interpret lectures during the training sessions and translate relevant documents afterwards. Training materials, especially the CPTM, were used to introduce the rules of engagement or civil military relations. Training in UN regulations and procedures helped liaison officers in behaving legally and ethically.

4.4.5 Training in cross-cultural communication

Like other peacekeepers in the CMUHU, liaison officers also received training courses during the Beijing session to improve their cross-culture communication skills. Instructors taught lectures concerning Sudan, including its culture, religion, customs, politics, economy, geography, and education. The six-hour course taught Sudan-deployed peacekeepers how to communicate with the local people effectively. In addition, these training programmes also provided psychological counselling for peacekeepers who would face uncertainties and clashes in an unfamiliar environment.

4.4.6 Liaison officers as instructors

Fundamental skills of communication in English is a basic requirement of UN peacekeeping forces. In UN assessments, a key criterion is the English listening and speaking ability of pilots and flight attendants, including conversation in English during helicopter fight and in daily life contexts. As mentioned above, other CMUHU members, especially pilots who had to frequently communicate and cooperate with other UN peacekeeping units or agencies, were required to improve their English speaking and writing capabilities.

The linguistic training for pilots was completed by liaison officers within the unit during their Beijing session. The liaison team conducted a questionnaire survey to understand the level of English proficiency and then prepared teaching plans and manuals for different groups, after which they provided daily intensive training courses in oral English to prepare pilots for future PKOs and exchanges in daily life occasions. To evaluate the effect of training, liaison officers conducted regular in-class tests for pilots with a focus on oral English in daily life and aviation situations (Wei 2021, 6).

While teaching the pilots English for aviation purposes, liaison officers stressed that some English words should be pronounced in a different manner due to the unique working conditions of pilots. Change in pronunciation was necessary because it would reduce listening mistakes in a noisy flight environment. For example, the number "3" was read in a loud voice as "tree" instead of "three," and the number "9" was read aloud as "niner" instead of "nine."

The CMUHU pilots were not confident in their English proficiency before the training started. However, they were enthusiastic about the PKOs and highly motivated and diligent in the training process. Finally, they made rapid progress and passed the assessment by a UN agency. According to Wei (2021, 6), "the training program presented a challenge to our teaching skills and improved our capability in using English. We were very proud that, on the whole, the training program ran smooth."

4.5 Roles of Chinese liaison officers

In the middle of August 2017, the CMUHU was deployed in Darfur, Sudan, where the liaison team played multiple roles for the peacekeeping mission in the conflict-ridden zone, including interpreter and flight attendant.

4.5.1 Working as interpreters and translators

The main task of a liaison officer was to provide interpreting and translation services for the following groups: CMUHU officers and soldiers deployed in Darfur, UNAMID officials, personnel from other peacekeeping troop-contributing countries and the local people in Darfur. The main purpose of interpreting and translation was to ensure communication and cooperation between CMUHU and other units, to help the CMUHU understand the mission mandates enacted by the UNAMID and to report the work of the CMUHU to the UNAMID. For example, the UNAMID would conduct quarterly inspections on peacekeeping units, including inspecting the CMUHU major equipment (e.g., helicopters [at the airport] and self-sustainment equipment [all facilities in the Chinese camp]). Liaison officers translated notices and requirements concerning the inspections and made reports to the unit commander. When the UN inspection team visited the Chinese camp, liaison officers provided translation and interpreting services for short preliminary meetings, group inspections, and summary meetings.

In the CMUHU, six liaison officers had a heavy workload of translation and interpreting. Facing To cope with a rather tight schedule, they had a general division of labour: some were responsible for the translation of logistics support, some interpreted in meetings for the unit commander, and some translated documents about transportation, medical treatment and the like. Whenever there was a complicated task, the liaison team helped each other in close cooperation. In most cases, Wei was responsible for translating and processing official emails, interpreting for UN officers when they visited the camp and interpreting for training courses in the classroom.

Liaison officers worked in both directions between English and Chinese. On the one hand, they translated relevant materials prepared by the CMUHU into English for UN agencies, including flight manuals, operation manuals, and maintenance records of other peacekeeping equipment. On the other hand, they translated into Chinese a large number of peacekeeping laws and regulations, SOPs, and security situation reports handed out by the UNAMID. For example, *The Manual for Military Aviation Units in United Nations Peacekeeping Missions* was translated before it was used as a reference. *The Assessment Report on Recent Attacks in the First Theater*, was also translated into Chinese to inform the unit of the critical conditions in Darfur. Some materials translated by the liaison officers are now used as training materials for Chinese peacekeeping personnel deployed in different missions. In addition, a large number of emails and messages sent through the local network between the super camps in Darfur were translated to ensure the fulfillment of tasks.

Translation was required more than interpreting in the beginning of the CMUHU PKOs in Darfur. Liaison officers provided full translation of the information requested and provided by the UN. When there was no flight mission, they handled official mails from UN agencies in a timely manner. Some emails contained long assessment reports or peace agreements, which required full and accurate translation so as to help the unit commander make reasonable judgments of the situation. As Wei (2021, 7) stated:

> When I was in the camp, I worked as a translator. My work included receiving, sending and translating UN peacekeeping emails; Called as "chief translator on duty" by the unit, I was responsible for proof-reading and revision before the final versions of all translations were made.

In later periods, interpreting was required more than translation. Escort interpreting took place in most cases, consecutive interpreting occasionally and simultaneous interpretation rarely. Liaison officers provided escort interpreting when there was oral or less official communication between the CMUHU commander and personnel from UN agencies or the units of other contributing countries. Consecutive interpretation was offered for formal meetings, most of which were large in size. Mu Shancheng, who was experienced in training foreign forces, interpreted most of the important meetings. When other members of the unit went out of the camp to perform tasks, Wei would go along and provide linguistic aid. When foreign troops visited or gave lectures in the camp, Wei acted as an escort or classroom interpreter. In August 2017, when guests from the UN aviation department visited for the first time after the unit arrived at the El Fasher super camp, Wei (2021) offered consecutive interpreting into English while Liu Guangcai interpreted into Chinese. As Wei (2021) remembers he had only one case of Simultaneous interpretation during his stay in Darfur, which took place when the first CMUHU batch held a medal-giving ceremony before ending the PKO in Sudan. Chang Yang was the interpreter when the CMUHU commander and Joint Special Representative (the highest rank officer of UNAMID) delivered speeches in Chinese and English, respectively.

One of the great challenges that CMUHU liaison officers faced was a large number of terms used in military, aviation and helicopter settings and the extensive use of abbreviations for these terms, especially in emails. Liaison officers were required to maintain consistency when translating the terms and their abbreviations, and, from time to time, they would use specially designed software for military terminology or consult e-dictionaries. For instance, the term "unit" appearing in peacekeeping materials was translated into "分队" in many cases; the word "mounted" was sometimes translated into "车载的." Taking another example, there are three abbreviations in the notice "Kenya MP coy team to arrive [at the] transit camp by 08:45 hrs": MP, coy and hrs. MP (military police) should be translated into "宪兵/纠察," coy (company) into "连" and hrs (hours) into "小时."

Another challenge was the local accents or dialects of UN peacekeepers, who came from different parts of the world. Their pronunciation of English words, greatly influenced by their mother tongue, sounded somewhat strange and brought about difficulties in interpreting. During the training in Beijing, because of the strong accent of a UN inspector from Argentina, the interpreting was laborious at the beginning, but, after several rounds of contact, it became easier. To facilitate communication, the interpreting was often accompanied by gestures, facial expressions, and/or pictures.

The third challenge that liaison officers encountered was disparities in linguistic expression. When Chinese peacekeeping liaison officers spoke English, they prioritised grammar; long, complicated sentences; and formal language. However, local employees and peacekeepers from many other countries in the super camp spoke succinctly and sometimes neglected English norms, resulting in a number of obstacles for interpreting and communication. In addition, an object can be referred to by different names in different languages. For instance, an UN inspector once came to Chinese barracks to check the communication equipment; he used the noun "plate" when referring to an antenna, while CMUHU personnel usually called it "锅盖" (pot cover), which sometimes led to difficulties in interpreting. Wei (2021, 9) reflected that:

When I was talking to a local black employee at El Fasher airport, he came up with some broken sentences which confused me, and he didn't know what I was talking about either. Later, we managed to come across some key words, then with gestures and guesses, we finally reached mutual understanding.

Another difficulty for liaison officers was the harsh working environment. The indoor working setting was acceptable because peacekeeping units had their own barracks, usually built with containers, but the outdoor environment were tough. Darfur is well-known for its harsh natural conditions and tropical desert climate, with an annual average temperature of 35 centigrade and frequent sandstorms. The effect of interpreting was severely undermined by the dark winds and devastating sandstorms. During the helicopter flight, liaison officers found it difficult to interpret because the cabin was narrow, muggy, and noisy; usually filled with a heavy fuel smell, and the helicopter itself was rather shaky due to air turbulence. To ensure communication, the helicopter pilots, passengers, and flight attendants had to wear headphones and relied frequently on body language and concise words. In addition, Darfur was plagued with frequent social turmoils and unrests; burnings, killings, and looting were commonplace.

4.5.2 Working as flight attendants

Liaison officers also acted as flight attendants. According to the regulations of the UNAMID aviation department, when a helicopter took off for a mission, four crew members were required on board: captain, co-pilot, air mechanic and flight attendant. The main responsibilities of flight attendants were to ensure the safety of people on board, and helicopters and to help the crew, passengers, and transportation management personnel communicate, sometimes by interpreting and other times by talking to foreign troops directly. In addition, liaison officers sent patients to secondary hospitals, borrowed vehicles from the transportation department, and worked with the supply or aviation department.

4.6 Conclusion

Our case study on CMUHU liaison officers deployed in Darfur has showcased that interpreting and translation play a critical role in the success of Chinese PKOs in conflict zones. As the English proficiency of most personnel in Chinese peacekeeping units was insufficient to communicate freely in formal occasions with UNAMID agencies as well as with friendly units from other troop-contributing countries and local personnel, the need for interpreting and translation was constant and great. Therefore, such demand for linguistic aid was satisfied by liaison officers who received training before deployment and in mission.

To prepare liaison officers for interpreting and translation and the duty of flight attendants, training courses longer than one year were offered in Beijing and in Darfur that demonstrated several positive traits. First, they followed the major ITS framework and training materials were complied in accordance UN requirements for mandatory training. Second, the training programmes were generic, as they were designed for peacekeeping personnel, civilians, the military, and the police, and they covered a wide range of issues included in UN pre-deployment specially in-mission training and functional training: military skills, linguistic competence, UN peacekeeping-related laws or regulations, and cross-cultural communication. Third, the training courses were interactive and practice few lectures were specially oriented, as liaison officers finished many translating and interpreting tasks in real life situations. Last but not least, judging from the afterward performance of CMUHU liaison officers in Darfur, the training programme was effective and well-designed for the most part.

However, there was much room for improvement if we consider the challenges liaison officers encountered. First, the training programme was not designed to improve their methods of interpreting and translation, since no focus was placed on guiding liaison officers in dealing with different types of interpreting and translation tasks in conflict scenarios. Issues concerning interpreter identity, ethics, and norms should be included as well. Second, cutting-edge technologies and tailored teaching methods should have been used; peacekeeping bilingual corpus should be established and utilised in the classroom and later in mission. Computer-aided translation tools and post-machine-translation editing techniques can be included to improve programme efficiency. Last but not least, instructors highly experienced in interpreting and translating for PKOs should be invited to facilitate effective down-to-earth training methods. With the above-mentioned issues properly addressed and with more resources and efforts invested, the training for China's peacekeeping liaison officers or interpreters is expected to experience a remarkable progress in the near future.

Acknowledgements

This work was supported by the National Social Science Foundation of China under Grant Number 17BYY200.

References

Baker, Catherine. 2012. "When Bosnia was a Commonwealth Country: British Forces and Their Interpreters in Republika Srpska 1995–2007." In *Languages and the Military: Alliances, Occupation and Peace Building*, edited by Hilary Footitt, and Michael Kelly, 100–114. Basingstoke and New York: Palgrave Macmillan.

Footitt, Hilary, and Michael Kelly. 2012. *Languages at War: Policies and Practices of Language Contacts in Conflict*. Basingstoke and New York: Palgrave Macmillan.

He, Ying. ed. 2014. *A Writing Course for Peacekeeping Police*. Beijing: People's Public Security University. [何银主编. 2014. 维和警察写作教程. 北京: 中国人民公安大学出版社.]

Kelly, Michael, and Catherine Baker. 2013. *Interpreting the Peace, Peace Operations, Conflict and Language in Bosnia-Herzegovina.* Basingstoke and New York: Palgrave Macmillan.

Li, Hongqian. 2009. "A Study on the Status of Chinese Military Peace-Keepers: Foreign Language Training and Their Language Proficiency-Taking UNIFIL as an Example." *Journal of Higher Education Research* 2: 38–40. [李洪乾. 2009.中国军事维和人员外语技能培养现状及其途径研究：以UNIFIL为例. *高等教育研究学报* 2: 38–40.]

Liu, Zhao. 1997. *Military English for UNPK.* Beijing: Military Translation Press. [刘钊. 1997. 联合国维持和平行动英语. 北京: 军事译文出版社]

Liu, Zhao. 1998. *Observation Course for UNM.* Beijing: Military Translation Press. [刘钊. 1998. 联合国军事观察员观察教程. 北京: 军事译文出版社.]

Liu, Zhao. 2003. *Communication Course for UNPKOS.* Beijing: Military Translation Press. [刘钊. 2003. 联合国维持和平行动通信教程. 北京: 军事译文出版社.]

Mu, Lei, and Xiangbing Wang. 2014. "Military Translation Research: Present and Future." *Foreign Languages Research* 1: 79–83. [穆雷、王祥兵. 2014.军事翻译研究的现状与展望. *外语研究* (1), 79–83.]

Ruiz Rosendo, Lucía, and Clementina Persaud. 2019. "On the Front Line: Mediating across Languages and Cultures in Peacekeeping Operations." *Armed Forces & Society* 45 (3): 472–490.

State Council Information Office of China. 2020. *China's Armed Forces: 30 Years of UN Peacekeeping Operations* (white paper book). Beijing: Foreign Languages Press.

UN Department of Peace Operations. 2021. UNAMID FACT SHEET https://peacekeeping.un.org/en/mission/unamid.

Wei, Zerong. 2021. "*Interview on Liaison Officers in China's Helicopter Unit for UN Peacekeeping Mission in Darfur*" by Tian Luo, 1–13. Chongqing, China. March 18–20.

Wu, Tong. eds. 2014. *English for UN CHINTPT.* Tianjing: Tianjing Science & Technology Translation & Publishing Co. Ltd. [吴彤主编. 2014. 维和运输分队实用英语. 天津: 天津科技翻译出版有限公司.]

Wu, Tong. eds. 2020. *English for Peacekeeping Contingents.* Tianjing: Science & Technology Translation & Publishing Co. Ltd. [吴彤主编. 2020. 维和分队实用英语. 天津: 天津科技翻译出版公司.]

Zhao, Chuang. 2016. "Three Abilities Required for Liaison Officer of UN Peacekeeping Forces." *The Guide of Science and Education* 8: 137–138. [赵闯. 2016. 联合国维和部队联络官应具备的三种能力. *科教导刊* (8):137–138.]

Zhang, Jian, and Ping Li. 2018. "Chinese Liaison Officers in UN Peacekeeping missions." *Army News* 17. [张健、李萍. 2018. 维和也精彩！谈谈走出国门的那些事儿. *陆军新闻*. 10月 17日]

PART II

Training interpreters in the context of international organisations and tribunals

5

DEVELOPING INTERPRETER COMPETENCE

Training interpreters servicing UNOG field missions

Alma Barghout and Lucía Ruiz Rosendo

This chapter will provide an overview of outreach and training activities provided by the United Nations Office at Geneva (UNOG) for interpreters servicing field missions. The United Nations (UN) has been present in the field since its inception, often with the assistance of interpreters. Since work in the field is very different from interpreting in UN conference settings, UNOG has organised a series of training activities aimed at addressing specific challenges encountered in the field. This contribution is part of ongoing mixed-methods research based on semi-structured interviews, focus groups, and surveys involving the participants of different training activities and UNOG's management and that aims to validate the effectiveness of said training initiatives. Drawing on the findings of this research, as well as on our experience as interpreters in the field and as interpreter trainers, we will discuss the following aspects in this chapter: the particularities of UN field missions; the functioning and the contents of the different training activities; and the need to design training activities that take the particularities of UN field missions into account. Our findings show that these programmes helped the participants to feel better equipped to face the challenges of interpreting in the field.

5.1 Introduction

Since the turn of the century, there has been an increasing awareness of the role of interpreters in conflict zones and expanding scholarly literature on the topic (see Ruiz Rosendo 2020 for a detailed literature review). Current academic interest is due to factors such as the greater visibility of interpreters and the increasing need for linguistic and cultural mediation in conflict and post-conflict situations. However, there remain few studies specifically addressing how interpreting skills are acquired in these settings; this hinders the comprehension of how interpreters develop their skills in the field. Moreover, there are ethical, cultural, and professional issues raised

DOI: 10.4324/9781003230359-7

by the involvement of untrained interpreters in conflicts; these issues have yet to be explored by academic institutions (Tipton 2011; Ruiz Rosendo 2022).

There are different categories of interpreters who work in these challenging contexts: untrained civilian interpreters working for the military, who are usually hired because they speak the relevant languages but who have not previously acquired the necessary skills to interpret adequately; untrained interpreters who are recruited by humanitarian organisations, such as the International Committee for the Red Cross (ICRC) or the United Nations High Commissioner for Refugees (UNHCR) (see Delgado Luchner and Kherbiche 2019); and military linguists, that is to say, military personnel who work as interpreters in the field. These latter interpreters are, first and foremost, military personnel, and as such they follow the principles and rules that apply to the military. Interpreters in the first two categories are people who happen to end up interpreting, rather than interpreters who happen to work in the military or the humanitarian field. There is yet another category of interpreters that has not been extensively studied (i.e., interpreters who work as professional interpreters at an international organisation, such as the United Nations [UN]) and who are deployed on mission to the field in what Tesseur and Footitt (2019) define as post-conflict scenarios. The main difference between this group and the others is that these interpreters have received specific training in conference interpreting and are acquainted with the ethical principles and values that apply to it (Ruiz Rosendo and Barea Muñoz 2017). They also differ in another respect: whereas locally recruited interpreters are often depicted, in various narratives, as belonging to a specific group that could potentially be considered the enemy and are therefore distrusted by different actors involved in the conflict (Packer 2007; Baker 2010), these professional interpreters are initially and generally considered by the users to be more reliable and trustworthy interlocutors, inasmuch as they are considered actors embedded in the organisation.

Whilst these professionals may be familiar with international organisations, work in the field is very different from interpreting in UN conference settings and requires additional skills. Interestingly, UN interpreters have rarely been trained for interpreting in this context (Ruiz Rosendo et al. 2021). In this sense, they share the lack of context-specific training that affects other categories of interpreters, and which has been remarked upon by some scholars (Baigorri Jalón 2011; Bos and Soeters 2006; Kelly and Baker 2013). Indeed, these authors have stated that there is little specific training for interpreters working in the field and that the necessary knowledge and skills have to be acquired through experience. Since interpreting is a situated practice (i.e., it depends on the context and setting in which it is practiced [Ruiz Rosendo 2021]), it is difficult (and probably inefficient) to design generic training schemes that do not take the particularities of the context into consideration. Along these lines, Todorova (2021, 311) argues that there is a real need "for specialised training that corresponds to the specific roles that [interpreters] perform and addresses the specific contexts in which they perform their duties." Indeed, this is one of the issues identified by Todorova and Ruiz Rosendo (2021) in their publication.

Against this backdrop, the object of inquiry in the present article concerns the nature of learning and the training programmes organised by the United Nations Office at Geneva (UNOG) to help conference interpreters acquire the necessary skills to work in the field. We draw on the analysis of the different initiatives organised and on data stemming from an ongoing mixed-methods research project based on semi-structured interviews, focus groups, and surveys involving the participants of different training activities and UNOG's management, and that aims to validate the effectiveness of said training initiatives.

With this chapter our purpose is to make two key contributions. Firstly, we aim to provide further evidence of the situated nature of learning in interpreting. Secondly, our intention is to highlight the difficulty of adopting a one-size-fits-all approach to interpreter training in the field, given the particularities of each context and the impact they have on the work undertaken by interpreters.

5.2 Context of UN field missions

The United Nations has an important presence in almost all countries around the world: in addition to the UN main duty stations in New York, Geneva, Vienna, and Nairobi, there are five Regional Commissions that have been established by different resolutions of the Economic and Social Council to promote regional development: Economic Commission for Africa (ECA); Economic Commission for Europe (ECE); Economic Commission for Latin America and the Caribbean (ECLAC); Economic and Social Commission for Asia and the Pacific (ESCAP); and Economic and Social Commission for Western Asia (ESCWA). The UN also has a large network of agencies and programmes. For example, the United Nations Development Programme (UNDP) has offices in 170 countries. Given that the UN has six official languages (English, French, Spanish, Russian, Arabic, and Chinese), for the smooth running of the UN's work, meetings and conferences, almost all UN agencies and entities make use of conference interpreters.

Interpreters, therefore, play essential roles in the multilingual character of the UN. There are two main categories of interpreters: staff members and freelance interpreters, who are recruited on a short-term basis for temporary assistance. These interpreters do not only work at the different headquarters, agencies, and offices around the world but are also deployed on field missions. Apart from peacekeeping operations, for which interpreters usually accompany national military contingents, the largest number of missions to the field are serviced by UNOG. A field mission is "where a team of interpreters accompanies a UN mission to locations outside of the four UN duty stations and which does not take place in a conference setting" (Ruiz Rosendo et al. 2021, 452). Most missions are conducted by the Special Procedures of the Human Rights Council (HRC), whose mandate-holders include Special Rapporteurs, Working Groups, and Independent Experts. Other missions include UN Commissions of Inquiry and Fact-Finding Missions and Investigations, which are established by the Security Council, the General Assembly, the HRC, its predecessor, the Commission on Human Rights, as well as country visits by the Secretary-General and the High Commissioner for Human Rights or their representatives. Their main purpose is to respond to situations of serious violations of International Humanitarian Law and International Human Rights Law and to promote accountability for such violations and to counter impunity (OHCHR n.d.).

UNOG has become a centre of excellence for servicing field missions due to its long experience and the fact that it hosts the Human Rights Council and the Office of the High Commissioner for Human Rights (OHCHR). This information was confirmed in a qualitative study[1] we carried out in 2020 that included semi-structured interviews with the senior management of the Division on Conference Management (DCM) and Chief Interpreters at multiple UN duty stations. They stated that Geneva is the duty station that services the majority of field missions and, consequently, recruits the highest number of interpreters to work in the field. To service these missions, interpreters are deployed from amongst the staff at duty stations, especially from UNOG for the reasons explained above, or they are recruited locally, regionally or internationally as freelance interpreters. To provide an idea of the number of field missions serviced and interpreters deployed by the UNOG Interpretation Service (IS), 96 missions were serviced with interpretation in 2017, with 27 UN staff interpreters and 175 freelance interpreters. In 2018, 90 missions were serviced with 22 staff interpreters and 163 freelance interpreters (see Ruiz Rosendo, Barghout and Martin 2021 for more information about field missions).

These interpreters, contrary to other categories of interpreters who work in the field in the context of humanitarian organisations or armed forces, are fully fledged conference interpreters who have passed a competitive examination, be it the former UN Language Competitive Examination (LCE) or the new Competitive Examination for Language Positions (CELP) for staff interpreters, or the freelance test, now named the Global Language Roster Examination. This attests that they do not need any training in languages or interpreting skills. However, over time, it has become increasingly evident that working in the field is entirely different to working in the booth, and interpreters face challenges they do not encounter at headquarters or in conference settings.

In terms of the interpreting skills, the main particularity of working in the field is the use of consecutive interpreting, voice-over, or interpreting with the *bidule* (a device composed of a wireless microphone and headsets for listeners, allowing for simultaneous interpretation without a booth). Indeed, interpreters work in different locations, such as a meeting room, a camp, a detention centre, a private house, an office, a hospital, or a tent, but rarely in a booth. Nevertheless, the real differences between working in the field and at headquarters are the settings, the environments, the security considerations, the working conditions, and being an integral part of the UN mission with all the ethical and psychological implications that this entails.

When deployed to the field, UN interpreters leave the safety of their booths in a conference setting and their comfort zone. Their working hours and conditions change radically. In the field, work can be unpredictable, spans very long hours, and involves a constant change of locations. Interpreters accompany the mission at all times and often travel long distances, at times in armoured vehicles. The mandate-holders or experts that the interpreters accompany usually hold meetings with government authorities, civil society, and individuals affected by the issues at hand. The subject matter can be very political and sensitive. It can also be very specialised, such as when meeting with prosecutors or judges. However, the most difficult work is often with the victims of human rights violations. The words in the statements that are interpreted over a microphone in a conference suddenly take life before the eyes of the interpreter in the field. Such interviews often present a tremendous emotional load (see Barea Muñoz 2021a, 2021b) as confirmed in the interviews conducted with senior management at DCM. Even though UN interpreters are professionals who know how to keep their calm and remain composed, they are not always equipped with the necessary coping mechanisms. Also, given that many of the situations they encounter are challenging and non-routine, making decisions when interpreting is not devoid of difficulties. This is because of the ethical implications of such encounters, which are not always reflected in the deontological codes governing the profession.

Even though there is usually a briefing with OHCHR colleagues before going to the field, this meeting does not actually prepare the interpreter to face such unfamiliar challenges. Consequently, prior to a mission, many consult with more experienced colleagues who have been deployed before them, preferably to the same country or to service the same mandate, as explained by chief interpreters in the interviews. Despite efforts by interpreters and others, all existing pre-field briefings fall short when it comes to preparing interpreters for these missions.

Given that work in the field is very different from interpreting in UN conference settings, and considering that Special Rapporteur missions are at the very heart of its mandate, over the last decade, UNOG has started to organise a series of training activities and initiatives aimed at addressing specific challenges encountered in the field, such as ethical, administrative, legal, security, and practical aspects, as well as psychological self-care.

5.3 Training interpreters to work in field missions

5.3.1 Paving the way: Initial steps

Whilst field missions had already been included in an outreach video (Isakov, n.d.) and in various presentations by experienced staff interpreters addressed to students from universities that have a Memorandum of Understanding with the UN (MoU universities), as well as students from non-MoU universities, it has only been in the last decade that the organisation has started to increasingly recognise the implications of interpreting in the field and to organise different initiatives, particularly after the DCM's recognition in 2013 of the psychological impact of field missions on interpreters. Indeed, given that field missions can take a toll on the interpreters, through exposure to horrific interviews on torture or violence against women, as well as first-hand experience of living conditions and human misery, DCM organised two courses in 2013 on "Mission Readiness and Wellness" for staff interpreters with the Staff Counsellor through the former Staff Development and Learning Section (SDLS), now called the Centre for Learning and Multilingualism (CLM). These self-care workshops helped UN interpreters to be more aware of the possible psychological implications of working in the field, including post-traumatic stress disorder (PTSD), and tips on preventing such consequences.

Another initial step was in the context of the induction courses organised by OHCHR for its rapid deployment roster. These periodic courses aim at preparing OHCHR staff to rapidly deploy when needed in the field. They are usually a week long and include one half-day session on working with interpreters. It is worth mentioning that similar sessions are also organised for newly appointed mandate-holders. For this purpose, senior staff interpreters were invited to give a presentation and answer questions on how to perform the required work when using the services of interpreters in the field, especially in interview settings. The last briefing, given by a senior interpreter to OHCHR, was in November 2019. Interpreters who participated in these sessions in the early stages noticed that the induction course for OHCHR colleagues included a session on psychological self-care. Upon the initiative of interpreters and with the agreement of the Chief of IS and of OHCHR, IS started sending a few interpreters to attend and benefit from this session every time it was held.

Despite the existence of these efforts, most initiatives have stemmed from the interpreters themselves. A case in point was a film that was recorded and edited by a senior staff interpreter at UNOG in 2018 (Osuna 2018). It is a collection of UNOG interpreters' testimonies that highlight some of the challenges and hardships encountered during Human Rights missions. The goal was to introduce interpretation students and other interested audiences to the world of Human Rights missions by presenting first-hand accounts of experiences in the field. In the film, staff interpreters speak candidly about the missions they have serviced and what they have entailed, as well as discussing the importance of preparation, including the subject matter and terminology, but also knowledge of the geography, history, political situation, and cultural sensitivities of the country concerned. They present practical tips on dealing with the long hours, difficult working conditions, and unfamiliar environments that are characteristic of field missions. Testimonies include real-life examples of the safety and security concerns that the interpreters encountered, some having found themselves in danger or even at gunpoint. Interpreters also mention the stress and psychological implications of such missions and present some coping mechanisms they have personally developed to deal with them.

In an interview that we conducted with the filmmaker in 2021, he explained that he made the film on his own initiative and on his own time to try and fill a gap in colleagues' preparation. He explained that interpreters do not know what to expect when they are first assigned to a field mission. Based on stories he had heard about the experiences of colleagues and his own field experience, he wanted to use the film to provide guidelines to interpreters on how to prepare for missions, how to behave in the field so as not to cross any red lines and not to get involved on a personal level with victims or give them unfounded hope. He also wanted to show the importance of interpreters remaining as objective as possible and provide insight on how to cope during and after a mission.

5.3.2 Fully-fledged courses

The increasing awareness of the challenges of interpreting in field missions materialised in the institutional organisation of a face-to-face course jointly organised by UNOG and the University of Geneva's Faculty of Translation and Interpreting (FTI) in January 2019 to attend to the needs of interpreters in challenging interpreting contexts, along the lines of the courses described by Bergunde and Pöllabauer (2019), Gez and Schuster (2018), and Delgado Luchner (2019) in their respective works. The general objective of the course was to provide training for permanent staff from all UNOG interpretation sections on the different practical matters and ethical, psychological, legal, administrative, and security implications when assigned to field missions.

The course combined interactive lectures and practical exercises and was divided into five components, each of them with specific expected outcomes: interpreting in the field; ethics and ethical situation management; psychological implications; legal and administrative implications; and security implications (for more information about the course, see Ruiz Rosendo et al. 2021). The pedagogical approach was fundamentally informed by situated learning and case-based learning (CBL), a method in which real case scenarios – drafted as problems that provide a background and supporting information – are used to integrate related concepts of professional practice, social behaviour, and ethics and to underpin and stimulate the acquisition of skills, knowledge and attitudes through collaborative learning. This means that one of the main elements of the course was the recurrent discussion of a series of case scenarios and the inclusion of role plays to discuss the role of the interpreter and the ethical implications of interpreting in some specific settings.

Regarding the procedure, the trainees were given a series of instructions before being given the case study material. They were asked to thoroughly read the case scenario and take into account some questions put forward by the trainers to guide their reading and analysis, which involved identifying what the dilemma was, what specific decision had to be made, who the stakeholders were, what the potential courses of action were and, most importantly, what the consequences of each course of action would be, along the lines of a teleological approach to ethics. The objective was to challenge the participants to grapple with the dilemma, formulate a decision, explain and defend that decision in order to elicit and test the ideas of the class, and ultimately gain a deeper understanding of the issues raised.

The trainers were practicing interpreters and interpreter trainers, senior interpreters, users of interpreting in the field, and subject matter experts (UN

Administrative staff, UN Security staff, experts in psychological health). The varied background of the session leaders in these activities testified to the different requirements of interpreters in different field situations, with the takeaway message that each situation encountered in the field must be considered individually.

Just after the completion of the course, the participants were asked to evaluate its effectiveness. A mixed-methods design was used, including questionnaires and focus groups. The findings showed that the course was considered to be essential to prepare for this kind of mission, particularly given its combination of academic and hands-on practical experiences through the theoretical presentations and the analysis of practical scenarios. The participants considered it essential that the trainers were professional interpreters with experience in working in UN field missions, as well as users and other stakeholders from the organisation or acquainted with the work it carries out.

Considering these findings and realising that the course contributed to filling a void in providing specific training to interpreters, UNOG management decided to build on this important step and organise further editions of this course. It was also planning on extending this training to include interpreters from other duty stations. Unfortunately, the onset of the COVID pandemic has delayed this work.

5.3.3 Integrating field missions in training schemes

After the UNOG-FTI course, UNOG has confirmed the idea that interpreting in field missions constitutes a training topic in itself that has to be integrated in the different courses organised by the organisation. Proof of this was the inclusion of a Workshop on UN Field Missions in the internship programme held in 2020 for the Arabic booth at UNOG. This internship enjoyed the cooperation of 28 trainers from all four duty stations. Considering the COVID situation and the impossibility of having an in-person internship or dummy booth practice, the internship was held online, for the first time ever, for a total duration of eight weeks (from 25 August to 23 October) with a one-week break in September for practice and assimilation of information.

The internship was advertised on Inspira, the UN's Human Resources Gateway, in order to cast a wide net. After a comprehensive screening of all applications and an online pre-selection interpretation test, 11 interns were accepted from all corners of the Arab world.

The workshop was organised during the last week of the Internship as "Master Classes" over two days. The first day included an introductory presentation by UNOG Staff Interpreters and two presentations by experts from OHCHR. They were followed by a Q&A session. On the second day of the workshop, UNOG staff interpreters gave a more practical presentation and showed a series of videos that were scripted and filmed for that purpose by IS and DCM, in which UNOG staff interpreters acted various scenarios based on real cases, following the CBL approach that had proven so successful at the FTI-UNOG course. Each video was followed by an interactive discussion. The duration of the first six short videos was of approximately 50 seconds each and showed the wrong and right versions of how to enter a room, where to sit, and how to behave when working in a field mission. They highlighted the importance of teamwork in a reproduction of real-life settings, including how to be alert and ready to take over from your colleague at all times. The last two videos were about four minutes each and were language specific. They focused on interview settings and touched on difficulties relating to dialects and again the importance of teamwork between the interpreters.

In order to assess the effectiveness of the workshop, an anonymous survey was conducted with the participants in May 2021. The survey was piloted by two interpreters who were members of the internship Steering Committee, have experience as interpreters working in the field and have an academic background. The response rate was 100%. All respondents held a university degree, nine in both interpretation and translation and two in either interpretation or translation. All have experience working as interpreters, and most of them (nine) reported having field experience, ranging from 1 to over 100 missions. However, prior to the Internship workshop, only one intern had received training related to interpreting in the field. The overall evaluation of the workshop was very positive and considered it "an eye-opening experience." Respondents particularly valued the short videos and subsequent discussions as an educational tool that helped them drive home important messages in a simple, easily remembered way, as well as the presentations given by professional interpreters with experience in field missions, in which they provided practical recommendations adapted to real situations.

All the respondents thought that interpreters need specific training for field missions. In fact, those who commented on any shortcomings would have liked a longer and in-depth training on field missions. The linguistic aspects mentioned in the comments referred mostly to dialects and terminology. We believe this confirms that interpreters at the UN level, even interns in this case, do not need training in interpretation *per se* but rather situated training for field settings.

5.4 Regulating the work of interpreters in the field

The rules that govern the work of interpreters at UNOG and during conferences away from headquarters do not necessarily apply during field missions. Therefore, when a team of interpreters is assigned to a field mission, the IS sends guidelines on working with interpreters to the UN entity organising the mission, which is usually the relevant mandate secretariat at OHCHR. These guidelines are a one-pager that includes matters relating to travel arrangements, working hours and working conditions for interpreters.

With time, it became apparent that these guidelines were not sufficient to regulate the work of the interpreters in the field. Issues arose including with regards to the language combinations needed, the number of interpreters assigned and their workload.

In order to formalise and standardise the rules that apply during field missions, the IS established a Working Group to draft two Standard Operating Procedures (SOPs)[2] on interpreters assigned to field missions. This work is currently in progress.

The first SOP aims at providing IS clients (that is, all those who organise, accompany and service the mission), staff and freelance interpreters and all other relevant stakeholders with procedures that apply to field missions, from the point of requesting interpretation services through to the return of interpreters to base. It includes practical instructions on how to request interpretation services, mission arrangements, working hours and conditions, interpretation equipment, confidentiality, security matters, and how to request separate translation services since translation work does not fall under the interpreters' professional responsibilities.

The second SOP is addressed to the interpreters themselves, staff and freelance alike. It includes details of all procedures to follow before, during and after a mission. Instructions provided are practical, administrative, ethical, and security- and confidentiality-related. Once these SOPs are approved and adopted by DCM and all relevant UN authorities, they will become mandatory and will be published on DCM's website.

The development of guidelines into full-fledged SOPs is yet another indication of UNOG's increasing awareness of the need to provide a framework adapted to the work of interpreters in the field. Another indication is the fact that there currently are two staff interpreters who are doing their doctoral work on interpreting in UN field missions, research that has received the authorisation and the support of the organisation.

5.5 Conclusions

The present study details the initiatives organised by UNOG to train staff and freelance conference interpreters who are deployed in field missions. This group presents different characteristics and faces different challenges compared to other categories of interpreters more present in the literature, such as untrained interpreters recruited by humanitarian organisations or by the armed forces.

The analysis of the different projects shows that there has been an increasing awareness on the part of the organisation as to the specific needs of interpreters who work in the field. Different stages are to be observed: at the beginning, most of the initiatives came from the interpreters themselves, particularly those with previous experience in the field who had realised that the usual training provided to conference interpreters did not equip them to work in these challenging settings. Therefore, they started to include the description of interpreting in field missions in outreach activities, such as presentations given to MoU and non-MoU universities and videos. In a second stage, and after thorough awareness-raising by the interpreters, the organisation agreed to organise a joint training programme with an academic institution, the University of Geneva's Faculty of Translation and Interpreting. In a third stage, the organisation confirmed the idea that interpreting in field missions constitutes a training topic in itself that has to be integrated in the different courses organised by the organisation, as well as to be the focus of specific SOPs. Therefore, the organisation convened a working group to prepare two SOPs, one addressed at users and another one at interpreters themselves, in an attempt to provide clear instructions on how to work with interpreters and on how to work in a field mission, respectively.

The validation of the different courses, as well as the interviews with DCM's senior management and Chief Interpreters at multiple UN duty stations, showed that specific training and extensive experience in conference interpreting does not mean that the interpreter is well equipped to work in the field, and the participants in the different courses considered that there is a need to design specific training courses to prepare interpreters for the particularities of the settings and challenges they will encounter. Along these lines, they believe that it is essential that the trainers are experts with experience as interpreters themselves or in working with UN interpreters. This leads us to believe that practical experience as an interpreter or as a user of interpretation in this specific setting is essential in order to design and plan relevant materials and lessons. This ultimately highlights the need to organise tailored training programmes focussing on specific groups. Even if one may argue that interpreting is, after all, interpreting, it is a situated practice, and learning is a social process which is situated in a cultural, historical and institutional context; it follows, therefore, that interpreting much depends on the context and setting in which it is practiced.

Disclaimer

The views expressed herein are those of the authors and do not necessarily reflect the views of the United Nations.

Notes

1 Data collection in the different studies referred to in the present paper has been undertaken in line with the ethical procedure of the Faculty of Translation and Interpreting of the University of Geneva (Directive relative à l'intégrité dans le domaine de la recherche scientifique et à la procédure à suivre en cas de manquement à l'intégrité) [Guidelines on Scientific Research Integrity and on the Procedure to Follow in the Case of Breach of Integrity].
2 A Standard Operating Procedure (SOP) is a document that provides clear-cut directions and instructions as to how teams and members within an organisation must go about completing certain processes.

References

Baigorri Jalón, Jesús. 2011. "Wars, Languages and the Role(s) of Interpreters." In *Les Liaisons Dangereuses: Langues, Traduction, Interprétation*, edited by Henri Awaiss, and Jarjoura Hardane, 173–204. Beirut: Sources-Cibles. Université Saint-Joseph.

Baker, Mona. 2010. "Interpreters and Translators in the War Zone." *The Translator* 16 (2): 197–222.

Barea Muñoz, Manuel. 2021a. *La interpretación en conflictos prolongados: el conflicto israeli-palestino*, PhD diss., University of Geneva.

Barea Muñoz, Manuel. 2021b. "Psychological Aspects of Interpreting Violence: A Narrative from the Israeli-Palestinian Conflict." In *Interpreting Conflict: A Comparative*

Framework, edited by Marija Todorova, and Lucía Ruiz Rosendo, 195–212. London: Palgrave MacMillan.

Bergunde, Annika, and Sonia Pöllabauer. 2019. "Curricular Design and Implementation of a Training Course for Interpreters in an Asylum Context." *Translation & Interpreting* 11 (1): 1–21.

Bos, Geesje, and Joseph Soeters. 2006. "Interpreters at Work: Experiences from Dutch and Belgian Peace Operations." *International Peacekeeping* 13 (2): 261–268.

Delgado Luchner, Carmen. 2019. *The Ethics of Interpreting in UN Field Missions* [PowerPoint slides, delivered in the course]

Delgado Luchner, Carmen, and Leila Kherbiche. 2019. "Ethics Training for Humanitarian Interpreters Working in Conflict and Post-Conflict Settings." *Journal of War & Culture Studies* 12 (3): 251–267.

Gez, Yonatan, and Michal Schuster. 2018. "Borders and Boundaries: Eritrean Graduates Reflect on Their Medical Interpreting Training." *The European Legacy* 23 (7–8): 821–836.

Isakov, Vadim. n.d. *Interpretation at UNOG.* http://vimeo.com/115696565

Kelly, Michael, and Catherine Baker. 2013. *Interpreting the Peace: Peace Operations, Conflict and Language in Bosnia-Herzegovina.* Basingstoke: Palgrave Macmillan.

OHCHR. n.d. *International Commissions of Inquiry, Commissions on Human Rights, Fact-Finding Missions and other Investigations.* www.ohchr.org/EN/HRBodies/HRC/Pages/COIs.aspx

Osuna, Cristóbal. 2018. *Interpreting in Human Rights Missions.* https://drive.google.com/file/d/13DYDhSUy6HjJF6BBnOrQ0liEMEGLhIOU/view?usp=sharing

Packer, George. 2007. "Betrayed: The Iraqis Who Trusted America the Most." *The New Yorker,* 26 March. www.newyorker.com/magazine/2007/03/26/betrayed-2

Ruiz Rosendo, Lucía. 2020. "Translating and Interpreting in Conflict." In *The Oxford Handbook of Translation and Social Practices,* edited by Meng Ji, and Sara Laviosa, 45–65. Oxford: Oxford University Press.

Ruiz Rosendo, Lucía. 2021. "Moving Boundaries in Interpreting in Conflict Zones." In *Interpreting Conflict: A Comparative Framework,* edited by Marija Todorova, and Lucía Ruiz Rosendo, 3–13. London: Palgrave MacMillan.

Ruiz Rosendo, Lucía. 2022. "Interpreting for the Military: Creating Communities of Practice." *JoSTrans* 37: 16–34.

Ruiz Rosendo, Lucía, Alma Barghout, and Conor H. Martin. 2021. "Interpreting on UN Field Missions: A Training Programme." *The Interpreter and Translator Trainer* 15 (4): 450–467.

Ruiz Rosendo, Lucía, and Manuel Barea Muñoz. 2017. "Towards a Typology of Interpreters in War-Related Scenarios in the Middle East." *Translation Spaces* 6 (2): 182–208.

Tesseur, Wine, and Hilary Footitt. 2019. "Professionalisms at War? Interpreting in Conflict and Post-Conflict Situations." *Journal of War & Cultural Studies* 12 (3): 268–284.

Tipton, Rebecca. 2011. "Relationships of Learning between Military Personnel and Interpreters in Situations of Violent Conflict." *The Interpreter and Translator Trainer* 5 (1): 15–40.

Todorova, Marija. 2021. "Pressing Issues and Future Directions for Interpreting in Conflict Zones." In *Interpreting Conflict: A Comparative Framework,* edited by Marija Todorova, and Lucía Ruiz Rosendo, 305–316. London: Palgrave MacMillan.

Todorova, Marija, and Lucía Ruiz Rosendo. 2021. *Interpreting Conflict: A Comparative Framework.* London: Palgrave MacMillan.

6

RESOURCEFULNESS WHEN RESOURCES ARE LACKING

A case study of field interpreters at the Office of the Prosecutor at the International Criminal Court

Nada Melhem, Nathalie Collart, and Dimitri Elman[1]

The International Criminal Court (ICC) operates in a number of countries where Languages of Lesser Diffusion (LLDs) are spoken. In the absence of formally trained interpreters for such languages, the need for training becomes indispensable. A chief challenge faced when training such interpreters is the lack of resources, namely, for legal terminology. This chapter examines the resources used by Field Interpreters (FIs) of LLDs working for the Office of the Prosecutor (OTP) at the ICC and explores the techniques that can be deployed when resources are found wanting. This exploratory study draws on years of experience by the Interpretation Team at the OTP's Language Services Unit in training FIs and the feedback garnered from the responses of some of these FIs to a questionnaire on legal resources.

6.1 Introduction

The International Criminal Court ("ICC" or "Court") is the first and only permanent international judiciary body that investigates and, where warranted, tries individuals charged with the gravest crimes of concern to the international community. Supported by more than 120 States Parties, the ICC fights against impunity from genocide, war crimes, crimes against humanity and the crime of aggression committed throughout the world, as a court of last resort and under specific legal conditions. This extensive territorial jurisdiction makes the language regime at the ICC extremely diverse (Constable 2016) and highly challenging as depicted by Swigart's (2019, 2020) ethnographic studies on the challenges of multilingualism at the ICC. While English and French are the Court's working languages, a vast array of "situation languages"[2] are needed for the running of the Court's activities ranging from investigations and proceedings to dealings with witnesses and outreach activities.

Acting independently as a separate organ of the ICC, the Office of the Prosecutor (OTP) conducts preliminary examinations, investigations and prosecution

DOI: 10.4324/9781003230359-8

of perpetrators of the four aforementioned crimes in accordance with its mandate under the Rome Statute. To uphold the independence of the OTP, the Language Services Unit (LSU) was established to provide language services, including field interpretation, for the OTP's activities, independently from other organs serviced by the Registry's Language Services Section (LSS). Field interpretation is provided by LSU in situation languages in combination with one of the ICC's working languages. Presently, the number of situation languages serviced by LSU field interpretation exceeds 50 languages. This number, however, may increase to cater for any potential new preliminary examinations or investigations and the language(s) in which the victims, witnesses and/or accused[3] choose to communicate. Most of these situation languages fit the description of Languages of Lesser Diffusion (LLDs) as encapsulated by Balogh, Salaets, and Van Schoor (2016). Building on a definition by three different scholars, namely Roat (2008), Skaaden and Wadensjö (2014) and Giambruno (2014) whereby an LLD is a language "that has relatively few speakers in one specific location or geographical area in relation to the population as a whole" (23), Balogh et al. (2016) add a few elements of relevance to our study, namely, that such language has often no official status, is often a non-standardised oral language with very few written resources, with its legal terminology seldom firmly established or even non-existent, and for which there is a lack of training resources and no university level interpreter training program available.

In the absence of formal training for such languages, the need to train interpreters for the Court's activities becomes indispensable. A chief challenge faced when training such interpreters is the lack of resources for ICC specific terminology extraction especially for languages with strong oral tradition. Interpreters of LLDs working for the ICC are faced with complex legal and procedural terminology on the one hand, and a scarcity or, at times, non-existence of resources for the extraction of such terminology on the other hand. Conventional resources may, at times, fail to provide interpreters of LLDs with equivalences. Thus, providing them with useful resources becomes "undoubtedly problematic" (Zekhnini 2016).

The topic of resources for training interpreters of LLDs especially for legal terminology has received scant research attention. Three significant contributions are worth mentioning in this regard. In "Trailld: Training in Languages of Lesser Diffusion: Training of legal interpreters" (Balogh et al. 2016), legal terminology is covered under Chapter 5 (Driesen 2016) but is addressed to translators rather than interpreters. Chapter 6 (Zekhnini 2016), which provides an overview on resources and materials for training legal interpreters of LLDs in court settings, offers great insight into the issue at hand, but deals chiefly with similarities and differences between various national legal systems, whereas the ICC operates in an international criminal law setting. The "Indigenous Interpreter Training Manual and Workbook" (Allen et al. 2018) contains one module on building indigenous language glossaries and another on legal interpreting for indigenous interpreters, but here again, the setting is national legal systems. The UNHCR "Handbook for

Interpreters in Asylum Procedures" (UNHCR Austria 2017) dedicates an entire unit to information mining with the aim of teaching interpreters how to identify their knowledge gaps and assess their knowledge needs, how to use resources to acquire knowledge about specific topics and research, and acquire relevant terminology. The handbook also provides specific information about asylum and practical resources for interpreters in asylum procedures.

This study examines the extent to which conventional interpreter training terminology resources apply to interpreters of LLDs working in the field for the OTP and explores other somewhat unconventional resources as well as techniques that can be deployed when resources are lacking. This study is divided into two parts: in the first part, we explore who the FIs at LSU are, whom they interpret for, and what they interpret, as well as the training they receive and resources they are provided with. The second part summarises the responses of some of LSU's FIs to a questionnaire on the most useful resources and their coping techniques when faced with complex terminological conundrums.

6.2 Field Interpreters (FIs) at LSU

6.2.1 FIs at LSU: Who are they?

FIs are independent freelancers engaged by LSU to provide consecutive interpretation in liaison settings on a short-term basis as and when required. In some cases, LSU staff members may be deployed as FIs. Even if contracted by LSU, FIs constitute an impartial aid to communication. They are expected to work in accordance with the internationally agreed-upon standards of the profession and the guidelines of the organisation, produce a faithful transmission of the message, commit to impartiality and confidentiality, and show professionalism.

Freelance FIs should ideally, though not necessarily, hold a university degree in Translation and Interpreting (T&I) or a related field, hold a professional qualification in T&I, and have previous experience as interpreters, particularly, in public service settings. However, the reality is that many of LSU's FIs are not trained as translators and/or interpreters in their LLD, do not necessarily have experience as interpreters, and are not necessarily linguists by trade. Among the other requirements, mother tongue proficiency in the situation language is a pre-requisite, and proficiency in English and/or French is also required. These two requirements are of the essence given the complexity of the task at hand; however, rarely do we find candidates equally proficient in both the LLD and relevant working language. FIs who originally come from the situation country but now live in a country where the target language (English or French) is spoken are usually more educated but less exposed to their native language and use it less frequently in their daily interactions. Conversely, those who stayed in their home country often studied English or French as a foreign or second language. Consequently, their weaker knowledge of the target language is counterbalanced by higher proficiency levels in the LLD.

6.2.2 FIs at LSU: Whom do they interpret for and what do they interpret?

FIs contracted by LSU provide interpretation for four main service users: investigators, trial lawyers, protection officers and psycho-social experts. Protection officers mainly deal with witness protection and security matters, and psycho-social experts inquire about the medical, social, and psychological wellbeing of witnesses. And while they may require the services of FIs to carry out their activities, the terminology involved in their line of work, albeit technical, will not necessarily pertain to international criminal law.

This leaves us with investigators and trial lawyers tasked with collecting and presenting evidence. The OTP's English or French-speaking officers interview victims, witnesses, insiders and suspects who speak situation languages, and subsequently require FIs to conduct their activities whether remotely or in situ. At the recipient's end, the profile of interviewees requiring interpretation varies significantly. Crime-base victims and witnesses are oftentimes poorly educated individuals living in a country where one strong national language is predominant and speaking a minority language that has no official status. Their understanding of legal language is already too weak. Protocol dictates that investigators cover procedure before starting the interview. Before the statement of a witness or victim is taken, the ICC's jurisdiction should be covered, and the principles of confidentiality and disclosure explained. For insider and suspect interviews, on the other hand, such a procedure is much more complex and is heavy with legal terminology and phraseology. Prior to being interviewed, the person is informed of his or her rights during an investigation under Article 55, paragraph 2 (a-d) of the Rome Statute and of the recording of the interview that is undertaken under Rules 111 and 112 of the Rules of Procedure and Evidence. Similarly, the closing procedure entails closing statements of a legal nature.

6.3 FIs at LSU: Training and resources

6.3.1 Induction and basic training for field interpreters

As noted above, LSU operates independently from the Registry's LSS. Both language services, however, engage jointly in the testing and training of FIs. A description of the joint accreditation process for FIs at the Court can be found in Swigart (2019). A vacancy announcement is published on the e-recruitment platform of the ICC and candidates who were actively sourced by both language services are invited to apply. The vacancy announcement attracts spontaneous applications as well. Shortlisted candidates who pass the language interview and interpretation test and obtain a positive security clearance are invited to participate in a monolingual group ICC Induction and Basic Training for Field Interpreters ("Induction") in French or English organised jointly by both language services. In the group Induction, interpreters learn about the ICC, the different types of assignments they may be called upon to do and are presented to the main clients of LSS and LSU. They are also taught the interpreter's role and turn-taking management, modules on memory and note-taking, terminology for FIs, and sight translation. Training also includes a number of role-play exercises in which participants are asked to interpret for Court officials in fictitious scenarios to give them a taste of the types of ICC assignments. Once they complete the Induction, interpreters are placed into a shared pool and either work for the OTP or the Registry.

Before their first deployment by LSU, FIs who have completed the ICC Induction are provided with reference materials, glossaries and templates needed for OTP-specific activities and, when needed, an OTP-specific Induction. Notwithstanding, the OTP may need to deploy FIs for a given situation in the early stages of activities, and LSU might have to organise Inductions for newly recruited FIs on very short notice with very limited resources and, at times, no glossaries for emerging LLDs. This has been the case for the Zaghawa, Luo, and Moore languages.

6.3.2 Legal terminology and resources

Field interpretation at the ICC requires, inter alia, the knowledge of specialised legal and procedural vocabulary that is very particular to the Court and its setting. A high level of accuracy is required in international criminal procedure and FIs need to be familiar not just with the legal terms but also the concepts that such terms denote. Since LLDs often have no official status, the legal language is often underdeveloped as it is seldom used in everyday speech and informal conversations. Basic ICC terms such as "prosecutor," "defence," and "investigator" may not have direct equivalents in many LLDs. The same applies to the crimes falling within the Court's jurisdiction. This task is further complicated by what Kelsall (2010) (as cited in Swigart 2020) refers to as "dissonance" between international criminal justice and non-Western languages and cultures. Concepts such as "reparations" are non-existent in national jurisdictions and finding an equivalent that does not strictly encompass "monetary compensation" but also "return of property, rehabilitation or symbolic measures such as apologies or memorials" could be challenging. And, unlike military/weaponry terminology or terminology on human anatomy or bodily injuries where images can be shown or drawings made to get the idea across, only through words can the idea be conveyed in legal terminology.

The ICC had to find "innovative strategies" for the development of legal lexicons in these LLDs through the establishment of 1) a glossary of key ICC terms; and 2) expert panels that mostly comprise linguists or academics specialised in the language to codify non-existent legal and judicial terms in some situation languages (Swigart 2019). These expert panels, however, do not convene systematically for all situation languages and even if they do, the process might be lengthy, and LSU might need to deploy FIs before the process is completed. It is the court interpreters of LLDs who mostly benefit from the expert panels' findings. By the time a case goes to court, a significant time has elapsed and more resources are available for the training of court interpreters of LLDs (see Constable (2016) for more information on the training of court interpreters of LLDs). This is unfortunately not the case for LSU's FIs who might be deployed on assignments early in the process, with minimum resources. LSU shares glossaries of key ICC terms with FIs who still have to validate the translations amongst native speakers. Similarly, OTP interview templates and other supporting materials are translated into LLDs and shared with the FIs before deployment. Those glossaries and templates, at times, have to be recorded in an audio format for non-written languages. A case in point is the Fur language, for which an audio glossary was created.

In the terminology module included in the Induction, FIs are introduced to conventional resources such as glossaries, translations, legal corpora, dictionaries, current affairs (local radio), background and parallel texts, the internet, and online search engines to the extent that they can be used. One suggestion that has not yet been implemented is to create a platform on the intranet for FIs to exchange term suggestions. In our experience training FIs, unconventional resources such as holy books served to find some basic legal terms such as those related to judgment, as religious books are amongst the most translated books in the world. Verses from the Bible on "judgment day" have been consulted to find an equivalent for the word "judgment" in Cebuano for instance. Direct solutions to terminology problems are also taught during the Induction, and these include neologisms and loanwords; indirect solutions such as explanation, paraphrase, general definition, and equivalent expression are subsequently covered.

The above reflects the experience of LSU's Field Interpretation team. What follows is the feedback of some of LSU's FIs garnered from their responses to a questionnaire on their most useful resources for ICC legal terminology.

6.4 FI resources for legal terminology

6.4.1 Data collection

In order to gather more information about the topic of the study, a questionnaire was set up using the model of Brinkman (2009) and sent out to LSU's FIs with the following languages: Bambara, Fulfulde, Fur, Kirundi, Sango, Songhai, and Tamasheq.[4] Interpreters for situation languages not deemed as LLDs such as Arabic and Swahili, *inter alia*, were not included in the sample. Similarly, languages that have larger speaker bases and trained linguists such as Georgian (Swigart 2019) were not considered for this study.

The questionnaire, drafted in English and translated into French, was divided into three sections, starting with a general introduction explaining the goal of the questionnaire, how the data will be collected and used, and the time needed to complete the questionnaire. The first section collects personal and professional data about the participants, using mostly a nominal scale and Yes/No questions. In the next sections, the participants were first asked about their linguistic profile, then their resources for legal terminology, using a mix of Likert-type questions and multiple-choice questions. The questionnaire ends with an open-ended question to give FIs the opportunity to share comments or add anything else they wish.

The questionnaire was emailed to 19 FIs, including two FIs who interpret two languages and were asked to complete one questionnaire per language. A total of 15 responses representative of all 7 LLDs was received – namely, one for Fulfulde, five for Sango, two for Songhai, three for Fur, two for Kirundi, one for Tamasheq, and one for Bambara. One of the respondents (from the Fur group) is an LSU staff member, whereas the remaining 14 respondents are accredited freelance contractors with the LSU.

6.4.2 Data analysis

The FIs were asked to fill out the questionnaire and return the responses by email. The returned questionnaires were processed by the Field Interpretation team using the SharePoint platform. The responses to all questions were manually entered into SharePoint, which provided a graphical summary of responses, allowing the team to conduct data analysis.

6.4.3 Results and discussion

The number of female respondents was half that of male respondents (5 versus 10), in keeping with the gender distribution amongst LSU's FIs for these languages. The average age of the respondents is 45.86 years old (from 31 to 67 years old). All the respondents hail from countries where the LLD in question is spoken, but fewer than half of them (five) are residing still in their home countries. With the exception of Kirundi and Sango, these LLDs are spoken by a limited number of speakers in a specific geographical area and have no official status as defined by Balogh et al. (2016). Most of the respondents (13) hold a university level degree, with 6 at a bachelor's level, 5 at a master's level and 2 PhD or higher, and 2 out of 15 respondents only completed secondary school. For the majority of respondents (nine), Interpreting or Translation is not the main occupation but rather a side job undertaken in addition to their main occupation as opposed to 40% of the respondents (six) who strictly perform interpreting or translation tasks. The average number of hours of interpretation provided per month is 43 (from 0.5 to 150 hours) with ten respondents providing interpretation on a part-time basis (under 50 hours), three providing interpretation on a half-time basis (50–90 hours) and two on a full-time basis (120–150 hours per month). The respondents have between 3 and 15+ years of experience in T&I, with 10 having less than 10 years and 5 above 10. The majority of the respondents (nine) have not received any formal training in T&I (apart from the ICC Induction). The remaining respondents (six) received formal training, including a university level degree in T&I for two respondents, T&I studied as a subject in a related field of study for two respondents (linguistics and language, and civilisation, respectively), and short training programmes for three respondents. It is noted, however, that such training does not pertain to the LLD in question. In the case of Fur interpreters, for example, training received was for the Arabic language in the absence of an established formal training in the Fur language. These findings are in line with Balogh et al. (2016) definition of LLD in that no university level training is available for interpreters of LLDs; some interpreters thus choose to receive T&I training in a third language in which they learn the principles of interpreting allowing them to extrapolate to the LLD in question. The majority of the respondents (nine) do not have a legal background. Those with a legal background (six) either hold an academic degree in law (three respondents) or have studied law as part of a university degree in a related field (translation for one respondent, court interpreting for one respondent and economics for one respondent). Here again, law, whether as a field or subject of study, was studied in a language other than the LLD.

In the next section, FIs were asked to provide further information about the language from and into which they interpret for the ICC. For all the respondents, save one, the selected language is their mother tongue. They have all acquired the language at home, with nine respondents learning it also by living in a community where the language is spoken, three as a subject at school, and two as a subject at university. The selected language was the language of schooling for one respondent only. As for the situations in which they use the language, all fifteen respondents said they use it with extended family and friends. Thirteen use it at home with immediate family, eleven at work or in a professional context (outside ICC activities) and eleven in the community. Thirteen respondents use this language in their daily life versus two who use it every week/occasionally. The majority of the respondents (13) stated that the selected language has a strong spoken tradition. Paradoxically, when asked whether written sources (such as dictionaries, newspapers, etc.) are available in the selected language, the majority of respondents (12) replied in the affirmative, whereas the remaining 3 respondents pointed out the lack of written sources in their language. On a scale from 1 to 5, where 1 is underdeveloped and 5 is well-developed, almost half of the respondents (47%) rated the development of legal terminology in the selected language as average, 13% rated it as 1 and 2, respectively, 7% as 4 and 20% as 5. The divergence of opinion could not be linked to the written versus spoken status of the language nor to the LLD in question being the national language as initially suspected. This finding seems to be subjective and warrants further investigation.

The third section included questions pertaining to legal terminology resources. Participants were asked about their familiarity with ICC terminology prior to being contracted by LSU, and 60% of the respondents (nine) confirmed being familiar with the ICC's legal terminology before working for the ICC, perhaps owing to their legal background or their preparation for the ICC accreditation test. It could also be that they come from a situation country where the ICC is known and often appears in the news. When asked if the glossaries provided by the ICC contain all the legal terms that the FIs encounter in the field, a staggering 60% of the respondents (nine) answered in the negative. This finding warrants further investigation and potential courses of action include establishing a list of additional terms to be added to the glossary of the ICC's core legal terminology or combining the terms extracted from the templates with the glossaries if missing to make it easier for the FIs to locate them.

The nine respondents who said that the glossaries provided by the ICC do not contain all the terms they encounter in the field were then asked what they do when a legal term does not figure in the glossaries, and the most common strategies cited by the respondents are explanation and paraphrase. Both explanation and paraphrase are covered in the Induction as indirect solutions for terminology problems. In the case of explanation, FIs are told to explain the word, not the concept for they might not grasp the concept in its entirety and fail to produce a sound explanation of the concept itself. In addition to explanation and paraphrase, two respondents note down the term and look it up later to find a better equivalent. One respondent consults dictionaries, local lawyers, or the local radio, and another uses a loanword from a third language if it is understood by the interviewee, more specifically, borrowing from the Arabic language if the Fur equivalent is lacking.

The respondents were asked to rate how often target language equivalents provided in the LSU glossaries are understood by the interviewees on a 5-point Likert scale ranging from very rarely to always, and close to half of the respondents (47%) said often, another 47% replied by saying very often (27%) and always (20%) respectively. Only 7% said rarely. This highlights the key role that FIs play in validating the terms passed on to them as explained in the first part of this chapter. In a follow-up question, participants were asked to explain their course of action when the interviewees do not understand the equivalents used by the FI or if the equivalent is unsatisfactory. Here again the most common strategies used by the respondents are explanation (12) followed by paraphrasing (8), and generalisation (2), in line with what they are taught in the Induction. Other coping strategies mentioned by individual respondents include the following: asking the interviewer to rephrase; using a loanword from a third language (Arabic in the case of interpretation into Fur); presenting the information in simpler terms; and giving the interlocutor examples leading to a better understanding of the term. While rephrasing, borrowing and simplifying could constitute potential solutions to terminology problems, giving the interlocutor examples can be a dangerous endeavour as such examples might be deemed leading, misleading or might not necessarily be accurate. FIs were asked to give examples of legal terms that do not have direct equivalents in the target language, and these included some core ICC terms such as the crimes falling within the Court's jurisdiction (genocide and crimes against humanity were specifically cited), "registry," "lawyer," "investigator," "prosecutor," "trial," "justice" and "defence." Some of the examples mentioned by the French-speaking interpreters are *"justice islamique," "juge d'instruction," "garde à vue,"* and *"mandat de dépôt."* This ties in with what was covered in the first part of this chapter whereby what is basic terminology for the ICC is not necessarily basic for our FIs. Once again, the common strategy cited by FIs for interpreting such terms is explanation. In the case of Bambara and Fur interpreters, another common strategy is to use loanwords from French and Arabic, respectively.

FIs were asked to give examples of legal concepts that do not correspond to the realities on the ground, and once again the crimes that the Court investigates were mentioned. Other concepts such as "complementarity" and "reparations" that are specific to the ICC were cited, as well as certain common legal terms such as "presumption of innocence" and "legal representative." As previously explained, witnesses with these LLDs are often poorly educated with rudimentary to non-existent legal knowledge. Even if FIs were to find equivalents, witnesses may not necessarily understand them. Here again, the common strategy to interpret such terms seems to be explanation. Bambara and Fur interpreters would use French and Arabic loanwords, respectively.

Lastly, the participants were asked about the resources they consult to build their own legal glossary and enrich their knowledge of legal terms and rate the frequency for using such resources. Despite them not containing all the terms that FIs encounter in the field, LSU glossaries seem to be the top resource very often consulted by the FIs (60%). Dictionaries and current affairs (radio, newspaper, TV, etc.) come second (at 40% each), followed by background texts on the case/situation (33%) and self-made glossaries (33%). Internet and online search engines are said to be used often by 27% of the respondents, such a low percentage being potentially attributed to the oral nature of the language, whereas legal corpora are sometimes used by 33%, translated texts and parallel texts sometimes used by 27%. Consulting peers/native speakers is sometimes used by 20% and often by another 20%, and lastly, direct contact with experts is only rarely used by 27%.

In the last question, participants were asked to share comments or add anything else they wished. One comment made by a Songhai interpreter stated that the legal terminology in her mother tongue is still under construction and, thus, inaccessible for uneducated native speakers. Therefore, interpreters have to rely on their own experience to paraphrase or use explanatory terms in the local language in order to convey the message. This comment dovetails with the responses provided by the FIs especially to the last section of this questionnaire. It alludes, however, to the role that the interpreter's personal experience plays in successfully paraphrasing or explaining the terms.

There were a few suggestions worth considering mostly revolving around two main themes, namely, 1) Setting up better synergy between freelance contractors and ICC linguists for the translation of certain legal terms and concepts; and 2) Reviewing the translation of certain terms to present them in a more simplified and accessible form. Under the first theme, it was suggested to connect FIs to in-house ICC translators for a better harmonisation of key terms, a suggestion echoed by another interpreter who proposed to bring together FIs and language experts in a virtual meeting to discuss the translation of certain key terms and concepts. Under the second theme, there was a suggestion that the legal terms and concepts for which no equivalences exist in the LLD be explained or presented in simpler terms to allow interpreters to find equivalences closer to the intended meaning. Along the same lines, one of the respondents suggested that LSU glossaries be updated by replacing the translation of certain terms with more simplified equivalences and finding suitable equivalences for words which have none. A final suggestion that would be harder to implement is to set up awareness sessions to explain to potential witnesses in their mother tongue about the OTP, its work as well as the judicial procedure so when OTP-specific terminology is used, such witnesses know what it refers to. It is noted that outreach sessions do exist but do not necessarily reach potential witnesses to be interviewed by the OTP.

6.5 Conclusion

The role that FIs play in the OTP's activities is of critical importance, a role that does not come without challenges, namely, the absence of (written) resources and terms that denote international legal concepts and crimes (Swigart 2019, 2020). Additionally, the high level of accuracy required in international criminal law places additional responsibility on the FIs at the ICC as opposed to other organisations such as the United Nations, where untrained FIs of LLDs are used as language assistants in their dealings with local communities within the framework of peacekeeping missions. This study shows that the glossaries provided by LSU, albeit essential, are not sufficient and that more consultation is needed with our FIs to further populate the glossaries and update the translations of certain terms. Including in the glossaries direct equivalents for key legal terms as well as paraphrased versions thereof would give the FIs a point of reference should the direct equivalents not be understood by the interviewee. Presenting the legal concepts in simpler terms would also make them more understandable and accessible for the FIs and the recipients of interpretation alike, an endeavour that the ICC could undertake to make the job of its FIs slightly less challenging.

Notes

1 The views expressed in this chapter are those of the authors and do not necessarily represent those of the ICC and OTP.
2 A term used to describe the languages needed at any stage of the proceedings.
3 Article 67 of the Rome Statute provides for the right of the accused "to be informed of the nature, cause and content of the charge, in a language which the accused fully understands and speaks" and "to have, free of any cost, the assistance of a competent interpreter."
4 The most requested LLDs at the time of the survey were for the following countries: Mali, Central African Republic, Burundi, and Sudan.

References

Allen, Katharine, Victor Sosa, Angelica Isidoro, and Marjory A. Bancroft. 2018. *The Indigenous Interpreter®: A Training Manual for Indigenous Language Interpreting*. Salinas, California: Natividad Medical Foundation.

Balogh, Katalin, Heidi Salaets, and Dominique Van Schoor. 2016. *Trailld: Training in Languages of Lesser Diffusion: Training of Legal Interpreters in Llds*. Belgium: Lannoo Publishers.

Brinkman, Willem-Paul. 2009. "Design of a Questionnaire Instrument." In *Handbook of Mobile Technology Research Methods*, edited by Steve Love, 31–57. New York: Nova Science Publishers.

Constable, Andrew. 2016. "Methodologies and Techniques Used in Training Simultaneous Interpreters of Languages of Lesser Diffusion at the International Criminal Court." In

Trailld: Training in Languages of Lesser Diffusion: Training of Legal Interpreters in Llds, edited by Katalin Balogh, Heidi Salaets, and Dominique Van Schoor, 69–79. Tielt: Lannoo Publishers.

Driesen, Christiane. 2016. "Chapter 5. Legal Translation and Terminology." In *Trailld: Training in Languages of Lesser Diffusion: Training of Legal Interpreters in Llds*, edited by Katalin Balogh, Heidi Salaets, and Dominique Van Schoor, 101–116. Tielt: Lannoo Publishers.

Giambruno, Cynthia S. 2014. "Dealing with Languages of Lesser Diffusion." In *Assessing Legal Interpreter Quality through Testing and Certification: The Qualitas Project*, edited by Cynthia S. Giambruno, 93–107. Alicante: Universidad de Alicante.

Kelsall, Tim. 2010. "International Criminal Justice and Non-Western Cultures." *Oxford Transitional Justice Working Paper*. www.law.ox.ac.uk/sites/files/oxlaw/kelsall_internationalcriminaljustice_final1.pdf.

Roat, Cynthia. 2008. Personal communication. "Language Access Webinar 1." Addressing the Language Access Barrier when Serving Refugee Patients. Refugee Health Technical Assistance Centre. Massachusets, 28 March.

Skaaden, Hanne, and Cecilia Wadensjö. 2014. "Some Considerations on the Testing of Interpreting Skills." In *Assessing Legal Interpreter Quality through Testing and Certification: The Qualitas Project*, edited by Cynthia S. Giambruno, 17–26. Alicante: Universidad de Alicante.

Swigart, Leigh. 2019. "Unseen and Unsung: Language Services at the International Criminal Court and Their Impact on Institutional Legitimacy." In *Legitimacy of Unseen Actors in International Adjudication*, edited by Freya Baetens, 272–296. Studies on International Courts and Tribunals. Cambridge: Cambridge University Press.

Swigart, Leigh. 2020. "Now You See It, Now You Don't: Culture at the International Criminal Court." In *Interactions of Law and Culture at the International Criminal Court*, edited by Julie Fraser, and Brianne McGonigle Leyh, 14–36. Cheltenham; Northampton, Cambridge, MA: Edward Elgar Publishing Limited.

UNHCR Austria. 2017. *UN High Commissioner for Refugees (UNHCR) Handbook for Interpreters in Asylum Procedures*, edited by Annika Bergunde, and Sonja Pöllabauer, 194. www.refworld.org/docid/59c8b3be4.html.

Zekhnini, Ahmed. 2016. "Chapter 6. Resources and Materials for Training Legal Interpreters in Languages of Lesser Diffusion." In *Trailld: Training in Languages of Lesser Diffusion: Training of Legal Interpreters in Llds*, edited by Katalin Balogh, Heidi Salaets, and Dominique Van Schoor, 117–121. Tielt: Lannoo Publishers.

7

THE MAIN CHALLENGES OF INTERPRETING IN THE CONTEXT OF THE INTERNATIONAL PROTECTION DETERMINATION PROCEDURE

Michele Arcella

This contribution focuses on the management of the main challenges posed by the work of interpretating in the context of the international protection determination procedure in Italy, in particular before the commissions responsible for interviewing asylum seekers. This procedural step is crucial to assess the international protection needs of the claimants, and the role of interpreters is essential to ensure effective communication between asylum seekers and interviewers and to allow the collection of information that is as detailed and reliable as possible as the basis of a fair and efficient decision-making process. This contribution describes the actions undertaken in the context of the refugee status determination (RSD) system in Italy in order to address the challenges that can affect the quality of the procedure. In particular, the contribution provides a description of the main tools used, such as training plans that are tailored on the interpreters' learning needs with greater involvement of the caseworkers as facilitators; guidelines for commissions designed to clarify the interpreters' functions; and consultation tools to collect the interpreters' viewpoint about the quality of the procedure and the main difficulties they faced within their working environment.

7.1 Introduction

Refugee status determination, or RSD, is the legal or administrative process by which governments or UNHCR determine whether a person seeking international protection is considered a refugee under international, regional or national law. Since oral accounts and the establishment and assessment of relevant facts by the officers are the main basis for the decision, interpreters play a decisive and complex role within the asylum procedure, in particular in the context of the RSD interview (Pöllabauer and Schumacher 2004, 21–29). During this interview, asylum seekers, who in most cases do not speak the language of the country of asylum,

DOI: 10.4324/9781003230359-9

are asked to explain the reasons why they left their country of origin through an oral account that includes all the details they deem necessary to have their application accepted. For their part, interviewers are responsible for collecting all the elements identified by international protection law as relevant to reach a fair decision in the most effective way.

Interpreters are called upon to ensure a smooth flow of communication in a complex multicultural communication environment, populated by individuals, interviewers, and asylum seekers with very different expectations and characterised by an unbalance of power. At the same time, interpreters must adhere to the principles that govern their profession, such as impartiality and confidentiality, and possess specific skills, such as linguistic and cultural knowledge, interpreting accuracy, and skills such as empathy – namely, the capacity to understand and share the feelings of another person. While compliance with these principles might seem obvious in theory, in practice it poses several challenges, especially when the need to have a very large number of interpreters available to cover a wide range of languages often leads to the recruitment of people who are not trained for this job (Pöllabauer 2004, 145) and who therefore unavoidably face substantial difficulties. Moreover, these difficulties increase if interpreters are not provided with detailed instructions and training about their roles in such a complex working environment.

This contribution addresses the need for the professionalisation of interpreters in the asylum context, illustrating how this issue is being addresses by the Italian asylum authorities in conjunction with United Nations High Commissioner for Refugees (UNHCR) and the companies that provide interpretation services, in light of the specific challenges presented by the Italian asylum system.

7.2 The role of interpreters in the Italian asylum system

The role of interpreter in the procedure for the determination of international protection in Italy is first mentioned in Presidential Decree no. 303 of 2004 (i.e., the implementation regulation of Law no. 189 of 2002). This regulation establishes that all communications regarding the procedure for the recognition of international protection are made to the applicants in the first language indicated in their asylum requests, or, if this is not possible, in English, French, Spanish, or Arabic, according to their preference. However, the presence of an interpreter during the registration of the application for asylum is not yet considered necessary by the legislator. Between 2007 and 2008, Italy equipped itself with its first systematic legislation in the field of asylum, through the transposition of the European Directives on qualifications and procedures for determining international protection and reception, and the rules on interpretation within this procedure were also updated (Directive 2011/95/EU of the European Parliament and of the Council of 13 December 2011 on standards for the qualification of third-country nationals or stateless persons as beneficiaries of international protection, for a uniform status for refugees or for persons eligible for subsidiary protection, and for the content of the protection granted [recast], OJ L 337, 20.12.2011).

In particular, Italian Legislative Decree no. 25 of 2008 established that at all stages of the procedure related to the registration and examination of the application, applicants are guaranteed the assistance of an interpreter in their own language or another language they understand and that, where necessary, the documentation they produce at every stage of the procedure is translated. With respect to the RSD activity, it was established that the record of the interview is read back to the applicant by the interpreter after the hearing and is signed by the latter, the interviewer and the applicant. The legislation also made the National Commission, the coordinating body of the international protection determination system in Italy, responsible for training interpreters.

The law does not further regulate the role and the tasks of the interpreter in the context of the asylum interview. Interpreters are not part of the staff of the Italian national asylum authorities, but are recruited through a call for tenders to identify companies providing interpretation services to the Territorial Commissions (hereinafter TCs), the authorities in charge of the RSD interviews.

In 2004 there were only 7 TCs, and 9,800 asylum requests were lodged (Department of Civil Liberties and Immigration, National Commission for the Right to Asylum 2004). However, in the following years, the number of TCs grew, in line with the increase in arrivals of asylum seekers and applications for international protection in Italy. In 2019[1] more than 43,000 asylum requests (Eurostat 2019) were lodged and the TCs were fifty-five. According to the information provided by one of the companies involved in this service provision for TCs, in 2019 approximately 920 interpreters worked in 21 out of 55 TCs, using more than 110 languages and dialects (data provided via e-mail on 25 March 2022 by Marta Bernardini, intercultural mediation sector manager of CIES, one of these service providers). These companies found themselves having to provide on a daily basis an increasing number of interpreters for an ever-growing range of languages to be used in the context of RSD interviews handled by TCs (according to the same aforementioned source the most used languages in 21 out of 55 TCs in 2019 were, in decreasing order: English, Arabic, Bangla, Urdu, Pidgin-English, Bambara, French, Mandinka, Spanish, Wolof).

In addition to the difficulties related to the growing demands of the asylum system, another challenge is represented by the lack of recognition of the professional role of the RSD interpreter and, more in general, of the intercultural mediator in Italy. In fact, these figures do not fall into the category of professional interpreting, and they are mainly employed by non-profit entities that try to define a deontological frame of reference through *ad hoc* tools, such as specific codes of conduct, and to promote their professional development through specific trainings carried out in cooperation with UNHCR and national authorities. This lack of professional recognition of RSD interpreters contributed to their traditionally low rates of pay and consequently to their very high turnover in the commissions responsible for the RSD procedure.

The combination of these factors is recurrent in many European countries, with a general negative impact on the quality of the service provided (Jiménez-Ivars

2021; Martin-Ruano 2017; Pöllabauer 2004; Pym et al. 2012; UNHCR 2017). The following paragraphs describe how the Italian asylum system has addressed these challenges.

7.3 Training the interpreters

Starting in 2004, when the first Territorial Commissions began to operate at local level, UNHCR, in agreement with the National Commission, organised and delivered, together with the companies providing interpreting services, specific training for interpreters.

The training included presentations focusing on the key elements of international protection, namely: the definitions of refugee and beneficiary of subsidiary protection contained in the 1951 Geneva Convention and in European legislation, and the Italian asylum procedure and the role of interpreters within this context, with particular attention given to the principles to be respected and skills required during RSD interviews, as set out in relevant UNHCR documents (UNHCR, 2009).

The training also included sessions on the principles enshrined in the codes of conduct adopted by the companies hiring the interpreters (the code of conduct drawn up by CIES, one of the companies providing the interpreting services to TCs, can be consulted at www.cies.it/wp-content/uploads/2022/04/Codice_Deontologico_COMMISSIONI-TERRITORIALI), as well as on interpreting modalities and skills (consecutive and simultaneous interpreting, note taking). Moreover, role-playing sessions were used to allow the interpreters to identify with asylum seekers and interviewers in order to better understand their specific needs and point of view in the context of recurrent RSD interview situations. Other practical exercises were also organised to discuss and guide the interpreters' choices in complex scenarios testing the aforementioned principles and skills.

All the sessions were set-up in a very interactive way in order to allow the interpreters to raise concerns related to the interpretation of key concepts of international protection and the practical implementation of the principles and skills required in this particular working environment. The increasing involvement of RSD interviewers in the training over the years ensured that these sessions were even more interactive. Interviewers have been involved as trainers since 2018, but they also regularly attend the sessions as participants and interact with the interpreters when they raise the issues that will be described in the following section.

As regards the key concepts of asylum, the training sessions aimed at breaking down the definitions of the two forms of international protection foreseen by the Italian legal framework, namely refugee status and subsidiary protection. These sessions required the trainers to use simple language in order to make legal notions and terminology accessible to people without a legal background (for example, persecution, particular social group, or inhuman or degrading treatment). The frequent use of examples from recurrent claims, historical events in certain countries and issues repeatedly mentioned by asylum seekers proved to be an effective way to explain complex words and meanings to interpreters, especially those who were already familiar with some topics due to their initial experience of RSD interviews. Moreover, this approach proved to be an effective way to reduce the misunderstandings related to the use of these words with asylum seekers (Wurzel 1993, 101–125).

The most challenging part of the training sessions involved explaining the role interpreters are expected to play in the context of the RSD interview. While in general participants had no real difficulty in understanding that their task would be to facilitate communication between asylum seekers and interviewers, illustrating the principles that they would have to abide by and the skills that they would need to develop in this working environment proved much more complex. In fact, during the sessions, when confronted with the examples given by the trainers to explain concepts such as knowledge of language and accuracy of interpretation, impartiality, empathy and confidentiality, many described situations involving difficult and challenging choices in order to comply with the principles and skills required.

As regards knowledge of language and accuracy (UNHCR 2009), the training sessions focused on the interpreters' responsibility to constantly improve the quality of their service through use of dictionaries and glossaries, in-depth study after work, including of the cultural attributes expressed through language, personal note-taking on terminology and meaning, and regular practice, in order to ensure a good command of the working languages and the ability to interpret consecutively in two directions. As regards the accuracy of the interpretation, it was stressed that interpreters should strive to transmit each communication without omissions, additions, distortions or any other changes to the original message; this implies that they should interpret everything (verbal and non-verbal communication) without changing anything of what the applicants or the caseworkers say, using the same register and language employed by the applicants, while avoiding summarising or omitting, adding or completing their sentences.

While the importance of self-study and practice in order to improve command of language were never questioned, the interpreters often raised concerns about the concept of accuracy. In fact, many of the interpreters explained how this requirement was extremely difficult to meet in several situations (as highlighted by translation and interpretation literature; see, e.g., Rudvin and Spinzi [2015, 92] on this subject) and created some moral dilemmas (Morris 1995, 25–46).

During the question-and-answer sessions interpreters pointed out specific difficulties related to the fact that applicants come from countries other than their own, with a variety of expressions and idioms that are simply unknown to them. Other difficulties emerged concerning the very low level of education of some asylum seekers and the consequent poor command of some languages or certain political or institutional terms (Wurzel 1993, 101–125), a fact that many interpreters realise only at the beginning of the interview. More generally, many of the interpreters stressed that the lack of information about applicants' claims and the limited possibility of familiarising with their language except in the few minutes before the interview, when they provide the applicants with preliminary information, puts them in the position of having to adapt their interpretation to very complex communicative contexts without knowing about these difficulties beforehand. Many interpreters therefore stressed the importance of having more opportunity to point out these difficulties to interviewers, possibly agreeing on interventions to clarify applicants' statements, in order to achieve more effective communication. Other interpreters asked for more time before the interview to talk to applicants, both to explain their role and the structure and functioning of the communication during the interview, and to familiarise themselves with their linguistic style. Finally, they asked to have some basic information about applicants' profiles and claims before the interview, in order to avoid having to improvise interpretation in relation to basic aspects of the claim that only emerge once the interview has begun. This was considered particularly important when interviewing asylum seekers with particular vulnerabilities (for instance, highly traumatised persons, minors) that can have a direct and strong impact on their ability to communicate.

As regards the principle of impartiality and the skill of empathy (UNHCR 2009), during the training sessions it was stressed that interpreters do not represent either applicants or authorities, and therefore that they must remain neutral, refraining from favoring or damaging either party and limiting themselves to facilitating the exchange between the participants in the interview. At the same time, the trainers underlined the importance of avoiding making negative comments about the participants or during their statements, as well as being judgmental, and the fact that interpreters must commit to setting boundaries to their role, avoiding personal involvement and refraining from acting as an interpreter if there is a conflict of interest (e.g., if they know the applicant personally). Also, in line with the principle of impartiality, interpreters were instructed to abstain from providing a service for applicants at one stage of the procedure, within the reception environment prior to the RSD interview, and then interpret for the same applicants before the commission responsible for determining their international protection needs, in order to avoid misperception of their neutral role. As regards the skill of empathy, it was stressed that interpreters must understand the communicative vulnerability of the applicant but at the same time find the right distance in order to avoid personal involvement.

Many interpreters mentioned several problematic situations that are often not perceived by the asylum authorities, highlighting tense situations with asylum seekers due to a lack of understanding of their role. The use of the first person in the interpretation of the questions asked by interviewers, required during the training sessions, contributes, if not well explained, to convincing some applicants that interpreters are responsible for deciding which questions to ask, giving them a responsibility that they do not have in the management of the hearing and consequently in the decision about their asylum application. Interpreters also pointed out that other specific activities or phases of work in the RSD environment risk undermining their neutral role if not conducted properly. Some said that the initial phase before starting the interview, dedicated to providing key information to applicants about the RSD procedure, could result in the interpreter being attributed an involvement in the decision-making process if this activity is not carried out properly or is carried out in the absence of interviewers. Other difficult situations mentioned by interpreters included when the transcript of the interview is read back to the applicant. At this point, many applicants unload their tension on the interpreters, blaming them for the lack of understanding of some parts of their statements. The interpreters have difficulty in managing this phase in the absence of interviewers.

With regard to these challenges, the interpreters stressed how important it is for them that the principle of impartiality be always explicitly explained to applicants by interviewers during the initial information phase, in order to reduce possible misunderstanding about their involvement in the decision-making process, and to make the message more authoritative since it comes from the representatives of the asylum authorities. Some interpreters also asked for activities such as the initial information phase and the re-reading of the interview transcript to the applicants to always be conducted in the presence of the interviewers, so that they can intervene directly on technical matters.

As regards the principle of confidentiality (UNHCR 2009), the trainers explained the importance of the interpreter not disclosing or commenting on information gained during the interview to parties outside the procedure, in order to protect applicants and their families, both in the country of asylum and in the country of origin. It was also emphasised that confidentiality reinforces the mutual trust between the applicant and other subjects involved in the procedure and applicants' freedom of choice. Therefore, interpreters must sign a confidentiality agreement in both the National Commission's Code of Conduct and that of their employer (i.e., the company providing the interpreting service).

With regard to this issue, many interpreters mentioned those situations in which confidentiality (and at the same time their neutral role) is tested by applicants who share with them aspects of their personal claims that could affect the assessment of their application. For example, they mentioned the initial information phase or the re-reading of the interview transcript, when applicants and interpreters may find themselves interacting in the absence of the interviewer. This circumstance may contribute to applicants' requests for support from interpreters, who are seen as fellow countrymen capable of helping them. Some interpreters described situations in which applicants revealed to them specific details of their very intimate story, linked in some cases to trauma suffered in the country of origin or during their journey, and explained their reluctance to talk about these details in front of interviewers, but they did not share these elements during the interview.

The opposite occurs when applicants perceive interpreters as belonging to their community, as fellow countrymen, and fear both being judged morally and that having details of their story revealed to the aforementioned community in the country of destination. Consequently, they are reluctant to talk about certain issues during the interview, especially if related to sexuality, religion, or certain family events.

Regarding these situations, interpreters once again stressed the importance of being supported by interviewers in reiterating to applicants that the principle of confidentiality also applies to interpreters and that their personal claims will not be revealed. Once again interpreters confirmed the importance of the presence of interviewers during the performance of specific activities, in order to avoid situations in which applicants reveal crucial details of their case to the interpreters alone, giving them a role that they do not have and creating strong dilemmas regarding the respect of the principle of confidentiality and impartiality.

Reflection by the interpreters on these concepts and principles facilitated their cooperation with the interviewers, through an increased understanding of the rationale behind the exploration of specific topics and the use of specific questions during the interviews or of the reasons why certain questions are asked repeatedly or rephrased. In addition, the training sessions held in recent years have included content that is increasingly aimed at addressing the problematic situations and gray areas (Killman 2020, 85) mentioned above, with examples drawn from the interpreters' own experience. Moreover, the regular inclusion in the training sessions of a section devoted to the operational techniques used by interviewers for managing the RSD interview proved to be very effective. In fact, the description of the interview techniques contributed to a greater understanding by interpreters of both the methodology used to explore the claims and the importance of cooperating in applying these communication techniques, involving distinct interview phases, open and closed questions, clarification, and reflection questions, all with the aim of achieving effective communication.

By the same token, the last few years have witnessed the progressive inclusion of interpreters in training sessions carried out at the local level for interviewers, on topics such as interviews and referrals of potential victims of trafficking, interviews of people with claims related to persecution on religious grounds or for their sexual orientation and gender identity. The involvement of interpreters in this kind of initiative was a development consistent with the training courses described above, characterised by the attempt to make the interpreters increasingly involved in the complexity of the work carried out by interviewers at RSD interviews.

Finally, as mentioned above, the increasing participation since 2018 of interviewers in the training contributed to the creation of more frequent opportunities for discussion in a neutral space where interpreters could at last explore the most effective ways to achieve real cooperation, allowing them to meet the needs of the asylum system while at the same time safeguarding their role and respecting the principles mentioned above. To this end, the specific requests made by interpreters on the management of certain activities in the RSD working environment contributed to create rules and tools to better regulate the relationship between interpreters, applicants and interviewers.

7.4 The contribution provided by interpreters to the quality of the system

The feedback provided by interpreters in the context of the training events contributed to raising awareness with the national authorities about the importance of their inclusion in the growth and professionalisation of the asylum system. Another clear indication of the need for an inclusive approach emerged from the activities carried out since 2015 within the quality monitoring activities of the National Commission for the Right of Asylum, conducted in collaboration with UNHCR. Alongside traditional tools to monitor the quality of asylum interviews and decisions handed down by TCs, quality monitoring activities included a participatory monitoring approach aiming at gathering the point of view of asylum seekers, as well as institutional and para-institutional actors involved in the asylum procedure. Several focus group discussions were held engaging dozens of interpreters involved with the TCs, who were asked to give their point of view about the main difficulties and best practices of their work within RSD interviews as well as about cross-cultural communication.

During the focus group discussions, interpreters gave examples from their own experience to further highlight difficulties in applying the aforementioned principles and skills, while also proposing practical solutions to overcome them.

At the same time, the monitoring activities also directly observed the quality of the interpreting services within the context of RSD interviews through checklists with specific quality indicators, which have evolved over the years to reflect and promote the improvement of interpreting services in line with the feedback provided by interpreters during exchanges with quality experts, trainers and interviewers. New indicators have in fact been included to ascertain the interpreters' ability to intervene during the interview to clarify terminological issues related to cultural variables and to point out factors that might undermine correct interpretation, through interventions coordinated with interviewers and, more in general, the respect of rules to avoid role reversal with the interviewer.

Since 2015, the findings of these monitoring activities have contributed to providing an external point of view about the quality of interpreters' work and their ability to engage with interviewers and applicants in a professional manner. At the same time, these findings have supported the development of training sessions that are better tailored to interpreters' needs and more focused on critical aspects of their work – and, thus, are more effective in providing key messages chosen, thanks to the direct observation of RSD interviews.

7.5 Codifying the rules

Several best practices for promotion in the RSD interpreting context were identified thanks to the interpreters' feedback and findings that emerged during the training sessions and monitoring activities. These best practices have been gathered and included in operational guidelines for the TCs providing practical indications about the management of the different phases and activities of the international protection determination procedure.

The guidelines also provide indications about the interpreter's role and the importance of cooperation between interpreters, applicants, and interviewers in order to foster a climate of mutual trust and achieve smooth communication, thereby reducing as much as possible linguistic and cultural misunderstandings that can compromise the quality of the RSD interview (Kälin 1986).

To this end, a list has been drawn up of correct behaviors to be followed by both the interpreters and the interviewers during the activities involving interpretation. The guidelines recommended activities such as briefings between interviewers and interpreters before the interviews, particularly the more complex ones; the routine presentation by interviewers of the interpreter's role, highlighting their impartiality; the routine check by interviewers of mutual understanding between interpreters and applicants during the interviews. A template document in Italian has also been created to give asylum seekers key information while waiting for the interview, which interpreters can also use to understand whether communication is fluent, also depending on the level of education and more generally on the claimants' profile. Moreover, interpreters are encouraged to point out difficulties in understanding the language spoken by applicants to the interviewers and are made to understand the importance of coordinating all interventions aimed at clarifying the meaning of applicants' statements with the interviewer, avoiding separate conversations with the latter. Finally, interpreters and interviewers are encouraged to exchange feedback at the end of the interview in order to improve the quality of their communication.

7.6 Conclusion: A possible way forward

The development of interpreters' training, thanks to its participatory nature, allowed interpreters to have very important moments of exchange with facilitators and interviewers and encouraged a critical reflection about their own actions (UNHCR 2017, 44). These exchanges contributed to creating increasingly effective training interventions, with a positive impact on the most problematic issues of their work in the RSD environment, in relation to both purely communicative aspects and to those concerning key principles underpinning applicants' access to their rights.

This type of training, as well as the consultation of interpreters through other channels more generally, was also an opportunity for institutions to improve the quality of the asylum system in a very complex operational context. The interpreters' privileged position in the context of the RSD interview allowed them to provide important feedback on the management of certain activities and fostered a reflection on the relationship between interpreters and interviewers, leading to the revision and promotion of operational tools.

This approach led to the reevaluation of the cultural mediation aspect of the interpreter's role to reach effective intercultural communication, while also favouring the establishment of clearer rules to enable a coordinated and therefore professional interaction between the actors of the RSD interview.

This path also led to the greater involvement of interpreters in some trainings for interviewers, with an implicit recognition of the fact that the specialisation of the asylum system's institutional actors must be accompanied by the interpreting service's professional growth to express its full potential and be truly effective. This inclusive approach should also be supported by additional interventions that demonstrate the same kind of attention to interpreters' role, but which are also characterised by flexibility, sustainability, and innovation.

Induction training packages should be created for new interpreters to gradually introduce them into the RSD environment, so they can operate properly in the context of interviews with asylum seekers from the outset. This type of intervention would also address the challenges represented by the continuous rotation of interpreters in this environment, ensuring a minimum standard of quality for the interpreting service despite the frequent staff turnover.

At the same time, setting up *ad hoc* monitoring mechanisms to assess the quality of crucial aspects of the interpreting service would allow its strengths and weaknesses to be identified and further contribute to developing training events tailored specifically to the identified areas of improvement.

A further contribution to increase the quality of interpreting service in the asylum context could be given from professional interpreters and academia. Promoting an exchange with these subjects could be key to develop the national asylum authorities' reflection about the management of interpreting activity in the RSD procedure through private tenders.

Finally, capacity development tools and resources for interpreters implemented on IT platforms might also contribute to achieving sustainable professional growth through an innovative approach.

Some crucial issues such as the recognition of the role of intercultural mediators and RSD interpreters need to be addressed and resolved in order to ensure their professional growth accompanied by their job stability. Nevertheless, the path described in the previous paragraphs offers concrete examples of how some elements are crucial, even in a context lacking the aforementioned professional recognition, to contributing to the professionalisation of interpreters while at the same time promoting a mature RSD system.

Disclaimer

The opinions expressed by the author are personal and attributable to him alone; they do not necessarily represent the position of UNHCR or the United Nations.

Note

1 2019 has been chosen because it is the last year that realistically reflects the volume of asylum claims lodged in Italy, before the COVID-19 pandemic, which had a very strong impact on the number of asylum requests and consequently on asylum hearings and related interpreting services.

References

Department of Civil Liberties and Immigration, National Commission for the Right to Asylum. 2004. *I numeri dell'asilo. Quaderno Statistico per gli anni 1990–2020. Richieste di asilo* (16). www.libertaciviliimmigrazione.dlci.interno.gov.it/sites/default/files/allegati/quaderno_statistico_per_gli_anni_1990_2020.pdf

Directive 2011/95/EU of the European Parliament and of the Council of 13 December 2011 on Standards for the Qualification of Third-Country Nationals or Stateless

Persons as Beneficiaries of International Protection, for a Uniform Status for Refugees or for Persons Eligible for Subsidiary Protection, and for the Content of the Protection Granted (Recast), *OJ L 337, 20.12.20116*). https://eur-lex.europa.eu/legal-content/EN/TXT/?uri=celex%3A32011L0095

Eurostat. 2019. *Asylum Applicants by Type of Applicant, Citizenship, Age and Sex – Annual Aggregated Data.* https://appsso.eurostat.ec.europa.eu/nui/submitViewTableAction.do

Jiménez-Ivars, Amparo. 2021. "Telephone Interpreting for Asylum Seekers in the UD: A Corpus-Based Study." *JoSTrans* 140: 125–146.

Kälin, Walter. 1986. "Troubled Communication: Cross-Cultural Misunderstanding in the Asylum-Hearing." *International Migration Review* 20 (2), 230–241.

Killman, Jeffrey. 2020. "Interpreting for Asylum Seekers and their Attorneys: The Challenge of Agency." *Perspectives* 28 (1): 73–89. https://doi.org/10.1080/0907676X.2019.1615518.

Martin-Ruano, María R. 2017. "Developing Public Service Translation and Interpreting under the Paradigm of Recognition: Towards Diversity-Sensitive Discourses on Ethics in PSIT." In *Ideology, Ethics and Policy Development in Public Service Interpreting and Translation*, edited by Carmen Valero Garcés, and Rebecca Tipton, 21–37. Bristol: Multilingual Matters.

Morris, Ruth. 1995. "The Moral Dilemmas of Court Interpreting." *The Translator* 1 (1): 25–46.

Pöllabauer, Sonja. 2004. "Interpreting in Asylum Hearings. Issues of Role, Responsibility and Power." *Interpreting* 6 (2): 143–180. htpps://doi.org/10.1075/intp.6.2.03pol.

Pöllabauer, Sonja, and Sebastian Schumacher. 2004. "Kommunikationsprobleme und Neuerungsverbot im Asylverfahren." *Migralex* 1: 21–29.

Pym, Anthony, François Grin, Claudio Sfreddo, and A. L. J. Chan. 2012. *The Status of the Translation Profession in the European Union: Final Report.* Luxembourg: European Commission.

Rudvin, Mette, and Cinzia Spinzi. 2015. *L'interprete giuridico: Profilo professionale e metodologie di lavoro.* Roma: Carocci.

UN High Commissioner for Refugees (UNHCR). 2009. *Self-Study Module 3: Interpreting in a Refugee Context.* www.refworld.org/docid/49b6314d2.html.

UN High Commissioner for Refugees (UNHCR). 2017. *Handbook for Interpreters in Asylum Procedures.* www.unhcr.org/dach/wp-content/uploads/sites/27/2017/09/AUT_Handbook-Asylum-Interpreting_en.pdf.

Wurzel, Petra. 1993. "Über die sprachlichen und kulturellen Ursachen von Mißverständnissen und Widersprüchen in Asylverfahren aus der Sicht des Dolmetschers." *Zeitschrift für Türkeistudien* 6 (1): 101–125.

PART III

Training interpreters to work with refugees in national and regional contexts

8

INTERPRETERS' TRAINING NEEDS IN REFUGEE HUMANITARIAN CRISES

Perceptions from Cameroon

Ebenezer Tedjouong and Marija Todorova

In the current state of the world, when we are witnessing ever-increasing numbers of refugee crises around the globe, the need for professionally trained interpreters who will work alongside protection and humanitarian personnel is significant. However, because of the urgency of the crises, the interpreters are often engaged for their language skills without having received any training, and sometimes they share the refugee experience themselves. This article will look at the specific issues that arise from the work of interpreters in the refugee context, including neutrality, empathy, and trust-related matters and will propose approaches to address those through adequate training. Data will be based on interviews with practising interpreters and humanitarian workers who use interpreters. These will be cross-referenced with existing training for community interpreters and interpreters in a refugee context.

8.1 Introduction

Interpreting for refugees in humanitarian emergencies is one of the least studied and most under-recognised types of interpreting. Previously, the work of interpreters in refugee camps has been studied through the lenses of mediation theory and practice, as the role of interpreters in such humanitarian crises involves significantly more than just enabling communication between the refugees and the assistance providers (Todorova 2016, 2017, 2019, 2021b). These studies, based on field data from refugee emergencies such as the Boat People emergency in Hong Kong 1975–2000, the Kosovo conflict in 1999–2000, and the EU refugee crisis of 2014–2015, considered interpreters' work in the often-overlooked context of supporting emergency management of large groups of refugees crossing the border or temporarily sheltered in refugee camps. Interview-based research found that interpreters working in refugee emergencies have specific roles and that these are

DOI: 10.4324/9781003230359-11

different from the roles taken by community interpreters in peaceful circumstances, thus requiring specific training suitable to perform these duties and roles. While the international staff of international humanitarian organisations have been trained how to work in an emergency, the locally employed interpreters often have a good knowledge of one of the languages (usually their mother tongue) but (sometimes only a basic) knowledge of the other language which they use to interpret, with little or no experience as interpreters before finding themselves in a position of interpreting for refugees. Moser-Mercer et al. (2014, 143) have built on their prior experience in the field of language acquisition to offer some insights in the need for training for language actors working in conflict, post-conflict, and humanitarian settings.

Research in the field (Salama-Carr 2007; Inghilleri 2008; Kujamäki 2012; Todorova 2019) has identified that most interpreters engaged in emergencies are not trained professional interpreters; instead, they are engineers or medical doctors with knowledge of the language spoken by the refugees (Baker 2010) often belonging to the humanitarian aid workers or the beneficiaries (Delgado Luchner and Kherbiche 2018). Due to this lack of specialised training, regardless of whether they have received some kind of interpreting training or not, interpreters in humanitarian settings are more often than not supposed to communicate in situations that had not been carefully defined or explained for them in any formal or informal training and can sometimes even run contrary to any instructions or preparation they received. Specifically, interpreters are trained to remain neutral, unbiased, and invisible. However, recent studies comparing interpreters with mediators have shown that while interpreters working in refugee contexts are expected to be impartial, such an expectation is impossible to meet in real-life scenarios (Todorova 2020). Therefore, this lack of adequate, real-life, and context-specific training can be identified as the main reason behind many of the challenges interpreters face in conflict, related to their position, expected neutrality, and heightened levels of stress.

Another distinctive characteristic of interpreting in emergencies arising from the iterative and prolonged contact with individual refugees and the highly emotional content of the mediated communication resulting from the trauma of conflict and forced migration is the experiencing of vicarious trauma. While working under "circumstances in which it would be difficult for any human being to remain unperturbed" (Martin and Valero-Garcés 2008, 2), humanitarian interpreters perform their work with a pronounced amount of empathy as a vital foundation for establishing a working relationship of trust between the interpreter and the refugee (Todorova 2019). In addition, many people working as interpreters within refugee emergencies are former refugees themselves; they are exposed to a significant amount of emotional trauma that accompanies witnessing or hearing atrocities (Pillen 2016). Barea Muñoz (2021) notes the emotional effect of the interpreting assignment on the interpreter who is situated inside the conflict. The emotional stress that arises from interpreting raises the need to offer psychological assistance designed specifically for humanitarian interpreters working in refugee situations.

Besides these specific roles and characteristics of interpreting in refugee crises settings resulting from conflict, "no provision has been made for training interpreters specifically to work in those settings, with few exceptions" (Ruiz Rosendo and Persaud 2016, 28). Training developed thus far for interpreters working in emergencies includes the technology-focused module by the Centre for Interpreting in Conflict Zones (InZone) and the self-study module for interpreting for refugees developed by UNHCR (2009). A joint programme organised by the University of Geneva's Faculty of Translation and Interpreting and the International Committee of the Red Cross (ICRC), as well as the joint initiative by University of Geneva's Faculty of Translation and Interpreting and the Centre of Competence on Humanitarian Negotiation (CCHN) focused on the role of interpreters in humanitarian negotiations (Erni and Espinosa Mooser 2021). More recently, Yarmouk University in Jordan and the University of Nairobi in Kenya introduced formal Diploma programmes in humanitarian interpreting and translation (Moser-Mercer et al. 2021), while the University of Glasgow offers an online asynchronous course for interpreters working with refugees. Ruiz Rosendo et al. (2021) provide a detailed study on a tailored training to for UN staff interpreters servicing field missions. However, more research is needed to evaluate the effectiveness of these programmes, their suitability for various localities and their implementation in the practice of interpreting in emergency refugee situations.

Research in this field (Todorova 2021a) shows that more training is needed to ensure that interpreters are ready to handle the unique environment of refugee emergencies. Specifically, non-professional interpreters need to be trained in interpreting, but other forms of preparation are just as crucial when working in emergencies. According to Moser-Mercer and Bali (2008), they lack both essential technical skills and ethics to perform as interpreters.

Interpreters that dealt with conflict and post-conflict situations in their line of work had the same complaint: a lack of specialised training for their specific role (Todorova 2021a). They needed instruction that matched the types of situations where they performed their duties. In this article, we will take the discussion further by considering the training needs for interpreters in humanitarian crises as identified by both interpreters and humanitarian workers who use interpreters with a particular focus on the situation in Cameroon.

8.2 Interpreting for refugees in Cameroon

In the world at large, but especially in Africa, unfortunately, interpreting in conflict zones and providing interpreting services in the many refugee camps that come into existence as a result of conflict is a frequently required mode of work for interpreters. Working in refugee camps is a complex and ever-changing encounter between the providers or facilitators of humanitarian aid (international organisations and their staff, international and local NGOs and their staff, etc.), the *ad hoc* or expert providers of language services, and the beneficiaries of language mediation (local communities, refugees, host governments and organisations, etc.). In this complex arena, the perceptions of interpretation and its skill requirements may vary from one group of stakeholders to the other. Taking a deep dive into the Cameroon based refugee camps has led to the exploration of both similarities and differences in perspectives between the various groups.

Cameroon is currently plagued by conflicts within and out of its borders. Apart from the crisis going on in the Northwest and Southwest regions of Cameroon, the major conflict zones are located in the Northern regions (Adamawa, North, and the Far North) and in the East region, an area that shares borders with the politically unstable Central African Republic (CAR). Over the past decade, the Islamist armed group Boko Haram has stepped up attacks on civilians in towns and villages in the Northern regions of Cameroon, causing large numbers of internally displaced people.[1]

The group has also looted hundreds of homes in the region, thus waging war on the people of Cameroon at a shocking human cost. Furthermore, apart from the various conflicts happening within its borders, the political instability in CAR has caused around 290,000 Central African citizens to flee to Cameroon, where they mostly live in refugee camps.

According to the United Nations Office for the Coordination of Humanitarian Affairs (OCHA), Cameroon is affected by three concurrent complex humanitarian crises, namely, the Boko Haram crisis in the Lake Chad Basin that impacts the three Northern regions of the country, socio-political violence in the Northwest and Southwest regions and the presence of over 280,000 refugees from the Central African Republic (CAR) in the eastern regions (East, Adamawa, and North). Central African refugees and the populations that host them share cultural, religious and linguistic similarities. The Fulani, Gbayas, Hausa, and Mboums from CAR have bonds of brotherhood and secular alliances with their Cameroonian hosts. They share the same sociocultural characteristics that strengthen the integration of refugees and the local Cameroonian population together. The major refugee camps are located in the Far North (Minawao) and the East (Lolo). Just as a way of illustration, the Minawao camp is jointly managed by local and international organisations. With a surface area of about 623 hectares, it hosts more than 60,000 refugees.

In the process of conflict management and provision of humanitarian aid, local and international NGOs deploy staff and resources in the refugee camps. In these camps, language diversity makes language mediation a must, and language services are provided by various actors. However, as we can see from the discussion below, very often, the people engaged in providing interpreting are non-professional and belong to the community of refugees. Moreover, they are often not formally trained in interpreting.

The University of Buea in Cameroon offers a programme for the training of translators and interpreters. The programme was structured to answer the needs of the government at the central administration level with the objective of progressively taking into account the needs of decentralised administration. Before the implementation of the programme could fulfil the needs at a decentralised level, the government declared that the civil service was saturated with interpreters. The civil service is structured around conference interpreting to the detriment of other forms of interpreting. The form of interpreting chosen is one that serves the elites in the administration. Conference interpreting is offered with only English and French as possible languages. In fact, the policymakers worried first about making it possible for the government to communicate with the citizens, thus neglecting the interactive nature of every communication act. To make communication a public good in the multilingual landscape of Cameroon, it would have been necessary to integrate other forms of interpreting, known as community interpreting, to fulfil the needs of the police, the courts, the hospitals, the councils, and other remote public spaces of interaction such as refugee camps. Apart from English and French, there is a greater need to offer other locally used languages. Exclusion of local languages such as Ewondo, Douala, and Bassa, and the lingua francas, such as Pidgin and Fulfulde, entails the exclusion from public debate and development of all members of the population who are not literate in the official languages. This also means a nonrecognition of the cultural identities that go with the different local languages.

In the refugee camps of the East region, for example, the refugees come from a large number of linguistically diverse Chadian and Central African communities. Though Fufulde is shared by most refugees, it is not the language spoken by the majority of NGO staff who are relatively fluent in English and/or French. Intelligibility among the speakers of different languages in the humanitarian assistance landscape is not easily achieved. Organisations such as the Red Cross would therefore adopt a working strategy based on recruitment of volunteers around and in the communities of refugees to ensure communication, including through language mediation. The working strategy is also based on multitasking. A logistic staff identified as having a pertinent dual language proficiency would be briefed on how to mediate conversations between two parties.

To understand the training needs of interpreters working in refugee camps, we collected data primarily based on semi-structured interviews (Baker 2019). Moreover, in order to compare the training requirements for interpreters working in refugee camps, we interviewed two groups of participants: those who interpreted and those who were employers of interpreters in the refugee camps. In total, we interviewed three interpreters and three employers of interpreters. During the interviews, we examined the training that interpreters had received, challenging and rewarding aspects of their work, their perceptions of the role of interpreters in the refugee assistance process, the impact of interpreting on their personality, the institutional support provided for their work, and the areas in which they believed refugee interpreters should receive training. On the other hand, employers were interviewed in order to identify their needs for interpreting, language combinations, challenges when working with an interpreter, as well as interpreter's training needs in order to perform communication with refugees. Because the participants in this study lived in geographically distant regions, it was necessary to conduct many of the interviews by Skype.

The approach to data presentation adopted here is that of narrating the participants' experiences with deliberate determination to stick to the storyline provided by the participant in the interview. To protect their identity, interviewees will be referred by names that are not their real names. Using a paradigmatic narrative approach to present the interviews (Delgado Luchner and Kherbiche 2018), the subsequent data analysis will dwell on the paradigmatic constituents of interpreter training and compare them within and across the groups of research participants.

8.3 The perceptions of employers

Mirabelle works as humanitarian staff for the International Red Cross organisations and has organised several sensitisation campaigns in refugee camps in the Northern regions of Cameroon. She speaks French, English, Kenyang, and Pidgin English. She works with a stakeholder management approach, including when she needs interpreters to mediate conversations in the camps. Interpreters are selected among the trained volunteers of the Red Cross organisation who the International Red Cross trains to serve as community workers.

In the Minawao refugee camp where Mirabelle works, interpreting comes in when they assess the needs of the population or collect data to communicate on specific situations in the camps. In general, volunteers are members of communities in the camps who are refugees themselves. The advantage is to have volunteers who at the same time are immersed in the context and have language proficiency that makes it possible for them to work as interpreters.

Mirabelle stresses that one of the most important criteria for selecting interpreters is "to use people with good records at the community level so as to make sure not to hire people who constitute not an aid but a hindrance in the communication process" since "if you were to choose a drunkard as an interpreter or simply someone who does not have a positive reputation within the community, people will likely not to listen to him/her."

Sometimes the International Red Cross may use persons from the host or refugee community with adequate language proficiency. It is part of the strategy to identify people with specific skills in the community and have them contribute to the crisis management and the humanitarian needs it entails. The choice of the interpreters is oriented or influenced by those who master the context and the stakeholders in presence. Before the interpreters perform their work, they are given some communication tips. The employers also insist that the interpreter communicates the message as is without adding or subtracting anything. This is done during briefing sessions in which the activities are presented. The interpreter is given all contextual elements on objectives, stakes, and challenges. If the job is to interview a family, for example, the interpreter is provided with the interview guide, and Mirabelle makes sure that the interpreter has understood the implications. Sometimes bilingual people from the audience are used to check the quality of interpreting and make sure that the interpreters focus on the message and nothing but the message.

If Mirabelle were to provide training for interpreters tailored to conflict zones or refugee camps, she would emphasise communication skills that help communicate the message, such as confidentiality, and the need for the interpreter to convey the same message. Some training in local languages may also be required. Gender considerations are important in the choice of the interpreter. This choice is to be guided by local cultural requirements. For example, in the Muslim community, it is not acceptable that women teach a community of men. Therefore, having a female interpreter in such a setting is a possible source of communication disruption. Immediate briefing is an important on-the-job training as it gives an overview of stakes, stakeholders and key messages.

Minawao refugee camp is on the far North of the country close to the border with Nigeria, while on the Southeast, on the very border with the Central African Republic is the Lolo refugee camp.

Joki worked in various refugee camps during 2014. He has served as a Communication Officer for the International Red Cross, the National Red Cross, and Save Cameroon Refugees. One of these was the Lolo refugee camp, where numerous Central African refugees did not speak the language of aid providers. Describing the experience of working with interpreters, Joki identified the major risk as having "an interpreter who says what he wants and not what the speaker says." This risk is further compounded by language varieties. For example, in the area where the camp is located, both the Cameroonians belonging to the host community and the Central African refugees speak Fufulde. But the language varieties of Fufulde spoken by the two communities are not the same.

To avoid communication blunders, Joki chooses interpreters both from the refugee community and from the host community based on the specific need. This reduces the risk of under-translation or over-translation. Interpreters are selected with the assistance of community leaders: the youth leader, the women leader, and the central president of the community of refugees. The same approach is adopted in the host community, where the leaders are requested to provide names of persons and their skills; the suggestions coming from leaders from both communities facilitate ownership of and inclusion in the process. During meetings, speeches are interpreted into Sango, Bororo, and/or Fufulde. Sango is widely spoken in the Central African Republic, whereas Bororo and Fufulde are languages spoken by diverse communities of Cameroon (Northern and Eastern regions), Nigeria and the Central African Republic. Sometimes, Joki may need two interpreters so that one interprets, and the other relays the message into the third language. One interpreter may also do the work in all languages involved. The risk is always for the interpreter not to understand the stakes and consequently add to the message or make omissions. This happened with so many interpreters during the emergency phase. The way the interpreters are selected, the level of language knowledge, and the mastery of interpreting skills have proved satisfactory. However, since some organisers had some understanding of the source language, they would request that the utterance be repeated for the interpreter to render the message accurately.

In general, Joki is content with the interpreters who could understand the languages and faithfully interpret under the supervision of community leaders.

However, if Joki were to train interpreters, he would emphasise essential communication, community mobilisation, and interpretation methodology. Regarding communication tips, the essence of training would be to focus on the basics of communication, the role of the different actors in the communication process, the contribution of non-verbal language, ways of reformulation, etc. Interpretation methodology would focus on note-taking, sight translation, and other exercises that boost multitasking and make possible a fluid and accurate rendition of the message based on a deep analysis of the original utterances. Another essential component of training is knowledge of the cultural context regarding community values and beliefs. This will enable the interpreter to work while being aware of cultural nuances and the consequences of the message for refugees. For example, in the Munka (an ethnicity of the West region of Cameroon) culture, lowering one's voice at a given moment of a conversation is synonymous with threatening the other party. The interpreter, therefore, needs a sound understanding of the cultural context and its implications in the communication process.

Apart from the International Red Cross, there are many other humanitarian organisations providing services in refugee camps in Cameroon, and they all require interpreters in order to provide humanitarian assistance to the refugees.

Alain also worked in organising aid provision at the Lolo camp. In the first attempt to solve language issues, he approached the Professional Association of Translators and interpreters (APTIC), whose headquarters are in Yaoundé, Cameroon. He thought it would be far better to work with professionals. Unfortunately, despite long hours of discussions with trained and certified interpreters, he could not get to an agreement on work and payment modalities. Professionals request for a minimum working day pay set by the professional association and to operate in teams of at least two interpreters.

Moreover, because they will be working out of a booth, interpreters request a salary increase of about 50%. Consecutive interpreting is more expensive than simultaneous in Cameroon. Even when Alain would get the funds from the European Union to pay the fees requested, it is almost impossible to get professionals with the required language combinations. Most of the interpreters trained by APTIC interpret from English to French and/or vice-versa. Their knowledge of the local languages is relatively poor. So, Alain ended up using the services of a bilingual teacher who works for a government school in the East. Though the interpreter had an acceptable level of fluency in Sango, Fufulde, and French, he sometimes battled with words and was contradicted by people from the audience who could understand the languages but doubted their speaking proficiency. Alain noticed that "it could be perceived by the audience that [interpreter's] proficiency in local languages was just average. He fought with words, and some of his utterances either shocked the participants or plunged them into laughter."

If Alain were asked to organise training for interpreters in the refugee camps, he would choose people with high contextual knowledge and a sound mastery of the local languages involved. The training will focus on background information on the conflict, communication and the pedagogy of interpreting. Courses will be organised in the form of short seminars with identified participants who are either from the refugee camps or interact with refugees on a daily basis.

8.4 The perceptions of interpreters

Brigitte is a professional interpreter. She has provided interpreting service at hundreds of meetings with the African Union, WHO, and other UN institutions. Before getting trained, she worked as an interpreter for an NGO in Meiganga (a town close to the Lolo refugee camp at the border between Cameroon and CAR). The NGO was carrying out surveys on reproductive health hazards in refugee camps. Her employers also sought to sensitise and train women on using female contraception. She worked in a team where she interpreted from English to French, and another interpreter relayed the message into the local language. It was a training session, and she had content knowledge as the same organisation previously used her as a peer educator. As she says herself, "When I did not understand what the trainer said, I just behaved as if I was the trainer myself, and I filled the gaps." In this endeavour, she now thinks she was deficient in using the appropriate phraseology. She had no concern for contextual equivalence. She would express things in a very "raw language" in the perspective of receivers, just because she followed the structures and the ways of saying something in the source language. This often shocked the beneficiaries of interpretation who were of a Muslim background.

If Brigitte were to train interpreters for refugee camps, she would emphasise interpreters' behaviour. In this setting, dressing as a conference interpreter would create a blockage. The interpreter must dress very modestly, use elementary language, argotic language if possible. Brigitte would give interpreters training on the basics of note-taking and make sure they have the required tools. In one of her encounters, they met with a young girl who was 15 years or so. The topic was the use of female preservatives. However, her parents insisted on being present. Brigitte thought that with the mother's presence, she would be using one stone to shoot two birds: training the daughter and the mother at the same time. In the course of the conversation the trainer mentioned coitus interruptus, and Brigitte did not know how to express it in French. So, she said "coït interrompu" and the teenager asked what this was. So, the trainer paused and asked Brigitte to explain the concept to the teenager. While she was explaining, she said the concept refers to "when the male wants to introduce his penis into your vagina, . . ." The mother of the teenager was so shocked that she interrupted the whole session, arguing that they were corrupting her child, teaching her bad manners. This incident brought so many other participants to abstain from attending future sessions. Brigitte therefore would want interpreters in the refugee camps to add empathy to any communication strategy that they use.

Some of the interpreters engaged to work in refugee camps identify equally with the humanitarian workers as well as an interpreter (Delgado Luchner and Kherbiche 2018) even when they have been trained and socialised as interpreters.

Eleonore also interpreted in the Meiganga refugee camp. She equally was employed by (local and international) NGOs who advocated against rape and other kinds of sexual violence among refugees. The NGOs employing her organised training sessions in the camps. Eleonore was a Year 3 English and French undergraduate student at the time. She was chosen for her bilingual proficiency. Her employers trained her on the use of written material to communicate the messages to the target audience. Once she proved to have understood the messages, she would be given English or French written material. She used the material to present the content to the audience in Fufulde or in Sango. She worked as trainer-interpreter, and her results were very appreciated by the organisers of the training. But one day she had to formally interpret consecutively during a training session. The speakers were from Britain and knew no words in the local languages. Eleonore reports that "one day the trainer used the word *survey*, and I translated by *surveiller* because I did not know how put it in French." The trainer explained that the objective is to carry out a survey on sexual reproduction. Eleonore was very embarrassed and simply said, "L'objectif est de *surveiller* la reproduction parmi les refugiés." [The objective is to carry out a *monitoring* of reproduction among refugees] (translation and emphases provided by the author). Unfortunately, one participant said he had heard the word "sexual." So, Eleonore said the objective is to "surveiller la sexualité" [monitor sexualities]. The male participant burst into anger, wondering "how people can travel all the way from Britain to come and watch over sexual reproduction in refugee camps." This rather unfortunate anecdote was used by Eleonore to stress the need for interpreters in refugee camps to have a good mastery of working languages. Because interpretation is done in refugee camps, says Eleonore, it does not make it low quality interpreting. What makes the huge difference is mostly the languages in presence and the context of emergency. The other requirements remain the same.

Even though trained interpreters are sometimes engaged by humanitarian organisations, very often the interpreters in refugee camps are not trained in interpreting (Todorova 2019).

Ejani was hired as an interpreter in the Far North region. The NGO that hired her was interviewing refugees on Boko Haram violence in the Nigerian and Cameroonian villages. In this area of Cameroon, there are many internally displaced persons and refugees who are hosted in the 623-hectare Minawao camp. She was hired for her English/French/Fufulde proficiency and did not have any training in interpreting. Her work included oral translation of written documents, consecutive interpreting, and drafting of written documents on the basis of oral renditions. Ejani found it very difficult to orally translate written documents and thinks each interpreter must be trained in this skill. "I personally think each interpreter also needs to be trained in note-taking. I always find it difficult to interrupt the speaker repeatedly so as to be able to interpret," says Ejani. Another area of training, according to Ejani, is a general presentation of the context and the issues at stake. If she had to train interpreters for refugee camps, she would focus on sight interpreting or translation, note-taking, and a presentation of contextual framework.

8.5 Conclusion

This research attempted to identify the training needs of interpreters working in refugee camps in Cameroon by comparing perceptions of employers to the ones of interpreters. From the data that has been presented, we can draw several conclusions. Firstly, the refugee camps are a less formalised context than the conference rooms where interpreting generally takes place. However, this does not make them less challenging and does require equally expert language knowledge.

Interpreting in refugee camps is a context that requires a mixture of written and oral translation. Working in refugee camps often incorporates working on sensitive topics with vulnerable population that requires training in specialised knowledge and empathy. Because of the nature of this context, interpreters will most often than not be hired on an ad hoc basis with consideration of their language skills and their knowledge of the context. Knowledge of local languages and multiple varieties of a language is required, alongside good command of English and French language. Training therefore would be in the form of short courses and integrate content provided on site rather than in formal education setting (see Chapter 10).

We therefore are concluding that, in the refugee camps, the need is rather for multitasking multilingual speakers skilled in both oral and written forms of language practice to ease interlingual communication. The need has equally been confirmed by the research participants of the two categories who called for a "user-oriented training" tailored to the needs of stakeholders.

Based on the above, interpreting in emergency context and refugee camps is preferably performed by non-professional ad-hoc interpreters who belong to the refugee or the local host community and, thus, bring their knowledge of the community and their social capital that enables trust. The need to provide them with the appropriate professional training in interpreting, including note-taking and short-term memory (see Chapter 15) was seen as helpful to perform their roles with more expertise.

Some participants pointed to the need of training interpreters who are capable of empathy in sensitive environments. Such emergency interpreters often find themselves in situations they have no clear understanding of, having to rely on their own estimates on how to act while working under the most challenging conditions. This in turn can have psychological implications on interpreters who need to be trained in self-care (see Chapter 16).

Finally, we want to point that the general training needs of interpreters in refugee camps and humanitarian refugee emergencies seem to be shared across various time periods and locations which is helpful in providing specialised training courses whenever and wherever a need arises.

Note

1   Internally displaced persons (IDPs), according to the *United Nations Guiding Principles on Internal Displacement,* are "persons or groups of persons who have been forced or obliged to flee or to leave their homes or places of habitual residence, in particular as a result of

or in order to avoid the effects of armed conflict, situations of generalized violence, violations of human rights or natural or human-made disasters, and who have not crossed an internationally recognized state border." (UNHCR Emergency Handbook 2022, https://emergency.unhcr.org)

References

Baker, Catherine. 2019. "Interviewing for Research on Languages and War." In *The Palgrave Handbook of Languages and Conflict*, edited by Michael Kelly, Hilary Footitt, and Myriam Salama-Carr, 157–179. Cham: Springer International.

Baker, Mona. 2010. "Interpreters and Translators in the War Zone." *The Translator* 16 (2): 197–122.

Barea Muñoz, Manuel. 2021. "Psychological Aspects of Interpreting Violence: A Narrative from the Israeli-Palestinian Conflict." In *Interpreting Conflict: A Comparative Framework*, edited by Marija Todorova, and Lucía Ruiz Rosendo. Cham: Springer.

Delgado Luchner, Carmen, and Leïla Kherbiche. 2018. "Without Fear or Favour? The Positionality of ICRC and UNHCR Interpreters in the Humanitarian Field." *Target* 30 (3): 415–438.

Erni, Fiorella, and Ana P. Espinosa Mooser. 2021. *Negotiating with Interpreters and Interpreting during Negotiations: Listening Tour with Humanitarian Negotiators and Interpreters*. Geneva: The Centre of Competence on Humanitarian Negotiation (CCHN).

Inghilleri, Moira. 2008. "The Ethical Task of the Translator in the Geo-Political Arena." *Translation Studies* 1 (2): 212–223.

Kujamäki, Pekka. 2012. "Mediating for the Third Reich: On Military Translation Cultures in World War II in Northern Finland." In *Languages and the Military. Alliances, Occupation and Peace Building*, edited by Hilary Footitt, and Michael Kelly, 86–99. Basingstoke: Palgrave Macmillan.

Martin, Anne, and Carmen Valero-Garcés. eds. 2008. *Crossing Borders in Community Interpreting: Definitions and Dilemmas*. Amsterdam: John Benjamins.

Moser-Mercer, Barbara, and Grégoire Bali. 2008. "Interpreting in zones of crisis and war." *AIIC*. https://web.archive.org/web/20160622064324/http://aiic.net/p/2979.

Moser-Mercer, Barbara, Leila Kherbiche, and Barbara Class. 2014. "Interpreting Conflict: Training Challenges in Humanitarian Field Interpreting." *Journal of Human Rights Practice* 6 (1): 140–158.

Moser-Mercer, Barbara, Somia Qudah, Mona Nabeel Ali Malkawi, Jayne Mutiga, and Mohammed Al-Batineh. 2021. "Beyond Aid: Sustainable Responses to Meeting Language Communication Needs in Humanitarian Contexts." *Interpreting and Society* 1 (1): 5–27.

Pillen, Alex. 2016. "Language, Translation, Trauma." *Annual Review of Anthropology* 45: 95–111.

Ruiz Rosendo, Lucía, Alma Barghout, and Conor Martin. 2021. "Interpreting on UN Field Missions: A Training Programme." *The Interpreter and Translator Trainer* 15 (4): 450–467.

Ruiz Rosendo, Lucía, and Clementina Persaud. 2016. "Interpreters and Interpreting in Conflict Zones and Scenarios: A Historical Perspective." *Linguistica Antverpiensia* 15: 1–35.

Salama-Carr, Myriam. 2007. *Translating and Interpreting Conflict*. Amsterdam: Rodopi.

Todorova, Marija. 2016. "Interpreting Conflict Mediation in Kosovo and Macedonia." *Linguistica Antverpiensia* 15: 227–240.

Todorova, Marija. 2017. "Interpreting at the Border: 'Shuttle Interpreting' for UNHCR." *CLINA* 3 (2): 115–129.

Todorova, Marija. 2019. "Interpreting for Refugees: Empathy and Activism." In *Intercultural Crisis Communication: Translation, Interpreting, and Languages in Local Crises*, edited by Federico Federici, and Christophe Declercq, 153–171. London: Bloomsbury Academics.

Todorova, Marija. 2020. "Interpreting for refugees: Lessons learned from the field." In *Interpreting in Legal and Healthcare Settings*, edited by Eva Ng, and Ineke Crezee, 63–82. London/Amsterdam/New York: John Benjamins.

Todorova, Marija. 2021a. "Pressing Issues and Future Directions for Interpreting in Conflict Zones." In *Interpreting Conflict: A Comparative Framework*, edited by Marija Todorova, and Lucía Ruiz Rosendo. Cham: Palgrave MacMillan.

Todorova, Marija. 2021b. "Interpreting for Refugees in Hong Kong." In *Interpreting Conflict: A Comparative Framework*, edited by Marija Todorova, and Lucía Ruiz Rosendo, Cham: Palgrave MacMillan.

UNHCR. 2009. *Self-Study Module 3: Interpreting in a Refugee Context.* www.refworld.org/docid/49b6314d2.html.

9

INTERPRETING FOR VULNERABLE POPULATIONS

Training and education of interpreters working with refugee children in the United States

Indira Sultanić

In the United States, interpreting for refugee children asylum seekers has, to date, been minimally explored. Moreover, the availability of educational and training opportunities, tailored for these groups, has been limited and underexplored in the context of interpreter readiness for asylum settings, especially those involving minors. This chapter offers an overview of interpreter education and training as relates to vulnerable populations and makes recommendations for further professionalisation of asylum interpreting as a specialisation within community and legal interpreting in the US context. It does so while recognising the contributing factors such as the current language access policies and practices on both the systemic and legislative levels. Finally, it aims to contribute to the growing body of research on interpreting in asylum and refugee services, more specifically, to literature on interpreting for vulnerable groups in the United States and beyond.

9.1 Introduction

Asylum interpreting, for adults and children alike, is a demanding task. It is, in its essence, emotional labour. In addition to the emotional aspect, it is complicated by several factors such as the setting or the environment, organisational requirements, or lack thereof, mode, modality, and the linguistic and cultural background of the interlocutors. Though interpreters are no strangers to the many facets of everyday interpreting tasks and the ever-changing nature of the communicative event, in asylum settings they face additional challenges. Those may include the asylee's often traumatic lived experiences, the laws and policies of the host country, the interviewer's expertise and disposition, and the interpreter's overall training, education, and readiness. When one of the interlocutors in the communicative event is a child, the task of the interpreter becomes significantly more difficult. The age and level of language acquisition of the child, in addition to the child's lived experiences

DOI: 10.4324/9781003230359-12

and cultural background, are all important considerations. Therefore, to successfully manage an interpreted event and the flow of communication between the parties, of which one is a minor, training, education, skill, and understanding of the interpreter's role in the interaction, as well as the ability to interpret the meaning from the nuances of both verbal and non-verbal communication are paramount.

Interpreting in asylum settings in the US, depending on the stage of the asylum process and the context, falls either into the category of community or legal interpreting. It resides at the intersection of the two. These settings have also been referred to as "quasi-judicial" (Wallace and Hernández 2017), and a "gray zone" (Bancroft et al. 2013). This intersection calls for special inquiry into what type of education and training currently exist for interpreters working with vulnerable populations in the US. What skills, knowledge, and/or credentials are currently available, and what considerations are still needed for improvement and further professionalisation of this field. Therefore, this chapter examines the education, training, and skills required in interpreting for refugee children asylum seekers in the United States; specifically for those interpreters working at the US–Mexico border, given that most unaccompanied children asylum seekers come through this port of entry. It does so by first providing an overview of the US context and briefly explaining the asylum process and language access policy as pertains to children and other vulnerable groups. It then considers the existing literature on asylum interpreting for adults and minors. Next, it discusses the type and the availability of interpreter training programs designed specifically for interpreter-mediated interactions with vulnerable groups. Finally, it makes further recommendations for interpreter education and training, especially of those working with refugee children in the US context.

9.2 Unaccompanied children

An unaccompanied child (UC), also known as an unaccompanied alien child (UAC), according to US Department of Health and Human Services (HHS) is an individual who "has no lawful immigration status in the United States, is under 18 years of age, has no parent or legal guardian in the United States or no parent or legal guardian in the United States is available to provide care and physical custody." (HHS n.d.). According to the Congressional Research Service Report, in 2020 and 2021 combined, a total of 142,749 UCs crossed the border. In the first ten months of 2021 alone, there were 112,192 reported UC "encounters" (The Congressional Research Service Report 2021, 4). Upon crossing the border, children are first apprehended and processed by the Customs and Border Patrol (CBP) and put in temporary holds (The Congressional Research Service Report 2021, 6). They are then "referred to the federal Office of Refugee Resettlement" (MPI 2021). Since the implementation of the Unaccompanied Children Program,[1] Office of Refugee Resettlement (ORR) has provided services and "cared for more than 175,000 children" in their facilities. According to the ORR fact sheet, in October of 2021, around 10,680 UCs were in the care of HHS (The Congressional

Research Service Report 2021, 2). Pro bono legal representation is one of the services provided by ORR, and one that is of most interest to the present topic in that interpreters, in addition to working with advocates, work closely with legal representatives and attorneys at different stages of the asylum process.

9.3 Asylum in the US context

In the US, eligibility for asylum is determined based on the Credible Fear Interview (CFI) conducted by CBP officers at the port of entry, during which an individual must demonstrate fear of returning to their home country (see Wallace and Hernández 2017; and Killman 2020). Asylum is granted in two ways: through the "affirmative process", by "submitting Form I-589, Application for Asylum and for Withholding of Removal", and the "defensive process", "a defense against removal from the United States", available only to individuals who are already "in removal proceedings in immigration court with the Executive Office for Immigration Review (EOIR)" (USCIS n.d.). Before they are transferred to ORR, unaccompanied minors are subject to the CFI. According to USCIS, the interviewing of minors by CBP officers is conducted following "child appropriate" interview techniques set forth in the *Guidelines for Children's Asylum Claims*. In these interviews, the asylum officer considers the child's "age, stage of language development, background, and level of sophistication" (USCIS n.d.).

In asylum cases, the right to legal counsel, due process, and consequently access to an interpreter depend on whether one is applying for asylum through the affirmative or defensive process (see Wallace and Hernández 2017; and Ragan 2020). Because of the laws and regulations, and as Ragan has argued, asylum seekers at the US-Mexico border "sit caught between a catch-22 of civil and criminal court" (2020, 20). In criminal court proceedings, legal representation is guaranteed, while in civil cases, especially asylum or immigration, individuals seeking asylum rely on pro bono legal representation, and volunteer interpreters.

Although it is not the focus of the present chapter, it is important to note, and could be argued that the anti-immigration policies in the US are a contributing factor in the rise of volunteerism. According to the National Immigrant Justice Center (NIJC) report, migration, or rather, unauthorized entry and reentry into the US has been criminalised for nearly a century (2020, 2). The treatment of asylum seekers at the US-Mexico border, the often inhumane conditions of the detention centres, length of stay in different border facilities, the behaviours of and the treatment of asylum seekers by CBP officers, are all a result of existing anti-immigration policies (see NIJC 2020 for more). For interpreters and language assistants alike, these policies and practices, may lead them to offer their services out of moral obligation or "a sense of duty" (Ragan 2020, 23). It may also lead to, or it may further exacerbate any existing ethical stress (see Hubscher-Davidson 2021). Especially for those interpreters working with unaccompanied children who are among the most vulnerable.

9.4 Language access and asylum

In the United States, language access is mandated under Title VI of the Civil Rights Act of 1964 and Executive Order 13166.[2,3] Organizations receiving federal funding are required to ensure access to their services in the language of the service seeker (HHS n.d.). As such, U.S. Department of Homeland Security (DHS) is required to ensure access to their services to Limited English Proficient (LEP) individuals; yet language access is provided by professional and non-professional interpreters, bilingual staff, and other volunteers. According to the DHS 2019 Language Access Plan, the USCIS takes the necessary steps to ensure access to information in languages other than English and provides interpreting services. In asylum cases however, according to the same plan, asylum seekers who do not speak English are expected to bring their own interpreter to the asylum interview with the following stipulations:

> Asylum applicants must provide their own interpreter who is at least 18 years of age and fluent in English and a language spoken by the applicant. The interpreter may be a family member, friend, or other person associated with the LEP person, but cannot be the applicant's attorney or representative, a representative or employee of the applicant's country of nationality or last habitual residence, an individual with a pending asylum application or a witness testifying on behalf of the applicant.
>
> *(DHS, Language Access Plan 2019, 11)*

On the one hand, these stipulations are problematic in that there is no guarantee that the individual who will serve as the interpreter will have the requisite interpreting knowledge, ability to remain impartial, or may render critical information both incomplete and inaccurate. They may also be someone with a lived experience and at a higher risk of being (re)traumatised by the content of the children's narratives. Furthermore, unlike a professional or an experienced interpreter, they may experience a higher level of ethical stress (Hubscher-Davidson 2021). On the other hand, those serving as interpreters may possess greater contextual knowledge to convey the information with completeness and empathy.

The Asylum Division also provides telephonic interpretation. In addition to using "telephonic interpretation service to monitor asylum interviews to ensure the quality and integrity of the interpretation", it also "provides telephonic interpretation services to individuals in credible fear, reasonable fear, and safe third-country screenings, and for asylum interviews related to applications filed by Unaccompanied Alien Children (UAC)." However, applicants who are under NACARA 203[4] and do not speak English, "must provide a competent interpreter" (DHS Language Access Plan 2019, 12). When bringing an interpreter, the same eligibility conditions (as described above) apply.

Per the DHS language access plan, they rely on third party vendors, therefore releasing them from any liability with regards to quality or need to ensure proper training and credentialing of interpreters who work on asylum cases, a concern raised by Wallace and Hernández (2017). In addition to these practices, once the children are in ORR facilities, where they are provided with pro-bono represen-tation, language provision, which as stated above is not mandated, thus becomes a volunteer-driven and volunteer-dependent endeavour. However, it is worthy of mention that among the volunteers there are also professional and trained inter-preters with appropriate expertise to ensure accurate and complete testimony and access to requisite services in addition to other bilingual language assistants.

To meet the needs of the growing number of asylum seekers requiring legal rep-resentation and language services at the US-Mexico border, it is not surprising that an all-hands-on deck approach has been adopted and led to utilisation of anyone who is willing and able to serve as a language assistant—professional or otherwise. There are those interpreters who have had minimal training on working with vul-nerable groups, including those who have never been trained on how to properly participate in an interpreted encounter yet serve as interpreters and language assis-tants. Although this may suggest that interpreter credentials, training and education are secondary, it highlights the fact that many volunteer interpreters feel a moral obligation to lend a hand in the face of "legal and physical barriers being enacted against asylum seekers" (Regan 2020, 23–24).

9.5 Interpreting in asylum settings

Interpreting in asylum hearings and the role of the interpreter has been explored by Inghilleri (2005, 2012), asylum settings, and the interpreter-mediated asy-lum interview (Maryns 2015; Inghilleri and Maryns 2019), interpreter agency in asylum hearings in the US (Killman 2020), interpreting for asylum hearings and asylum proceedings (Kolb and Pöchhacker 2008; Pöllabauer 2004, 2015), and language of the asylum procedure (Maryns 2006). Most recent studies also include those aspects related to language access and its impact on due process in asylum interviews (Dadhania 2020), and language access in detention centres in Texas (Wallace and Hernández 2017). Interpreting in contexts involving unac-companied minors has been explored in several studies on interpreter-mediated hearings for unaccompanied children in Sweden (Keselman et al. 2008, 2010a, 2010b), on interpreter-mediated questioning of minors (Salaets and Balogh 2015; Böser and La Rooy 2018), rapport between children and interpreters in the ques-tioning of minors (Salaets and Balogh 2019), and on interviewing of traumatised refugee children asylum seekers (Jain and Lee 2018). In the United States, as of this writing, interpreting for unaccompanied refugee children asylum seekers has only recently been explored by Sultanić (2021). The study conducted by Sultanić (2021) examines the effects on the interpreter of exposure to traumatic narratives told by children, the challenges that arise from these interactions, and coping strategies employed by interpreters. The findings of this study show that the strategies used to cope with the traumatic narratives were seldom formally taught to the interpreters working in these settings, yet all interpreters employed some mechanism to cope during and following difficult encounters. Training and education were not the primary area of interest in Sultanić's study (2021);

nevertheless, participants' answers on the type of training received were recorded, and a portion of that previously unpublished data will be discussed in the training and education section.

9.5.1 Interpreting for minors

Various important works indicate that several factors must be considered when interpreting for minors. The study on *Interpreter-mediated questioning of minors* (ImQM) conducted by Salaets and Balogh (2019) in several European countries, and their seminal work on *Children and Justice* (2015) are two such examples. Although their studies were not based on observations of real-time interpreted events, the findings are significant for developing best practices for interpreted-mediated interactions with minors. In the study on the questioning of minors, the authors demonstrate many important aspects that need not be overlooked when interpreting in settings involving children. These are categorised into: children's understanding of the role of the interpreter, participant's spatial relationship, preferences for language-concordant vs. interpreted interaction, preference and adjustment of interpreting mode, rapport building, and briefing of and with all stakeholders.

It is arguable that all of these aspects, in an interpreter-mediated communicative event, begin with briefing. Salaets and Balogh propose that briefing with clear explanation of everyone's role is necessary, and "can be achieved through joint training" of all stakeholders (2019, 39). As their study showed, explaining the role of the interpreter to the children, negotiating the mode of interpreting (simultaneous, chuchotage, consecutive, etc.) at the beginning of the session, determining where each person should be positioned, is all part of rapport building. In rapport building, Salaets and Balogh also remind us of the children's understanding of "confidentiality" and "gender" preferences, all of which should be considered (2019, 36–37).

Similarly, trust in the interpreter is required from all stakeholders and can also be achieved through briefing. For the other professionals to trust the interpreter, Salaets and Balogh argue that they "must be sure the interpreter is a trained and certified professional, as they are" (2019, 38). Briefing is also important to ensure that interpreters will respect the autonomy of the interlocutors by maintaining professional boundary and not leading or taking on the role of interviewer. In learning to collaborate with an interpreter, the power dynamics of the interaction become easier to navigate as well. Of course, it is important to mention that, though children are vulnerable, their vulnerability "should not be confused with children being naïve or ignorant" (Salaets and Balogh 2019, 38). As elucidated by the Belgian UNICEF report referenced in Salaets and Balogh 2019, "children know very well when interpreters are interfering or overstepping their role," and, thus, professionalism is vital. Undoubtedly, the child's ability to make such an observation will depend on the age, level of language acquisition of the child, and their conceptualisation of the world around them.

9.6 Training and education in the US

The rise of volunteerism, out of an urgent need for language assistance, especially at the US–Mexico border in recent years, has solidified the need for training and education of interpreters working with vulnerable populations, especially children, to be brought to the forefront. Nilsen has argued that "most of the interpreter's assignments in the public sector involve interpreting between adults," though "interpreting for young children is nevertheless an important field" (2013, 14). This is reflected in the curricula of different interpreter training programs as most tend to focus on interactions between adult service seekers and service providers. In the United States, training and education of interpreters in community or public service settings is still primarily divided into legal, medical, and educational. These trainings and education modules are available in many academic and para-academic settings (see, e.g., Sultanić 2018, 2020). All of these trainings and educational models are designed with their respective contexts in mind, though some aspects of the professional and ethical principles overlap.

An online survey of existing interpreter training programs revealed a significant shortage and yielded no substantial results with regards to specific training for interpreting for refugee children in the US. Moreover, asylum interpreting in the US context has not to date been established as its own area of expertise but rather exists, as previously stated, and observed by Bancroft et al. (2013) and Wallace and Hernández (2017), under the general umbrella of either legal or community interpreting, or at the cross-section of the two. This is in large part due to language policies. The trainings for working with refugees and vulnerable populations in the US that do exist have primarily been offered through organisations for immigrant integration, and typically comprise some variation of trauma-informed interpreting. The most notable programs are described below.

The most comprehensive, free trauma-informed interpreting curriculum developed in the US to date is *Breaking Silence: Interpreting for Victim Services*. This curriculum was developed by Bancroft et al. (2016), a project of Ayuda,[5] in partnership with the District of Columbia's Office of Victim Services and Justice Grants (OVSJG). It is a training program on "victim-centered, trauma-informed interpreting" with a focus on "interpreting for victims of violent crime, domestic violence, sexual assault and child abuse" (Ayuda 2016). This program was first offered as a pilot, and later made available for free through Ayuda's website.

Prior to the *Breaking Silence* curriculum, another similar training, which also focused on interpreting for survivors of trauma and torture in different social service settings called *The Voice of Love: Interpreting Compassion*, was pioneered by Bancroft in 2012, and delivered first as a pilot, then as a recurring training. *The Voice of Love* was established as a non-profit organisation which has since been dissolved according to The Open Database of the Corporate World.[6] A training manual called "Healing Voices" was also developed. The one thing that both programs have in common is that the training modules, or rather the educational components, are built on the premise of trauma-informed interpreting. Both are also centred around interpreting for adults. Though much of the content focused on the emotional fortitude and vicarious trauma, it could be adapted to any interpreted event or situation where traumatic narrative is introduced. Still, in the US these programs are not mandated for interpreters working with refugees or otherwise vulnerable groups, unless the interpreters are working for the organisation providing these services to refugees and/or unaccompanied children, as is the case with those working with Ayuda. Ayuda curates a *Community Legal Interpreter Bank*, and a *Victims Services Interpreter Bank*, and requires that the interpreters on their roster have a foundational 40 hour interpreter training (the minimum required for one to be a qualified healthcare or community interpreter in the US as of this writing), and to have completed *Breaking Silence*, or a similar trauma-informed curriculum for working with survivors of "sexual assault, domestic violence, human trafficking, hate crimes" and others (Ayuda 2016, 1).

Bridging Refugee Youth and Children's Services (BRYCS) is another organisation that offers a series of workshops for the different stakeholders working with minors. Their trainings include workshops on how to work with an interpreter, how to access a remote interpreter, how to setup a session using proper equipment and troubleshoot technical issues, and how to access real-time interpreters in several languages. They later build networks or curate lists of interpreters and translators working with other refugee and migrant-serving organisations. BRYCS offers training to providers working with interpreters on how to interview refugee and immigrant children and their families, as well as education on the importance of briefing with the interpreter. Additionally, they provide access to translated materials. Neither Ayuda nor BRYCS are specifically tailored for interpreting for unaccompanied minor asylum seekers, but they recognise the value of training and education of all stakeholders on properly engaging with one another to serve the best interest of those needing access to their services in a language other than English.

In the study on the effects, challenges and strategies used when interpreting traumatic narratives of children in the United States conducted by Sultanić (2021, 233), in which she interviewed 21 interpreters, a total of 15 had received some form of interpreter training while six had no formal training yet all worked with minors during the different stages of the asylum process. Interpreters provided language services in different settings (asylum offices, detention centres, immigration court and Special Immigration Juvenile Status (SIJ) hearings, during the application process, story-gathering with attorneys and clients, during CBP interviews, in shelters, etc.), and in different modalities (in-person and OPI) (Sultanić 2021, 233). As Bancroft has argued, in the US, as is the case in other countries, interpreting in legal settings outside of the courtroom "is still very likely to be performed by interpreters with very little or no training in the field or by interpreters whose training and experience has focused almost exclusively on non-legal sectors (community, conference, and business inter-preting)" (2013, 98). The findings from the Sultanić (2021) study, corroborate this. The portion of the unpublished data from the Sultanić (2021) study shows that, out of the 16 who had prior interpreter training, only six received some training on interpreting for vulnerable populations. When probed to describe the type of training, the range varied from those participants who completed a two-day (one) to a week-long training (one) to those who received a crash course during their general interpreter training, with the longest being a three-hour training on responding to and describing trauma. For two participants, the training consisted of some practice scenarios, but they expressed that prior work experience with vulnerable populations provided some context for their ability to interpret for unaccompanied children. Another participant shared that the training they received was for advocacy work with vulnerable populations, and though not interpreting specific, it was applicable to interpreted events. Several responses exemplify the participants' overall belief that even a general training on and understanding of trauma can have more specific applications with one participant sharing that:

> I have taken webinars for how to deal with vicarious trauma, and the vicari-ous trauma can be applied to many different aspects of interpreting. It can be applied to people who work in healthcare, and end-of-life interpreting assignments. You can apply it to these unaccompanied refugee minor cases. You can apply it in many different areas depending upon where you work as an interpreter.

One participant cited *Breaking Silence*, the program described earlier, as the training they completed to interpret for vulnerable populations in different settings. For this participant, the most beneficial aspect of the training was having the specialists teach them the importance of "what happens, why it's important not to touch the child in an interview, why it's important not to cry" since they have the expertise in this area. Their experience was like that of the participant who completed a two-day workshop. They shared:

> It was really comprehensive. They had everything. They had different speak-ers who could speak to the different angles about what the kids went through. I think even a psychologist about what they were dealing with. They had other seasoned advocates themselves share their stories. We did group exer-cises where we kind of did case studies, so there were all those components, lots of discussion, so it was the experts, discussion, the case studies, all that. And on the job, in the trenches people.

This further demonstrates why specialised training and education of interpreters working with vulnerable populations, especially children, must be prioritised.

9.7 Recommendations for training and education for working with refugee children

Studies have shown that interpreting for vulnerable populations, whether it be groups that fled war and violence, torture, or other kinds of trauma and traumatic experiences, takes a toll on the interpreter and can lead to vicarious traumatisation, or re-traumatisation of the interpreter (see, e.g., Bancroft 2016; Lai et al. 2015; Lai and Costello 2020; and Figley 1995). Therefore, training and education of interpreters working with asylum seekers must at its centre be trauma-informed. Several aspects must be considered. Further professionalising the training and education of interpreters working with vulnerable populations in the US, especially those working with refugee children, is vital. The recommendations offered in this section draw on existing training in the US, namely the *Breaking Silence* curriculum and recommendations from Bancroft (2016), the research conducted by Salaets and Balogh (2015, 2019), discussed in this chapter, and the results from the Sultanić (2021) study. Bancroft (2016, 17–18) specifies that interpreters "working for victim services need to understand":

- The impact of crime on victims
- What trauma is and its impact
- Vicarious trauma
- Domestic violence, sexual assault, and child abuse
- How basic interpreter skills (such as mode switching, note-taking, sight translation, and simultaneous interpreting) are used in this field
- Where community (including medical) interpreting crosses the line into legal interpreting

Additionally, they need to be aware of their "unconscious bias" and be "emotionally prepared" to handle any situation (Bancroft 2016,18). All these components are essential to interpreting for unaccompanied minors, especially for those at the US–Mexico border, since interpreting takes place at several stages of the process, in different settings, and with different stakeholders. The emotional preparedness, however, needs to be assessed and techniques for handling the emotional labour that is interpreting need to be taught and evaluated. Detailed recommendations for what to do prior to, during, and following an interpreted event with traumatic content can be found in Bancroft (2016) and in the strategies utilised and shared by the participant in the study conducted by Sultanić (2021).

In addition to understanding trauma and its impact, as suggested by Bancroft (2016), and emotional strength, the following aspects, many of which have been proposed by Salaets and Balogh (2019), must also be considered in training modules, and when interpreting for unaccompanied children:

- The age of a child
- Language development or level of language acquisition

- Their understanding of the role of the interpreter
- Preferences of interpreting mode and ability to know how and when to switch between different modes (as proposed by Salaets and Balogh 2019, and Bancroft 2016)
- Preferences for gender
- Positioning or spatial relationships when in person, with special considerations and adjustments for remote modalities
- Rapport building between the child and the interviewer through an interpreter
- Briefing with all stakeholders prior to the event, including introducing the interpreter and their role to the child
- Normalising and implementing professional debriefing between the interviewer and the interpreter as an opportunity for the interpreter to safely process the difficult content, therefore reducing the risk of vicarious traumatisation, and re-traumatisation

Since accuracy is of utmost importance (Wallace and Hernández 2017) and errors in interpretation can lead to incorrect or incomplete information being recorded, especially during the CFI or the story-gathering process, knowledge of relevant asylum or immigration terminology and procedure is vital in that errors in interpretation can affect the outcome of an asylum's claim and be "tantamount to a death sentence" Pöllabauer (2004, 143–144), especially when an individual is fleeing war, violence, trafficking, or other crimes.

Training and education of interpreters working for unaccompanied children, or otherwise vulnerable minors, in any setting, can then broadly be categorised into: (1) background information and knowledge, (2) procedural knowledge, including understanding of the interview structure and techniques, (3) interpreting knowledge, (4) terminology knowledge, (5) emotional strength built on trauma-informed training with special strategies learnt for coping prior to, in-process, and post assignment, and (6) interprofessional training and collaboration. Interprofessional collaboration, also recommended by Salaets and Balogh (2019) is essential in achieving the mutual goal of access to services through interpreter-mediated interviews of asylum-seeking adults and minors.

Interpreters should be well-versed in the language of interviewing of minors, whether it be through training with therapists, advocates, or the forensic interviewing process, to understand how the questions are asked and their purpose in eliciting information. They must know the difference between closed- and open-ended questioning. It is only then when interpreters will have a deeper understanding of their role, and why role-boundary and turn-taking must be negotiated before an encounter, and sometimes even during the event. Though many of the volunteers working at the US–Mexico border are trained, professional, and often certified interpreters, in addition to the emotional fortitude and ability to perform long consecutive as it's been argued by Ragan (2020) as the only requirement for an interpreter to be able to do this job, interpreters must also have specialised training in language-brokering for children; especially since, when it comes to the CFI, the devil is in the details, and incorrect information collected during the story-gathering process could cost someone their life.

9.8 Conclusion

In conclusion, this chapter argues that interpreting for refugee children, a particularly vulnerable group, requires a high level of skill and knowledge. Training and education of interpreters working in settings involving minors requires special attention for the reasons described herein. Interactions involving children asylum seekers occur in a variety of settings, from social services, behavioural health, special education, medical, and legal. Each one of these settings, in addition to having its own set of rules, with regards to the ways in which information is communicated, or ways in which practitioners, experts, and other personnel interact with children in these settings, vary significantly. As a result, it places different demands on the interpreter to be able to ensure effective communication between the different stakeholders. This chapter establishes that not all interpreting programs, nor interpreters, are created equal, and that, while some training components of trainings designed for survivors of torture, trauma, and violence, offered through trauma-informed workshops, can be generalised and applied to interpreting for unaccompanied asylum seekers, specialised and tailored training is required to guarantee accuracy and, as Wallace and Hernández (2017) have argued, due process. Thus, and as previously stated, the rise of volunteerism has solidified the need for these conversations to take place, and for training and education of interpreters working with vulnerable populations, especially children, to take centre stage. Further education and training are needed, including standardisation of and consensus on asylum interpreter training content and its duration as pertains to different settings.

Notes

1 "The Unaccompanied Children (UC) Program (UC Program 2021) is managed by the Office of Refugee Resettlement (ORR 2021) within the Administration for Children and Families (ACF), an operational division of the U.S. Department of Health and Human Services (HHS)" (Fact Sheet, November 1, 2021, 1). For more see www.acf. hhs.gov/orr/programs/ucs/about

2 For more on Title VI see https://www.hhs.gov/civil-rights/for-individuals/special-topics/needy-families/civil-rights-requirements/index.html

3 For more on Executive Order 13166 see https://www.justice.gov/crt/executive-order-13166

4 "NACARA 203 allows certain individuals to apply for relief from USCIS https://www. uscis.gov/archive/nacara-203-nicaraguan-adjustment-and-central-american-relief-act even if they have not been placed in deportation (or removal) proceedings before an immigration judge." For more on NACARA 203 relief see uscis.gov.

5   "Ayuda provides legal, social, and language services to help low-income immigrants in our
     neighborhoods access justice and transform their lives." For more see www.ayuda.com/
6   For more see https://opencorporates.com/companies/us_md/D14037006

References

Ayuda. 2016. *Working with Interpreters Outside of the Courtroom: A Guide for Attorneys.* Wash-
    ington, DC. https://ayuda.com/wp-content/uploads/2017/06/Working_With_Inter-
    preters_2016.pdf.

Bancroft, Marjory A. 2016. "Breaking Silence: What Interpreters Need to Know About
    Victim Services Interpreting." *ATA Chronicle,* November/December 2016.

Bancroft, Marjory A., Lola Bendana, Jean Bruggeman, and Lois Feuerle. 2013. "Interpret-
    ing in the Gray Zone: Where Community and Legal Interpreting Intersect." *Translation
    and Interpreting* 5 (1): 94–113. https://doi.org/10.12807/ti.105201.2013.a05

Böser, Ursula, and David La Rooy. 2018. "Interpreter-Mediated Investigative Inter-
    views with Minors." *Translation and Interpreting Studies* 13 (2): 208–229. https://doi.
    org/10.1075/tis.00012.bos

Dadhania, Pooja R. 2020. "Language Access and Due Process in Asylum Interviews." 97
    Denver U. L. Rev. 707. https://scholarlycommons.law.cwsl.edu/fs/296

DHS (U.S. Department of Homeland Security). 2019. "USCIS Language Access Plan."
    www.uscis.gov/tools/multilingual-resource-center/uscis-language-access-plan

Figley, Charles R. ed. 1995. *Compassion Fatigue: Coping with Secondary Traumatic Stress Dis-
    order in Those who Treat the Traumatized.* Brunner/Mazel. New York and London: Rout-
    ledge (Taylor & Francis Group).

HHS. n.d. www.hhs.gov/civil-rights/for-individuals/special-topics/needy-families/civil-
    rights-requirements/index.html

Hubscher-Davidson, Séverine. 2021. "Ethical Stress in Translation and Interpreting." In
    The Routledge Handbook of Translation and Ethics, edited by Kaisa Koskinen, and Nike K.
    Pokorn, 1st ed., 415–430. London: Routledge.

Inghilleri, Moira. 2005. "Mediating Zones of Uncertainty: Interpreter Agency, the Inter-
    preting Habitus and Political Asylum Adjudication." *The Translator* 11 (1): 69–85.

Inghilleri, Moira 2012. *Interpreting Justice: Ethics, Politics and Language.* New York: Routledge.

Inghilleri, Moira, and Katrijn Maryns. 2019. "Asylum." In *Routledge Encyclopedia of Transla-
    tion Studies,* edited by Mona Baker, and Gabriela Saldanha, 3rd ed., 22–27. London/New
    York: Routledge.

Jain, Amit, and Joanne Lee. 2018. "Interviewing Refugee Children: Theory, Policy, and
    Practice with Traumatized Asylum Seekers." *Yale Journal of Law and Feminism* 29 (421):
    421–464. http://hdl.handle.net/20.500.13051/7095

Keselman, Olga, Ann Christin Cederborg, Michael E. Lamb, and Örjan Dahlström. 2008.
    "Mediated Communication with Minors in Asylum-seeking Hearings." *Journal of Refugee
    Studies* 21 (1): 103–116. https://doi.org/10.1093/jrs/fem051

Keselman, Olga, Ann Christin Cederborg, Michael E. Lamb, and Örjan Dahlström. 2010a.
    "Asylum-Seeking Minors in Interpreter-Mediated Interviews: What Do They Say and
    What Happens to Their Responses?" *Child and Family Social Work* 15 (3): 325–334.
    https://doi.org/10.1111/j.1365-2206.2010.00681.x

Keselman, Olga, Ann Christin Cederborg, and Per Linell. 2010b. ""That Is Not Necessary
    for You to Know!": Negotiation of Participation Status of Unaccompanied Children

in Interpreter-mediated Asylum Hearings." *Interpreting* 12 (1): 83–104. https://doi. org/10.1075/intp.12.1.04kes

Killman, Jeffrey. 2020. "Interpreting for Asylum Seekers and Their Attorneys: The Challenge of Agency." *Perspectives: Studies in Translation Theory and Practice* 28 (1): 73–89. https://doi.org/10.1080/0907676X.2019.1615518

Kolb, Waltraud, and Franz Pöchhacker. 2008. "Interpreting in Asylum Appeal Hearings: Roles and Norms Revisited." In *Interpreting in Legal Settings*, edited by Debra Russell, and Sandra Hale, 26–50. Washington, DC: Gallaudet University Press.

Lai, Miranda, and Georgina Heydon. 2015. "Vicarious Trauma Among Interpreters." *International Journal of Interpreter Education* 7 (1): 3–22.

Lai, Miranda, and Susie Costello. 2020. "Professional Interpreters and Vicarious Trauma: An Australian Perspective." *Qualitative Health Research* 31 (1): 70–85. https://doi. org/10.1177/1049732320951962

Maryns, Katrijn. 2006. *The Asylum Speaker: Language in the Belgian Asylum Procedure*. London: Routledge. https://doi.org/10.4324/9781315760285

Maryns, Katrijn. 2015. "Interpreting in Asylum Settings." In *Routledge Encyclopedia of Interpreting Studies*, edited by Franz Pöchhacker, Nadja Grbic, Peter Mead, and Robin Setton, 22–25. London, UK: Routledge.

MPI (The Migration Policy Institute). 2021. *Unaccompanied Children Released to Sponsors by State and County, FY 2014-Present*. www.migrationpolicy.org/programs/data-hub/ charts/unaccompanied-children-released-sponsors-state-and-county

Nilsen, Anne Birgitta. 2013. "Exploring Interpreting for Young Children." *Translation & Interpreting* 5 (2): 14–29.10.12807/ti.105202.2013.a02

ORR. n.d. *U.S. Department of Health and Human Services*. www.acf.hhs.gov/orr/programs/ ucs/about

Pöllabauer, Sonja. 2004. "Interpreting in Asylum Hearings: Issues of Role, Responsibility and Power." *Interpreting* 6 (2): 143–180. https://doi.org/10.1075/intp.6.2.03pol

Pöllabauer, Sonja. 2015. "Interpreting in Asylum Proceedings." In *The Routledge Handbook of Interpreting*, edited by Holly Mikkelson, and Renée Jourdenais, 202–216. London: Routledge.

Ragan, Robin. 2020. "Going All in to Help Asylum Seekers at the U.S.-Mexico Border." *The ATA Chronicle* (July/August), 2020.

Salaets, Heidi, and Katlin Balogh. eds. 2015. *Children and Justice: Overcoming Language Barriers*. Cambridge: Intersentia.

Salaets, Heidi, and Katalin Balogh. 2019. "Interpreter-Mediated Questioning of Minors (ImQM): The Voice of Children and Their Rapport with Interpreters." *Revista de Llengua i Dret, Journal of Language and Law* 71: 27–44. https://doi.org/10.2436/rld. i71.2019.3257

Sultanić, Indira. 2018. *Medical Interpreter Training and Readiness for the Hospital Environment*. Unpublished PhD diss., Kent, OH: Kent State University.

Sultanić, Indira. 2020. "Medical Interpreter Education and Training." In *The Oxford Handbook of Translation and Social Practices*, edited by Meng Ji, and Sara Laviosa, 357–377. Oxford: Oxford University Press.

Sultanić, Indira. 2021. "Interpreting Traumatic Narratives of Unaccompanied Child Migrants in the United States: Effects, Challenges and Strategies." *Linguistica Antverpiensia, New Series. Themes in Translation Studies* 20: 227–247. https://doi.org/10.52034/ lanstts.v20i.601.

The Congressional Research Service Report. 2021. https://crsreports.congress.gov/.

UC Program. 2021. *Fact Sheet*. www.hhs.gov/sites/default/files/uac-program-fact-sheet.pdf

USCIS (U.S. Citizenship and Immigration Services). n.d. www.uscis.gov/humanitarian/refugees-and-asylum/asylum/minor-children-applying-for-asylum-by-themselves

Wallace, Melissa, and Carlos Iván Hernández. 2017. "Language Access for Asylum Seekers in Borderland Detention Centers in Texas." *Revista de Llengua i Dret, Journal of Language and Law* 68: 143–156. https://doi.org/10.2436/rld.i68.2017.2940.

10

INTERPRETING IN AN ASYLUM CONTEXT

Interpreter training as the linchpin for improving procedural quality

Sonja Pöllabauer

This contribution investigates training in an asylum context as a particular domain of public service interpreting (PSI). It outlines specifics of interpreting in asylum procedures and the development of interpreter training and trends in this field, with a particular focus on PSI training, before addressing recent approaches to interpreting didactics. Based on a corpus of training curricula and descriptions that was compiled through a web and literature search and analysed qualitatively, it then takes a closer look at the training landscape of asylum interpreter training to examine trends, and differences between the range of training measures that are currently in place.

10.1 Introduction

Interpreting in an asylum context is a domain of interpreting that can be included within the field of public service interpreting (PSI). Ever since increased attention has been paid to interpreting outside traditional fields (conference, business, diplomatic interpreting), different labels have been used for interpreted encounters that take place in public service, law, and non-governmental settings (for instance, community interpreting, public service interpreting, dialogue interpreting) (Pöllabauer 2013, 1). In more fine-grained differentiations, asylum interpreting is most commonly included under legal interpreting (Monteoliva-Garcia 2018, 39) as a form of non-courtroom interpreting, which may be set against prototypical courtroom or judicial interpreting. Following Bancroft et al. (2013, 94), non-courtroom legal interpreting may be viewed as a "gray zone" where rules that are prevalent in other fields of interpreting "may mesh or collide," thus causing confusion about the job demands and strategies available to interpreters in such settings. This contribution focuses predominantly on interpreting in asylum adjudication procedures and largely neglects related fields such as humanitarian or conflict interpreting (for

DOI: 10.4324/9781003230359-13

instance, Delgado Luchner and Kherbiche 2018; Killman 2020; Moser-Mercer et al. 2021; Todorova 2021), though there are some obvious parallels in all of these fields (for instance, the emotionality, volatility and conflict-proneness of encounters in such a context, the heterogenous backgrounds of interactants, asymmetrical relationships, role conflicts, and lack of training of interpreters in these fields; for the latter, also see Todorova 2020); also with a focus on training, some particular content may be equally relevant for all of these volatile and fragile settings (see also other chapters in this volume). Interpreting in an asylum context is linked to interpreting in conflict and post-conflict settings, depending on how broadly or narrowly conflict interpreting is defined. Interpreting in (post-)conflict settings can be defined as a form of crisis translation (Federici and O'Brien 2019, 4). A crisis can be defined as "an event or series of events that are non-routine, pose a significant threat, and require a response to mitigate the harm often involving communication across multilingual barriers, or crisis translation" (Federici 2020, 177). Communication, including translation and interpreting is a relevant element of crisis management and may be viewed as a strategy for risk reduction (Federici and O'Brien 2019, 1), though there is often little awareness for the role of interpreters in humanitarian crises (Federici 2016, 3–4), and lack of awareness of adequate linguistic support may have a significant effect in cascading crises (Federici 2020, 177; see Čemerin 2020 for different low- or high-scale forms of communication in humanitarian crisis situations). Within conflict situations, we can distinguish different spaces of communication where translation is needed, from acute/emergency situations, situations with a focus on documenting and registering individuals, situations with a focus on admitting them into the system, or situations where individuals are required to seek specific social services. Asylum interpreting is needed when individuals officially apply to be admitted in and processed through a specific national asylum system, and it is this specific (post-)conflict context on which I focus in this contribution.

While throughout history interpreters have been needed in times of strife (Inglis and Thorpe 2020), interpreting in asylum determination procedures takes place in a specific system, with both clearly defined and unspoken routines. Interpreters are the linchpin in this communication environment that is shaped by institutional translation policies and discursive constraints and where decisions are based on oral narratives.

Most industrialised countries have established a system for determining refugee status (status of international protection) after World War II. Asylum determination is based on instruments of international and humanitarian law, and national asylum legislation. Applicants for international protection must pass through this system to be granted or refused refugee status. Individuals who flee from areas of conflict often cannot provide written evidence to substantiate their claims. Asylum authorities thus rely on in-person oral interviews to establish and assess the validity of applicants' assertions. These interviews are a complex and hierarchical form of expert-lay communication with a prototypical structure and an institutionalised question-answer format that is controlled by the institutional representatives. The burden of proof, however, mostly lies on the applicants, who are required to disclose relevant facts and present their claims in the best possible way to make their stories believable. Contradictions arising in this process may harm their credibility and thus threaten their chances of being granted protection. These oral accounts of events are reformulated in a complex process of "de- and recontextualization practices" (Blommaert 2001, 414) from a spoken-language format into a written format and preserved in written records (transcripts) of the interviews, which are the basis for the asylum officials' decisions.

Interpreters play a crucial role in this system as both sides need to rely on the interpreter to do his or her job professionally so that procedural safeguards can be upheld. The crux of the matter, however, is that the different parties in such encounters do not necessarily adhere to the same notions of what constitutes professional behaviour: officials are not always trained in working with interpreters, applicants may not know what is expected of them, and interpreters are also not necessarily trained for this task and may not be aware of the remits of their role while having to communicate in an atmosphere of institutional hierarchy and between speakers with often divergent backgrounds (for instance, different educational, sociocultural, religious backgrounds).

Interpreting in such an environment has received increased attention in interpreting studies over the last two decades (Pöllabauer 2015), though Monteoliva-Garcia (2018, 56) concludes in a recent review of legal interpreting literature that "asylum, immigration and police settings should receive further scholarly attention." From what is academically known, authors have arrived at similar conclusions: interpreters working in this field are not always (well enough) trained, and this lack of training may negatively impact the quality of asylum procedures (Pöllabauer forthcoming). Following Inghilleri (2003, 261), we can confirm that "the embodiment of distinctive, contradictory and conflicting habitus amongst the participants" makes interpreter-rendered communication particularly challenging. Interpreter training, and also the need for user training (institutional representatives, asylum officials), and particularly specialised training that is tailored to the specifics of interpreting in this fragile and sensitive framework, can thus be viewed as a cornerstone of improving interpreting quality and ultimately procedural quality.

The last decade has seen the emergence of training initiatives that focus on specialised training for public service interpreters, also including some for interpreters working in an asylum context. This contribution will consider the formats and content of a sample of such training measures and discuss how these are aligned with contemporary approaches to interpreter/translator training. Particular attention will be paid to the integration of topics that may be considered central to an asylum context but are often underrepresented in interpreter training, such as training for speakers of languages of limited diffusion (LLDs) (Lai and Mulayim 2013), interpreting for specifically vulnerable groups of applicants (Keselman et al. 2010) or dealing with emotions, empathy, vicarious traumatisation, coping and self-care (Bancroft et al. 2016). Remote interpreting is also a topic that has become more important in this context (Licoppe and Veyrier 2020), specifically with the onset of the COVID pandemic, and is challenging because of the nature of asylum interviews where trust may be perceived as paramount to enable disclosure of personal information. The personal and delicate nature of this field is also one of the reasons why it is difficult, if not sometimes near to impossible, to access (Monteoliva Garcia 2018, 56) as authorities are often reluctant to grant permission for research projects due to reasons of data protection but also because this is a field that is highly politicised and "loaded with strong ideologies" (Nikolaidou et al. 2019, 3); in addition, interpreters may be reluctant to participate in research projects for fear of committing "formal errors" in such an overly regulated context (ibid.). An overview of training options can thus, by its nature, not be exhaustive. In this analysis of such courses, the focus will lie on courses for which information is publicly available (see also some of the other chapters in this volume for more examples; see Ticca et al. forthcoming for an innovative approach to training outside the formal legal domain of asylum procedures).

10.2 Training public service interpreters

While interpreters have been needed since ancient times, the professionalisation and academisation of the field did not begin until the early and mid-20th century. In the beginning, interpreter training was geared mostly towards conference interpreting training, which was offered at newly established "interpreter schools" at different universities and aligned with the professional standards set up by the International Association of Conference Interpreters (AIIC) (Pöchhacker 2016, 2829). Training in the field of PSI has been lagging behind and has remained a low-level matter in many countries. In some countries, it was spurred by the introduction of legislative changes, for instance, the introduction of the US *Court Interpreters Act* in 1978, or the establishment of accreditation authorities, such as the National Accreditation Authority for Translators and Interpreters (NAATI) in Australia (Pöchhacker 2016, 30). Due to a lack of inclusive and institutionalised translation regimes in many countries (Ozolins 2010, 196–198), there was little awareness of the need for training or the willingness to offer or finance such training. Thus, in many countries, training programmes were developed through grassroots commitment and offered at a low level of formalisation.

In the past, little specific PSI training was offered at the university level, and for some countries, this still applies, though with the harmonisation of the higher education structure in the EU this seems to have changed in some countries (Pöchhacker 2016, 31). Nonetheless, even if university-based training is available, this is often still deemed too time- or cost-intensive (Pöllabauer 2020, 36), which is why many countries feature a diverse, sometimes confusing landscape of diverse and heterogeneous training formats (Bancroft 2015, 228). Factors that influence training provision often have more to do with financial considerations and less with quality assurance, and there is still little awareness of the need for training public service interpreters and little exchange between service providers (Pöllabauer 2020, 37 and 50).

On a positive note, however, there is a trend towards establishing more university-level courses on PSI, not only at BA but also MA level, and PSI training has also become a topic beyond the academic realm and has been taken up, for instance, by the European Commission's Knowledge Centre on Interpretation (European Commission 2021) or platforms such as the European Network for Public Service Interpreting (ENPSIT 2021). In university-level courses, there seems to be some consensus as regards competencies that need to be acquired and content to be imparted (Kadrić and Pöllabauer forthcoming).

If we take a closer look at non-university training initiatives for interpreters in an asylum context, however, there still is little institutionalisation or stand-ardisation of specific training offers (Bergunde and Pöllabauer 2019, 2). Even though the field has possibly been given more attention recently, particularly in the wake of recent geopolitical developments, the findings of a 2010 UNHCR report on asylum interpreting stating that "across the Member States in this research, the provision of training for interpreters is, at best, limited, and in many cases non-existent" (UNHCR 2010, 33) will presumably still apply in many countries.

10.2.1 Training for whom?

The provision of PSI training is made complicated by the heterogeneous back-grounds of the potential trainees. PSI takes place in a variety of different national settings for allochthonous speakers with often diverse backgrounds and frequently a low symbolic, cultural, and economic capital (Prunč 2017, 23–26). They are needed for a variety of languages, some of which will be languages of limited dif-fusion in the respective national context. There is often little recognition of the need for quality service provision and transparency in the sense of a "democratic translation culture" (Prunč 2017, 34–36; my translation). While conference inter-preting takes place on the premise that the "best is good enough" (Pöchhacker 2007, 136), with PSI institutional representatives often taking the stance that some sort of bilingualism, for which often no credentials may be asked or required, is sufficient, which understandably will not fuel motivation to invest both money and energy into pursuing training. Training has to cater for different groups of inter-preters, and not all training formats will be suitable, accessible or affordable for all potential interpreter students. So due to differing demands, the training landscape will necessarily need to be diverse, as long as there is no officially established and regulated national translation regime in place, which would have to be based upon stronger political commitment, increased financial acknowledgement, and fewer ideological qualms.

Following Bergunde and Pöllabauer (2019, 5) we can differentiate four groups of potential trainees. This grouping is made based on experiences with PSI training in Austria, but similar observations can be made for other regions (for instance, Maryns 2012, 309–310):

- Interpreters with a higher (tertiary)-education (university, college) training in interpreting, often for a traditional language canon with a focus on conference interpreting, and with little specialisation in asylum-related topics.
- Interpreters with recognition as sworn/certified court interpreters; depending on the respective national background, these will or, in some countries, will not have undergone some form of formal training and will or will not have passed a court interpreter exam.
- Semi-trained interpreters who have completed some form of shorter training offered either in-house or through academic or non-academic providers; such courses may either be offered for a specific language combination or be non-language specific and provide a generalist or specialist focus as regards content. Moreover, while such a format is often more flexible and cost-efficient, it may install a false "sense of complacency in governments and policy-makers" (Hale 2007, 169) as to what it can, in fact, deliver.
- Interpreters with no training whatsoever, who may be much needed for specific languages and thus may not perceive the necessity of pursuing training as they are recruited and remunerated in any case or, on the contrary, be in lesser demand and thus also will not view training as a priority.

10.2.2 Training formats

Regarding training, we can differentiate a variety of formats. How training is organised (for instance, short term, full-time, undergraduate, postgraduate, generalist vs. specialist focus, based on higher education entrance qualification or not) and what results it can deliver (sensitisation or more formal kind of training, with or without the awarding of a certificate, degree, certification/accreditation), depends on who provides the training. In an overview of the challenges community interpreting has faced on its road to professionalisation, Roberts (2002, 169–171) distinguishes between "university/college training," "training by organizations hiring community-based interpreters," and "distance education for community-based interpreters". University-based training, for instance, will naturally operate under different premises (curricular/organisational pre-sets) to training offered in-house or by nongovernmental or faith-based providers (also see Pöllabauer 2020). The latter category of "distance education," mentioned by Roberts, is in fact, not a classificatory category linked to the provider, but addresses a specific organisational facet of training. Regarding organisational aspects and based on a review of the training landscape in German-speaking countries, Iannone and Redl (2017, 131–136), for instance, observe an overall tendency towards shorter, cross-language and modular training, with elements of blended learning or e-learning. Since that they arrived at this conclusion before the onset of the pandemic, it may safely be assumed also that the ratio of distance training/elements will even have increased worldwide over the last two years. In what follows, I will use some of these descriptors to discuss examples of specific asylum-related interpreter training. In addition, attention will be paid to pedagogical considerations as far as these may be inferred from the corpus under review.

10.3 Interpreting didactics

Following Orlando and Gerber (2020, 202) changes in the global higher education landscape, the prevalence of English as a lingua franca or the need to integrate new technologies, as well as relevant findings from translation theory, are some of the prevalent challenges of translation education, "while at the same time [having to respond] to [vocational and] industry demands" (Kadrić and Pöllabauer forthcoming). To cope with these challenges, specific pedagogic competencies (Pokorn et al. 2020) and awareness of contemporary principles of andragogy, in our case with a focus on PSI education, are essential. As in translation education, critical constructivism has come to be an important principle in contemporary interpreting education. Forms of holistic teaching and learning have found their way into PSI didactics and become accepted as valid approaches to teaching to prepare and empower students for a field that is shaped by globalisation, political ideologies, and societal and technical changes. Graduates need to be prepared for these professional challenges and to be given the means to serve as self-reflective agents. Elements from theatre pedagogy (Bahadır 2010; Kadrić 2011), experiential and situated learning (Cirillo and Niemants 2017; González-Davies and Enríquez-Raido 2016; Pérez and Wilson 2011), or service-learning (Shaw 2013), both face-to-face or online (Mulayim and Lai 2015), have all been found to be useful for problem-based, self-reflective teaching, and learning. With a focus on holistic and constructional vocational learning, Ott (2011, 15; my translation) outlines four dimensions of holistic learning, which I will use to describe which areas of learning are addressed by the courses that are analysed below, which competencies they seek to impart, and how. These dimensions are 1) subject-related learning (acquiring subject competence), 2) methodological-operative learning (acquiring methodological competencies), 3) socio-communicative learning (acquiring social competencies), and 4) affective-ethical learning (acquiring individual competencies).

10.4 Examples of training interpreters for asylum procedures

10.4.1 Methodology and limitations

In what follows I will outline the formats, as well as parallels and differences, of a corpus of training initiatives.[1] As already mentioned, this list does not make claims to be exhaustive. Based on a literature and web search (search phrases in English) a corpus of course descriptions and syllabi of 13 training courses was compiled (see Annex), which will be briefly compared in what follows. A more detailed analysis, including quantitative elements (Pöllabauer 2020), would be desirable but remains beyond the scope of this contribution.

Inclusion criteria were programmes with a specific focus on the asylum/ immigration context. Courses with a broader focus on PSI or humanitarian interpreting were excluded, as were sites offering self-study material in the form of handbooks and guides.[2] Another limitation of the chosen approach is that the comprehensiveness of the available information varies, with only scarce information on some courses, which could be offset with follow-up interviews. A search in languages other than English might also yield additional results.

10.4.2 Comparative analysis

A comparison of these initiatives shows that there is a range of training approaches very much in line with what is known about the panoply of PSI training programmes. The overall number of specific courses is still low, however, possibly because this is a field where practitioners are trained in other fields of interpreting or learn on the job. The list is international and includes courses in Africa ("The Cairo Community Interpreter Project"), Asia (the "Korean Ministry of Justice" initiative), North America ("Immigration Interpreter Training," "Interpreter Training Series: Basics of the Asylum Process and Interpreter Sensitivity," "It breaks my heart"), online/blended-learning courses with an international target audience ("Interpreting for Refugees: Contexts, Practices and Ethics," the EASO[3] training, "Trainers' Seminar in Humanitarian Interpretation"), and Europe (the remainder of the courses, see Annex).[4]

For all courses under review, the *target group* is bilinguals working (or planning to work) in an immigration/asylum context; some are also open to immigration staff and volunteers ("Immigration Interpreter Training," "It breaks my heart") or interpreter trainers/educators ("Interpreting for Refugees: Contexts, Practices and Ethics," "Trainers' Seminar in Humanitarian Interpretation"). Some are only open to a specific clientele, for instance, interpreters who already work for asylum authorities and are invited by these to attend training (for instance, the EASO interpreters' module, which can be offered upon request of the EU member states' national asylum authorities, or an online video training for the German asylum authorities that was developed in cooperation with the German Federal Association of Translators and Interpreters).

Pre-attendance screening or specific prerequisites, though considered very important (Lee and Choi 2015, 45), seem to be in place with some though not all providers (for instance, "Asyltolkning" expects the completion of basic modules on dialogue interpreting; the "Immigration Interpreter Training" or "The Cairo Community Interpreter Project" require written and/or phone interview tests).

The majority of the training options are *cross-language*; only a small number of providers offer language-specific training, not only but also for LLDs ("Immigration Interpreter Training," "Interpreter Training" by the Irish Refugee Council). Additional *language proficiency instruction* is, for instance, offered by the Korean training initiatives (Lee and Choi 2015) or the Austrian QUADA training (Bergunde and Pöllabauer 2020).

The *duration* of the different training options ranges from 1.5 hours ("Basics of the Asylum Process and Interpreter Sensitivity") to between 40 and 50 hours (for instance, "Immigration Interpreter Training," "The Cairo Community Interpreter Training"). It is difficult to assess how frequently the different programmes are offered; most seem to be offered upon demand. The *costs* vary; some of the training options are free of charge ("Trainers' Seminar in Humanitarian Interpretation"), others anticipate course fees (ranging between EUR 20 to EUR 750, or $400 to $770); for some, no information on costs was available.

In line with recent trends in PSI training as outlined above, some of the courses have a *modular structure*, with basic modules on introductory/general content and follow-up modules on specialised content (for instance, "How to become an interpreter," EASO training "Interpreting in an Asylum Context," QUADA training) or an option of follow-up courses ("It breaks my heart," for instance, offers follow-up content on interpreting for rape survivors or interpreter safety and self-care).[5]

As with pre-attendance requirements, *course completion requirements* also vary. Some expect some form of a final test (the Korean training initiatives), others a certificate ("Asyltolkning," "It breaks my heart," "Trainers' Seminar in Humanitarian Interpretation," QUADA training, EASO training). For the remainder of the courses, no information on course completion requirements was given. None of these courses are elements of a specific accreditation procedure.[6]

As regards the *provider* landscape, we mostly find training initiatives that are offered by non-university providers. There is only one university-affiliated course: "The Cairo Community Interpreter Course" was developed by the Center for Migration and Refugee Studies at the American University in Cairo and has been offered frequently in different Asian and African countries. The "Interpreting for Refugees: Contexts, Practices and Ethics" is an online course hosted by the University Glasgow that was developed in the Inter4Ref project (https://inter4ref.eu/en/), as was the "Trainers' Seminar in Humanitarian Interpretation." As mentioned before, PSI has also come to be integrated in mainstream university training in some countries, either as a topic that is tackled individually in courses or as a specialisation at BA or MA level. Some countries also offer university-affiliated vocational courses at a post-graduate level (see, for instance, the course on public service and court interpreting [Dolmetschen für Gerichte und Behörden] offered at the Postgraduate Center of the University of Vienna [Postgraduate Center 2021]). The scope of this contribution does not allow for a more comprehensive focus on the integration of asylum interpreting in university interpreter curricula or in more general PSI training courses, but one specific example seems worth mentioning: the MA program in Intercultural Communication, Public Service Interpreting and Translation at the University of Alcalá anticipates a practicum that can also be taken at the Spanish Asylum and Refugee Office (Valero Garcés 2017). This is a (university) provider-user cooperation that seems unique in that it is generally very difficult to access the field and obtain first-hand information and experience.

The remainder of the courses is either offered by NGOs or charity organisations (Irish Refugee Council; Leipzig Refugee Law Clinic;), private companies (Cross-cultural communications, LLC; Language Connections, Inc), or adult education institutions (for instance "Asyltolkning" which is offered by the Swedish Folkuniversitetet, or the QUADA training, which is offered at an Austrian Volkshochschule).

In the case of the EASO training ("Interpreting in the Asylum Context" and "Operational Training on Interpreting in the Asylum Context") and the online video training used by the German asylum authorities, the providers are an EU organisation (EASO) and a national asylum authority in cooperation with a professional association of translators and interpreters (German Federal Association of Translators and Interpreters). The EASO training is special in that it was developed by an international group of experts (law, pedagogy, translation/interpreting) under the auspices of EASO. A considerable degree of exchange and consensus-building was required, as can be confirmed by the author who was part of that group; this will presumably also apply to the training and materials that were jointly developed by an international consortium of the Inter4Ref project ("Interpreting for Refugees: Contexts, Practices and Ethics," "Trainers' Seminar in Humanitarian Interpretation").

My search did not turn up concrete examples of in-house training, which is a common practice in other domains of PSI. In this case, either information on such activities is not made public or, and this seems more plausible, such kinds of training are not generally offered, as most asylum interpreters are freelancers and asylum authorities thus have no legal authority to offer such kind of training.

Regarding *training formats*, we find, not surprisingly, activities that are either offered face-to-face (for instance, "It breaks my heart," "The Cairo Community Interpreter Project"), in a blended learning format (for instance, the QUADA training) or only digitally, though it may be presumed that with the onset of the pandemic, most formats will either have been suspended or changed to a digital mode. The online courses are either self-study courses ("Basics of the Asylum Process & Interpreter Sensitivity," the German online video training), or interactive webinars ("Immigration Interpreter Training"; "Interpreting for Refugees: Contexts, Practises and Ethics"), which also offer feedback and instructor-led interaction with other trainees. Examples of blended learning formats are the EASO courses, which first offer a comprehensive but non-interactive online phase, followed by a two-day face-to-face workshop; a similar approach is also adopted by the QUADA training, though in this case, both the online and the face-to-face instruction phases are shorter in duration.

A different methodological approach would be needed to draw comprehensive conclusions about the pedagogical approaches that are taken in the various courses (for instance, participant observation of classroom activities, interviews with trainers, qualitative content analysis of course material and syllabi). What can, however, be inferred from the available corpus of course descriptions and syllabi, specifically with some of the face-to-face courses (for instance, "Asyltolkning," the EASO face-to-face workshops, "It breaks my heart," the QUADA training), is that hands-on experience, interaction, and activities (role-plays, simulations, videos) allowing for self-reflection in the sense of "critical education" (also see JRS Indonesia 2018 on the implementation of the "Cairo Community Interpreter Training" in Indonesia) seems to be supported.

As regards content, the curricula of all training options address content that falls under the subject-related dimension of learning (for instance, facts about the asylum system, integration, refugees' coping strategies, terminology, deontological codes and the profession), and at least also address topics that fall under methodological-operative dimension (skills, techniques, for instance interpreting techniques, notetaking, research skills) or the socio-communicative dimension of teaching (interactants' roles, interpretation-related coordination of talk, best practices) ("Immigration Interpreter Training," "Interpreter Training," the "Cairo Community Interpreter Project," the Korean courses, "Trainers' Seminar in Humanitarian Interpreting"), though with the shorter or online courses this can obviously only be addressed in a superficial manner. Some of the training initiatives, however, also pay particular attention to the affective ethical dimension, for instance dealing with ethical dilemmas, mental hygiene, self-care, empathy, trauma-informed interpreting (for instance, "It breaks my heart," the EASO and QUADA modules, "Interpreting for Refugees: Contexts Practices and Ethics"), Critical Whiteness and dealing with racism ("How to become an interpreter"), or LGBTIQ issues ("Asyltolkning").

10.5 Conclusion

This overview of training courses, with a particular focus on training measures for interpreters in an asylum context, shows that similarly to training courses with a more general focus on PSI, there is a choice of different formats that are geared specifically to an asylum context. These range from face-to-face to blended and online training, offered by different providers (from grassroots providers such as NGOs to university-affiliated providers or international organisations). Available training options in this specific context mostly seem to focus on bilinguals with no specific interpreter training, though some are also expressly open to additional target groups (trained interpreters, interpreter trainers, users of interpreters). Specific training for users of interpreters (institutional representatives, legal advisors), which is also frequently mentioned as another element for improving interpreting quality, does not yet seem to be comprehensively available, with the EASO Interview Techniques Module (EASO 2021) being one exception (this is also a matter where in-house awareness-raising measures might be in place in different countries). Though each individual training programme will of course have to consider national specifics and constraints, increased cooperation and international exchange might help to make users more aware of the need for (specific) training and how this may ultimately also help to improve procedural quality.

The available training measures differ in scope, but most are shorter training elements, some of which might more precisely be labelled "sensitisation measures" as some do not seem to fully comply with the criteria of training proper. The majority of providers, probably for reasons of cost, offer cross-language training, which serves as an indicator that the need for language-specific training for LLDs does not yet seem to be comprehensively covered; this also suggests that specific content such as, for instance, interpreting techniques, can only be discussed at a superficial cross-language level and that attendees will have to be willing to deepen their skills and hone specific techniques largely on their own, which might work for some but probably not for all.

Some general content is covered, not surprisingly, by all training options under review (asylum-specific subject matter, terminology, interpreters' role, basics of professional ethics), while additional more specific content, which is deemed particularly relevant for interpreting in an asylum context, is covered only by some (training for particularly vulnerable groups, dealing with emotions, empathy, racism, and traumatisation, self-care, and mental hygiene). Interestingly, (video) remote interpreting, so far, seems to have been largely neglected, even though it may be assumed that the Covid 19 pandemic has also brought about changes for the asylum context.[7] Generally, a stronger focus on minimum entrance and completion criteria might also be advisable and benefit the harmonisation of the available training options.

With regard to pedagogical issues, from what can be inferred from the different curricula, the more comprehensive face-to-face training elements, at least, also seem to strive to apply current principles of constructive and holistic teaching and learning. This, however, is a field that would merit more research. Particular attention might, in addition, also be paid to the qualification and backgrounds of trainers (also see Kadrić and Pöllabauer forthcoming).

By way of conclusion, it seems fair to say that over the years, this specific context of training seems to have attracted increased attention. Despite these attempts, however, more effort and lobbying at different levels (political, financial, ideological) would be needed to award this topic the attention it should rightly merit to guarantee those in need fair communication and the highest possible quality of interpreting.

Notes

1 Some of these are entitled "training," though, in face of their limited scope, they might more precisely be described as sensitisation measures.

2 I did not include The Voice of Love/MCIS Language Solutions, a US-based registered charity that had been offering short-term training for interpreters for survivors of trauma, war, torture, and sexual violence (http://voice-of-love.org), as the webpage has not been updated for at least two years. For some time, InZone, the Centre for Interpreting Conflict Zones (University of Geneva), had also been offering courses related to a humanitarian context. At the time of writing, the Centre seems to have redirected its focus to higher education for refugees (Centre for Interpreting in Conflict Zones, www.unige.ch/inzone/), though the former head of the centre is now involved with training programmes in Africa (see Moser-Mercer et al. 2021). Self-study material, such as an older (1993) UNHCR "training module" for "Interpreting in a Refugee Context"

(UNHCR 1993), or the resources provided by EURITA (European Resettlement & Integration Technical Assistance, www.ritaresources.org/resources/library/interpretation-language-access/) were also excluded.

3 EASO (European Asylum Support Office) has recently been renamed European Union Agency for Asylum (EUAA).

4 Some of these courses are offered online and target an international audience, others offer training in a specific national context (Austria, Egypt, Germany, Indonesia, Ireland, Korea, Sweden, United Kingdom of Great Britain, the United States).

5 A dual structure with a preparatory and a main course is also suggested by Lee and Choi (2015, 48–50) based on the experience gained through training in Korea; it remains unclear whether this proposed training model has been implemented.

6 Examples would be the UK Diploma in Public Service Interpreting (DPSI), which is a broad qualification/accreditation examination with also a focus on law (www.ciol.org.uk/dpsi), or the Australian NAATI certification scheme (www.naati.com.au).

7 The revised version of the German UNHCR handbook for training interpreters in an asylum context has recently had included a chapter on audio and video remote interpreting (UNHCR 2021). The 2nd edition of the English version of this handbook was published in 2022 (UNHCR 2022).

8 Renamed in 2022 to *Basislehrgang Dolmetschen (Asyl- und Polizeibereich)* [Basic course in interpreting (asylum and police context)].

References

Bahadır, Şebnem. 2010. *Dolmetschinszenierungen: Kulturen, Identitäten, Akteure.* Berlin: SAXA.

Bancroft, Marjory A. 2015. "Community Interpreting." In *The Routledge Handbook of Interpreting*, edited by Holly M. Mikkelson, and Renée Jourdenais, 217–235. Oxford: Routledge.

Bancroft, Marjory, Katharine Allen, Carola E. Green, and Lois M. Feuerle. 2016. *Breaking Silence. Interpreting for Victim Services. A Workbook of Role Plays and Exercises.* Washington, DC: Ayuda.

Bancroft, Marjory A., Lola Bendana, Jean Bruggeman, and Lois Feuerle. 2013. "Interpreting in the Gray Zone: Where Community and Legal Interpreting Intersect." *Translation & Interpreting* 5 (1): 94–113.

Bergunde, Annika, and Sonja Pöllabauer. 2019. "Curricular Design and Implementation of a Training Course for Interpreters in an Asylum Context." *Translation & Interpreting* 11 (1): 1–21.

Blommaert, Jan. 2001. "Investigating Narrative Inequality: African Asylum Seekers' Stories in Belgium." *Discourse & Society* 12 (4): 413–449.

Čemerin, Vedrana. 2020. "Language Mediation in Emergency Migration Contexts: A Case Study of the Migrant Crisis 2015 in Croatia." In *Intercultural Crisis Communication. Translation, Interpreting and Languages in Local Crises*, edited by Federico M. Federici, and Christophe Declercq, 39–62. London: Bloomsbury.

Cirillo, Letizia, and Natacha Niemants, eds. 2017. *Teaching Dialogue Interpreting.* Amsterdam: John Benjamins.

Delgado Luchner, Carmen, and Leïla Kherbiche. 2018. "Without Fear or Favour? The Positionality of ICRC and UNHCR Interpreters in the Humanitarian Field." *Target* 30 (3): 415–438.

EASO. 2021. *Training Curriculum.* Valletta: European Asylum Support Office.

ENPSIT. 2021. *European Network for Public Service Interpreting & Translation.* www.enpsit.org

European Commission. 2021. *Knowledge Centre on Interpretation.* https://ec.europa.eu/education/knowledge-centre-interpretation/knowledge-centre-interpretation_en

Federici, Federico. 2016. "Introduction." In *Mediating Emergencies and Conflicts. Frontline Translating and Interpreting*, edited by Federico Federici, 1–29. New York: Palgrave Macmillan.

Federici, Federico. 2020. "Translation in Contexts of Crisis." In *The Routledge Handbook of Translation and Globalization*, edited by Esperança Bielsa, and Dionysios Kapsaskis, 176–189. London: Routledge.

Federici, Federico, and Sharon O'Brien. 2019. "Cascading Crises. Translation as Risk Reduction." In *Translation in Cascading Crisis*, edited by Federico Federici, and Sharon O'Brien, 1–22. London: Taylor & Francis.

González-Davies, Maria, and Vanessa Enríquez-Raido. 2016. "Situated Learning in Translator and Interpreter Training: Bridging Research and Good Practice." *The Interpreter and Translator Trainer* 10 (1), 1–11.

Hale, Sandra B. 2007. *Community Interpreting*. Houndmills: Palgrave Macmillan.

Iannone, Elvira, and Katharina Redl. 2017. "Ausbildungstrends in der Professionalisierung von LaiendolmetscherInnen." In *Zum Umgang mit Migration. Zwischen Empörungsmodus und Lösungsorientierung*, edited by Ursula Gross-Dinter, Florian Feuser, and Carmen Ramos Méndez-Sahlender, 123–144. Bielefeld: Transcript.

Inghilleri, Moira. 2003. "Habitus, Field and Discourse. Interpreting as a Socially Situated Activity." *Target* 15 (2): 243–268.

Inglis, David, and Christopher Thorpe. 2020. "Translation Encounters and the History of Globalization." In *The Routledge Handbook of Translation and Globalization*, edited by Esperança Bielsa, and Dionysios Kapsaskis, 13–26. London: Routledge.

JRS (Jesuit Refugee Service) Indonesia. 2018. *More than Just Language*. Pringwulung, Sleman, Yogyakarta: JRS. http://jrs.or.id/wp-content/uploads/downloads/2019/01/20181221-JRS-LESSONS-LEARNED-INTERPRETER-ENGLISH-SMALLSIZE-E-BOOK.pdf

Kadrić, Mira. 2011. *Dialog als Prinzip: Für eine emanzipatorische Praxis und Didaktik des Dolmetschens*. Tübingen: Narr.

Kadrić, Mira, and Sonja Pöllabauer. forthcoming. "Education and Training of Public Service Interpreter Teachers." In *The Routledge Handbook on Public Service Interpreting*, edited by Laura Gavioli, and Cecilia Wadensjö. Oxford: Routledge.

Keselman, Olga, Ann-Christin Cederborg, and Per Linell. 2010. "'That is Not Necessary for You to Know!.' Negotiation of Participation Status of Unaccompanied Children in Interpreter-Mediated Asylum Hearings." *Interpreting* 12 (1): 83–104.

Killman, Jeffrey. 2020. "Interpreting for Asylum Seekers and their Attorneys: The Challenge of Agency." *Perspectives* 28 (1): 73–89.

Lai, Miranda, and Sedat Mulayim. 2013. "Training Interpreters in Rare and Emerging Languages. The Problems of Adjustment to a Tertiary Education Setting." In *Interpreting in a Changing Landscape. Selected papers from Critical Link 6*, edited by Christina Schäffner, Krzysztof Kredens, and Yvonne Fowler, 287–304. Amsterdam: John Benjamins.

Lee, Jieun, and Moonsum Choi. 2015. "Recommendations for Interpreter Training for Asylum Interview Settings: The South Korean Case." *International Journal of Interpreter Education* 7 (2): 39–54.

Licoppe, Christian, and Clair-Antoine Veyrier. 2020. "The Interpreter as a Sequential Coordinator in Courtroom Interaction. 'Chunking' and the Management of Turn Shifts in Extended Answers in Consecutively Interpreted Asylum Hearings with Remote Participants." *Interpreting* 22 (1): 56–86.

Maryns, Katrijn. 2012. "Multilingualism in Legal Settings." In *The Routledge Handbook of Multilingualism*, edited by Marilyn Martin-Jones, Adrian Blackledge, and Angela Creese, 297–313. London: Routledge.

Monteoliva-Garcia, Eloisa. 2018. "The Last Ten Years of Legal Interpreting Research (2008–2017). A Review of Research in the Field of Legal Interpreting." *Language and Law/Linguagem e Direito* 5 (1): 38–61.

Moser-Mercer, Barbara, Somia Qudah, Mona Nabeel Ali Malkawi, Jayne Mutiga, and Mohammed Al-Batineh. 2021. "Beyond Aid: Sustainable Responses to Meeting Language Communication Needs in Humanitarian Contexts." *Interpreting and Society* 1 (1): 5–27.

Mulayim, Sedat, and Miranda Lai. 2015. "The Community-of-Inquiry Framework in Online Interpreter Training." In *Interpreter Education in the Digital Age. Innovation, Access, and Change*, edited by Suzanne Ehrlich, and Jemina Napier, 95–124. Washington, DC: Gallaudet University Press.

Nikolaidou, Zoe, Hanna Sofia Rehnberg, and Cecilia Wadensjö. 2019. "Negotiating Access with Public Authorities in Research on Asylum." *Working Papers in Urban Language and Literacies* No 262.

Orlando, Marc, and Leah Gerber. 2020 "The Impact of Globalization on Translator and Interpreter Education." In *The Routledge Handbook of Translation and Globalization*, edited by Esperança Bielsa, and Dionysios Kapsaskis, 202–215. London: Routledge.

Ott, Bernd. 2011. *Grundlagen des beruflichen Lernens und Lehrens*. 4th ed. Berlin: Cornelsen.

Ozolins, Uldis. 2010. "Factors that Determine the Provision of Public Service Interpreting: Comparative Perspectives on Government Motivation and Language Service Implementation." *The Journal of Specialised Translation* 14: 194–215.

Pérez, Isabelle, and Christine Wilson. 2011. "The Interlinked Approach to Training for Interpreter Mediated Police Settings." In *Modelling the Field of Community Interpreting: Questions of Methodology in Research and Training,* edited by Claudia Kainz, Erich Prunc, and Rafael Schögler, 242–262. Vienna: LIT Verlag.

Pöchhacker, Franz. 2007. "Giving Access – Or Not: A Developing-Country Perspective on Healthcare Interpreting." In *Interpreting Studies and Beyond. A Tribute to Miriam Shlesinger*, edited by Franz Pöchhacker, A. Lykke Jakobsen, and Inger M. Mees, 121–138. Copenhagen, Samfundslitteratur Press.

Pöchhacker, Franz. 2016. *Introducing Interpreting Studies*. 2nd ed. London: Routledge.

Pokorn, K. Nike, Maurizio Viezzi, and Tatjana Radanović Felberg, eds. 2020. *Teacher Education for Community Interpreting and Intercultural Mediation: Selected Chapters.* Ljubljana: University Press. https://doi.org/10.4312/9789610604020

Pöllabauer, Sonja. 2013. "Community Interpreting." In *The Encyclopedia of Applied Linguistics*, edited by Carol A. Chapell. Oxford: Wiley-Blackwell.

Pöllabauer, Sonja. 2015. "Interpreting in Asylum Proceedings." In *The Routledge Handbook of Interpreting*, edited by Holly M. Mikkelson, and Renée Jourdenais, 202–216. Oxford: Routledge.

Pöllabauer, Sonja. 2020. "Does it all Boil Down to Money? The Herculean Task of Public Service Interpreter Training – A Quantitative Analysis of Training Initiatives in Austria." In *Training Public Service Interpreters and Translators: A European Perspective*, edited by Market Štefková, Koen Kerremans, and Benjamin Bossaert, 31–57. Bratislava: Univerzita Komenského v Bratislave.

Pöllabauer, Sonja. Forthcoming. "Research on Interpreter-Mediated Asylum Interviews." In *The Routledge Handbook on Public Service Interpreting*, edited by Laura Gavioli, and Cecilia Wadensjö. London: Routledge.

Postgraduate Center. 2021. "Behörden- und Gerichtsdolmetschen." www.postgraduatecenter.at/weiterbildungsprogramme/kommunikation-medien/dolmetschen-fuergerichte-und-behoerden/

Prunč, Erich. 2017. "Auf der Suche nach Aschenbrödels Schuh. Ethische Perspektiven des Kommunaldolmetschens." In *Interpreting Studies at the Crossroads of Disciplines*, edited by Simon Zupan, and Aleksandra Nuč, 21–42. Berlin: Frank & Timme.

Roberts, Roda P. 2002. "Community Interpreting. A Profession in Search of its Identity." In *Teaching Translation and Interpreting 4*, edited by Eva Hung, 157–175. Amsterdam/ Philadelphia: John Benjamins.

Shaw, Sherry. 2013. *Service Learning in Interpreter Education: Strategies for Extending Student Involvement in the Deaf Community*. Washington, DC: Gallaudet University Press.

Ticca, Anna Claudia, Véronique Traverso, and Emilie Jouin. forthcoming. "Training Interpreters in Asylum Settings: The REMILAS Project." In *The Routledge Handbook on Public Service Interpreting*, edited by Laura Gavioli, and Cecilia Wadensjö. London: Routledge.

Todorova, Marija. 2020. "Interpreting for Refugees. Lessons Learned from the Field." In *Interpreting in Legal and Healthcare Settings. Perspectives on Research and Training*, edited by Eva N. S. Ng, and Ineke H. M. Crezee, 63–81. Amsterdam: John Benjamins.

Todorova, Marija. 2021. "Interpreting for Refugees: Empathy and Activism." In *Intercultural Crisis Communication Translation, Interpreting and Languages in Local Crises*, edited by Christophe Declercq, and Federico M. Federici, 153–171. London: Bloomsbury.

UNHCR. 1993. "Interpreting in a Refugee Context (RLD 3)." www.unhcr.org/publications/legal/3ae6bd5f0/training-module-rld3-interpreting-refugee-context.html

UNHCR. 2010. *Improving Asylum Procedures. Comparative Analysis and Recommendations for Law and Practice*. www.unhcr.org/protection/operations/4ba9d99d9/improving-asylum-procedures-comparative-analysis-recommendations-law-practice.html

UNHCR. 2021. *Trainingshandbuch für DolmetscherInnen im Asylverfahren*. 2nd ed. Linz: Trauner.

UNHCR and Sonja Pöllabauer, ed. 2022. *Handbook for Interpreters in Asylum Procedures*. Berlin: Franz & Timme. www.refworld.org/docid/59c8b3be4.html

Valero Garcés, Carmen. 2017. "Training Interpreters and Translators in Spain's Asylum and Refugee O8ce (OAR): A Case Study." *International Journal of Interpreter Education* 9 (2), 5–20.

Annex: List of Training Programmes (alphabetically by course titles)

Asyltolkning/Migrationsgolkning [Asylum/migration interpreting], Folkuniversitetet. Accessed November 26, 2021. www.tolk.su.se/polopoly_fs/1.58397.1323765781!/asyltolkning.pdf

How to Become an Interpreter, Refugee Law Clinic Leipzig. Accessed November 26, 2021. https://rlcl.de/en-sprachvermittler

Immigration Interpreter Training, Language Connections, Inc. Accessed November 26, 2021. www.languageconnections.com/immigration-interpreter-training-program

Interpreter Training Series: Basics of the Asylum Process and Interpreter Sensitivity, Journey's End Refugee Services. Accessed November 26, 2021. www.jersbuffalo.org/interpreting-events/2021/8/24/interpreter-training-basics-of-the-asylum-process-amp-interpreter-sensitivity-zoom

Interpreter Training, Irish Refugee Council. Accessed November 26, 2021. www.irishrefugeecouncil.ie/interpreter-training

Interpreting for Refugees: Contexts, Practices and Ethics, University of Glasgow. Accessed November 26, 2021. www.futurelearn.com/courses/interpreting-for-refugees

Interpreting in the Asylum Context and *Operational Training on Interpreting in the Asylum Context*, European Asylum Support Office (EASO). Accessed November 26, 2021. https://op.europa.eu/webpub/easo/training-catalogue-2018/en/ https://op.europa.eu/webpub/easo/training-catalogue-2018/en/#chapter3

It Breaks my Heart, Cross-Cultural Communications, LLC. Accessed November 26, 2021. www.cultureandlanguage.net/trainings/it-breaks-my-heart-interpreting-for-trauma

Korean Ministry of Justice Training Initiative, Korean Ministry of Justice, UNHCR Korea, and Dongheon Legal Company. Accessed November 26, 2021. https://cit-asl.org/recommendations-for-interpreter-training-asylum-interview/

Online-Videotraining für Sprachmittler [Online Video Training for Interpreters], Bundesamt für Migration und Flüchtlinge [German Federal Asylum Authorities] and Bundesverband der Dolmetscher und Übersetzer (BDÜ) [Federal Association of Interpreters and Translators]. Accessed November 26, 2021. www.bamf.de/SharedDocs/Pressemitteilungen/DE/2017/20170928-033-pm-online-videotraining-sprachmittler.html

Qualitätsvolles Dolmetschen im Asylverfahren (QUADA) [Quality Interpreting in Asylum Procedures], Volkshochschule Wien-Alsergrund. Accessed November 26, 2021. www.vhs.at/de/e/alsergrund/quada[8]

The Cairo Community Interpreter Project (CCIP), The American University in Cairo/Center for Refugee and Migration Studies. Accessed November 26, 2021. https://sites.google.com/aucegypt.edu/ccip/

Trainers' Seminar in Humanitarian Interpretation, National Centre for Social Research and National Organization for the Certification of Qualifications & Vocational Guidance. Accessed November 26, 2021. https://inter4ref.eu/en/wp-content/uploads/2020/11/Trainer-Seminar-Syllabus.pdf

11

ETHICS AND TRAINING OF INTERPRETERS IN THE ASYLUM CONTEXT

Fabrizio Gallai

Asylum interpreters are required to faithfully interpret what is being said during the interview – a central tenet of their codes of ethics. They must not offer advice or express their views on matters being interpreted. However, they have often been found to act as 'principals', prompting applicants to respond, summarising a testimony, or editing out information. Researchers have partly attributed such deviations from ethical principles – such as neutrality and impartiality – to a lack of properly trained interpreters and interpreting service users. In many countries, short-term programmes have been developed without sufficient consultation with interpreter trainers and failed to deliver effective training, and few means are available for service quality management. This chapter explores the distinctive attitudes and narratives of asylum interpreters, whose role is no longer seen as a fixed notion as they adjust their positioning along a spectrum from invisibility to advocacy. In this context, it argues the need to engage more systematically with ethical issues in the context of interpreter (and interpreting service user) training, and that the responsibility of asylum interpreters extends beyond clients to include the wider community to which they belong.

11.1 Introduction

Asylum applicants, who after a potentially long and life-threatening journey from persecution find themselves in an unfamiliar country, might be feeling helpless and desperate, and need interpreters in order to be heard (UNHCR Austria 2017). The interpreter may even be seen as "a reassuring individual . . . representing a link to their language, culture and 'home'" (Pöllabauer 2015a, 204). It is in this complex communicative setting, as outlined in Chapter 10, that asylum interpreters work. Because applicants are rarely able to produce written evidence to back up their claims, their oral testimonies are frequently the only foundation for an

DOI: 10.4324/9781003230359-14

official's decision. The quality of the interpreters' translation and their professional behaviour have a major influence on the work of the interviewer, the decisions s/he takes, and the future of the asylum seeker.

As varied as the many responsibilities assigned to interpreters are, so are the backgrounds and training of those who work in such contexts. In terms of training, there are four types of interpreters: (a) those who have received formal training (at universities and colleges); (b) those who have received shorter interpreting training (general or specific training courses, in-house training); (c) sworn and court-certified interpreters (who may or may not have received training); and (d) interpreters with no training (UNHCR Austria 2017, 42). According to UNHCR Austria (2017), all four are frequently utilised in asylum proceedings. Due to the complexities of the linguistic situation in asylum proceedings, it may be necessary to utilise non-professional interpreters (i.e., type (c) or (d) above) for languages of limited diffusion (LLDs).

Countries differ in their level of quality assurance. Some have established registers which ensure some level of vetting (e.g., trained interpreters are given preference over untrained interpreters, specific training for interpreters working in asylum hearings is provided, and codes of ethics or standards of behaviour for interpreters are developed). However, interpreter training in many countries still mostly concentrates on conference interpreting, with little focus on other settings. When no training is available, interpreters are sometimes refugees themselves, having a similar background to the applicants they translate for. Interpreters for major languages may instead have a host nation background with no significant links to the applicants' native countries. According to reports (e.g., Pöllabauer 2004), both interpreter 'types' may offer benefits and drawbacks to the communication scenario.[1]

It seems self-evident that in such a critical scenario, a highly trained and professional interpreter with the necessary linguistic, cultural, and emotional abilities – as well as a clear understanding of their job and the great responsibility they hold toward the other parties involved – is required. However, "training and practice vary in quality and consistency according to the country" (Tipton and Furmanek 2016, 84). Interpreters' omissions, additions, distortions, and other (ethically) inappropriate behaviour – disrespect, prejudice, biased behaviour towards applicants and/or other interactants, and taking over other participants' roles – are well documented in publications and accounts (UNHCR 2010, 122–123).

This chapter responds to the need for qualified interpreters, which is evident in the asylum context both within the EU and beyond, by offering a theoretical insight into a variety of ethical issues in the context of asylum interpreting training. The first section focuses on the main ethical principles for asylum interpreting – which are "codified and reaffirmed collectively by its practitioners" (Pöchhacker 2016, 167) – while the second part provides an overview of the main themes and concerns that have been highlighted by (micro-interactional and macro-ideological) research on interpreting in asylum settings. Lastly, I will explore how this research can be incorporated in the asylum interpreters' curriculum.

11.2 Ethics in interpreter-mediated asylum interviews

The majority of research on interpreting in asylum settings (a sub-branch of legal interpreting) has focused on institutional encounters that are directly or indirectly related to the asylum application process, which is a legal-administrative procedure by which a country's authorities assess asylum claims based on the 1951 Geneva Convention and the 1967 Protocol (United Nations 1951/1967). Asylum seekers must present personal documentation and explain their motivation for seeking refuge in the country to which they are applying during this interview-based procedure.

The professional status of interpreters in the asylum system has been laid down in guidelines and accredited training programmes, both at national (e.g., EU countries) and international (e.g., UNHCR) levels. These prescriptive standards assert *objective neutrality* on the part of the interpreter: apart from "a competent command of the relevant languages," interpreters should have "adequate interpreting skills" such as "the ability to accurately and faithfully interpret what is said by the interviewer and applicant without omission, addition, comment, summarizing or embellishing" (UNHCR 2010, 33). Under the assumption of absolute equivalence of meaning between languages, interpreters are rendered *invisible* in this triadic interchange.

Principally, asylum interpreters' behaviour is governed by the basic tenets set out in professional codes of conduct (i.e., in terms of competence, confidentiality, neutrality and impartiality),[2] accuracy and completeness, as well as professional conduct with other participants in the communicative interaction (Hebenstreit et al. 2017). Finally, transparency has been put forward as a key principle in recent literature, although it appears only obliquely in the wording of existing codes. However, as highlighted by many scholars (e.g., Laster and Taylor 1994, Mikkelson 1998, Turner 2001), the constraints placed on interpreters in any legal setting are often at odds with the standards promoted by the interpreting profession as explained bellow.

11.2.1 Common and near-universal principles

11.2.1.1 Competence

Competence indicates a commitment to maintaining high standards of performance and requires the interpreter to ensure that s/he has the requisite skills and knowledge and adequate working conditions, including access to relevant information and documentation.

11.2.1.2 Confidentiality

Confidentiality – whereby interpreters must not pass on to others information gathered in interpreted interactions – is universally recognised as a key professional ethics principle for interpreters in all legal settings, though it is subject to legal constraints (such as the obligation to report criminal activity) or a higher moral imperative (such as the duty to save lives), as it is for everyone else.

11.2.1.3 Neutrality and impartiality

As evidenced by similar references in interpreter codes of ethics, impartiality is a key need of interpreters across the judicial system. Bias among interpreters for immigration (especially asylum) interviews and hearings may be particularly destructive. According to this principle, interpreters do not advocate for any of the participants in a conversation. Personal ideas, attitudes, value judgments, or other assumptions have no bearing on the quality or correctness of interpreters' interpretations.

11.2.1.4 Accuracy and completeness

Interpreters provide precise and thorough translations into the target language. The speakers' original messages should be rendered fully and completely, without distortions. All parts of the conversation and any written material referred to or used should be interpreted for the respective other participants. For example, standards outlined in an *UNHCR training module for interviewing applicants for refugee status* state that:

> Interpreters should understand that everything the interviewer and applicant say must be interpreted. It is not sufficient to summarize or embellish what is being said through filling in missing information. Nor should the interpreter try to improve on the words or phrases of the applicant in order to make him or her sound more coherent, credible or educated.
>
> *(UNHCR 1995, 5)*

Interpreters' responsibilities include providing culturally relevant background information and expressing the emotive meaning of interlocutors' speech (or signing) to enhance comprehension. It also entails being familiar with the procedures for which interpreting is required and aware of the officers' strategies for eliciting information (see Tipton and Furmanek 2016, 82–83).

11.2.1.5 Professional conduct: Integrity

Integrity entails honesty (avoiding or declaring conflicts of interest); responsibility (e.g., not cancelling bookings without cause); solidarity (cooperating and sharing knowledge with colleagues, affording colleagues moral assistance, etc.); and refusing any job or situation which might detract from the dignity of the profession or bring it into disrepute.

In this regard, a 'dilemma' situation may occur when a variety of courses of action appear to be conceivable based on certain values and obligations, but only one path of action can be pursued. What is vital in this context is the ability to look at the "right" and "wrong" courses of action and come to an unbiased conclusion based on clear and informed thinking. Common sense, as well as the capacity to think critically and self-critically, as well as rationally, are requirements (Smallwood 1995).

11.2.1.6 Transparency

The emphasis on user expectations, service provision conventions, and the require-ment for "ratification" are all consistent with upholding a transparency principle, requiring the interpreter to do his/her best to ensure that all parties to the commu-nication understand the interpreter's role and status, as well as the service expected. This satisfies the bare minimum of "not misleading" the user. However, proactive transparency, as described by Prunč (2008) as openness and clarity regarding the interpreter's techniques and choices, can help to satisfy all of the important ethical principles. Transparency, in general, has the ability to serve the higher-level ide-als of clarity, truth, and trust, described by Chesterman (1997) as underpinning a professional interpreter ethics.

11.2.2 Issues related to ethical principles

The difficulty in developing ethical guidelines for legal (and asylum) interpreters stems: (a) from the wide range of situations in which the profession is practiced – from highly regulated and codified settings to less structured events, and (b) from the wide range of participants' status, needs, and power relations.

Firstly, although certified interpreters are preferred, they are often not avail-able in certain refugee languages. In these contexts, freelance interpreters without any interpreting qualification are used. Research has identified some recurring problems with the employment of such interpreters in asylum settings, including issues of accuracy (Maryns 2006, Gómez Díez 2010, Keselman et al. 2010, Pölla-bauer 2004), language variation (Bögner et al. 2010, Maryns 2006), and neutrality (Bögner et al. 2010).

Secondly, Hale (2007) discovered widespread interpreters' apathy or scepti-cism regarding codes, which some interpreters regarded as overly vague or simple, or worthless in solving ethical quandaries in practice. Because of this commonly shared attitude, the issue has shifted to the interpreter's ability to apply judgment and take initiative. Tate and Turner (1997/2002) discovered that sign language interpreters in the UK frequently disregard the explicit prescriptions of their code of practice, relying on their own judgment and 'intervening' in various ways (e.g., to clarify). Tate and Turner suggest an ongoing "case law" annex that would codify new solutions to issues not fully covered by the Codes in order to fulfil practition-ers' demand for clear guidance. Cokely (2000) goes even farther, recommending a "rights-based" approach that emphasises interpreters' decision-making flexibility rather than prescriptions and constraints. Other scholars, such as Mikkelson (1998), have advocated for more empowerment of public service interpreters, particularly in legal situations, while Hale (2007) concludes that codes can only provide basic direction and that ethical conduct must be established primarily via training.

Whereas some codes – and authors – oriented towards legal interpreting typically exhibit a more conservative, mechanistic attitude, authors such as Niska (1995) and Mikkelson (1998) have advocated for the (legal) interpreter's emancipation, if not *empowerment*, as a responsible professional rather than an unobtrusive message converter. Similarly, Wadensjö's (1998) descriptive research revealed the insufficiency of the Swedish Code of Conduct in controlling the real-life dynamics of interpreter-mediated encounters. These authors' case studies show how tenets such as confidentiality, correctness and completeness, and client self-determination are difficult to uphold in specific interactions.

In particular, the principle of neutrality has long been seen as a key feature of a skilled interpretation. However, the notion has been challenged as impossible or undesirable by (a) sceptics, who believe that utterance comprehension is dependent on contextual disambiguation, which in turn implies that interpreters cannot construe meaning in a vacuum and are thus subject to the influence of their own background; and (b) activists, who believe that the interpreter's role should include *advocacy* (cf. Baker 2009; Boéri and Jerez 2011; Pöllabauer 2015a).

Tipton (2008) draws on Bourdieu's concept of *shared habitus* to claim that social practice is produced by 'structure' (the place or institution) as well as the actors engaged. Thus, neutrality cannot be attributed only to the interpreter. Baseline neutrality must be created and maintained, but it may also be challenged and restored by any of the participants involved, including the interpreter. In this regard, the interpreter is not described as a 'neutral agent' – neutrality being a fixed condition of the subject – but as an 'agent of neutrality,' leaving room for the interpreter's judgment.

To sum up, many authors recognise that ultimate, objective impartiality is unattainable since interpreters cannot completely separate themselves from their own background, opinions, and cultural prejudices. As a result, the criterion for neutrality is often understood as an attitude or disposition (Tipton 2008), something that all interpreters should strive towards in their pursuit of excellence (Chesterman 2001). Others advocate openness as an ethical safeguard, ensuring that all parties are informed of the interpreters' duties and functions in advance (Setton and Dawrant 2016) or the "basis and aims" of the interpreting process (Prunč 2008).

In the next section, we will see how this mismatch between deontology (normative norms and expectations) and professional practice is a common theme in empirical studies on asylum interpretation.

11.3 Research on asylum interpreting: Main training-related issues

Although the asylum procedure normally prioritises the interpreter's *conduit* function, empirical research – which mainly consists in field studies within particular national contexts[3] – has shown that suggested norms are not always mirrored by interpreters' actual behaviour in asylum settings. Scholars use different discourse analytical methods, with an emphasis on linguistic-anthropological and sociological approaches, and draw from a set of data-collection methods. The general reluctance to allow asylum interviews to be videotaped makes data collecting particularly challenging in this setting.[4] Nonetheless, there is a growing – micro-interactional and macro-ideological – body of research, which must inform asylum interpreters' training programmes.

11.3.1 Micro-interactional research

As seen above, interpreters are not merely conduits that translate words from one language to another, and they frequently play a considerably more *active* role than is usually imagined.

11.3.1.1 Role expectations, conflict and overload

Asylum hearing research provides us with a variety of theoretical role prescriptions and/or practical role constructions. The behaviour of the interpreters is guided by distinct, frequently contradictory or even mutually incompatible roles (Pöllabauer 2015b).

Despite the theoretically assumed role of interpreters as individuals who facilitate communication and help to forge understanding, some do not view the role of interpreters in asylum hearings favourably: interpreters are seen as a "problem" or even "obstacle" to communication, and are described as incompetent, distortional, and biased. Applicants may regard interpreters as "government collaborators" or even "traitors." In such a circumstance, the applicant's willingness to reveal all relevant data is understandably constrained. Interpreters, on the other hand, may be regarded as "helpers" by applicants – the first familiar figure in an unfamiliar setting.[5] These diverse labels and normative claims for the interpreter's role bear out Anderson's early assumption that the interpreter's role "is always partially undefined – that is, the role prescriptions are objectively inadequate" (Anderson 1976/2002, 211).

The emphasis on the adversarial dimension in asylum procedures – establishing the credibility of the asylum seeker's account – is key in this context. Interpreters tend to anticipate what is perceived as a bureaucratically valid account, that is, an account that meets specific formal genre characteristics – "coherent, plausible, consistent" (UNHCR 2005, 124) – which serve as a guiding principle for the asylum procedure. In this way, interpreters become "agents of institutional efficiency" (Kolb and Pöchhacker 2008) in the interviewing process, either as co-interviewers eliciting more institutionally appropriate answers (Keselman et al. 2010), or as co-producers of the written record (Maryns 2006; Pöchhacker and Kolb 2009). Donk (2000) also states that interpreters act as "co-interrogators" or "auxiliary officers," exhibiting biased behaviour – usually towards the applicants – and attempting to assist interviewers.

Pöllabauer's (2004) study of German/English hearings found that three interpreters assumed roles which were discrepant with the Code of conduct and were mainly determined by the officers' expectations. They shortened and paraphrased, provided explanations and intervened to solve face-threatening situations – often allying themselves with the institution and acting in ways that promote the institutional perspective and priorities. Pöllabauer (2004, 154) believes the motivation behind this tendency stems from the interpreters' "extensive knowledge of the archetypal structures and makeup" of the hearings that led them to know what information is relevant to officers at the various stages of the procedure. Further, motivation is influenced by the permissiveness of the officers, who are said to view interpreters as institutionally aligned. These findings were confirmed in Kolb and Pöchhacker's (2008) analysis of 14 appeal hearings, in which they highlighted the interpreters' active involvement in formulating the written record of the proceedings – in line with adjudicating officials' expectations.

To sum up, such evidence of *role conflict* and *role overload* in this unequal and asymmetrical interaction demonstrates that role performance is not only a matter of professionalism on the part of the interpreter. Rather, the latitude and power exercised by interpreters in carrying out their function is subject to setting-specific higher-order constraints at the interactional, socio-professional and institutional levels.

11.3.1.2 Linguistic aspects

Asylum applicants' language use and narratives may be difficult to grasp for interpreters who come from a different sociocultural background. Blommaert (2001, 423) maintains that the narratives of applicants show a particular pattern of coherence, which he calls "ethno-coherence." In particular, accounts at asylum hearings are used to contextualise geographical, social, political, or personal factors. This type of narrative is known as a "home narrative" (Blommaert 2001, 428), and is extremely complex, with frequently unexpected sequential and unified story patterns. To frame and contextualise events and arguments, specific spatial and temporal structures are adopted. Listeners who are unfamiliar with such narratives may find them perplexing and convoluted, and arguments that appear irrational or contradictory may be viewed as improbable. Such patterns should, therefore, be practiced in training.

Overlapping conversation and irregular turn-taking can also be challenging for interpreters. In such instances, they need extremely particular tactics to coordinate discourse and ensure they can translate all utterances.[6] Further, shifting forms of address used by participants (i.e., addressing the collocutor directly or indirectly) can sometimes pose a problem and necessitate specific interpreter strategies: by changing the form of address interpreters can make questions more specific, reformulate utterances in a less face-threatening manner, or detach themselves from the speech.

Another linguistic element of asylum hearings is code-switching and language mixing (Maryns and Blommaert 2001, 69), which may be motivated by preference for one language for a specific purpose, linguistic constraints, or automated processing functions. Interpreters may be required to determine the applicants' national origin, taking on the role of 'expert witness' or "auxiliary police officers" (Pöllabauer 2004) by assessing the characteristics of the applicants' speech.[7]

Lastly, the ambiguity inherent in the asylum interpreter's duty is most visible in the multimodality that characterises the interpreter's performance. While the interpreter is generally defined as a "oral translator" in the asylum process (UNHCR 2009, 18), the written word continues to pervade the interpreter's performance (Tipton and Furmanek 2016, 78). The applicants' 'stories', which are told in a very precise narrative style, are changed and rewritten into a succession of written texts (e.g., interview recordings and transcripts, notes, legal rulings) that adhere to specified genre formats. This conflict between oral and written text (Maryns 2006) also includes varied degrees of immediacy and replicability of the rendering: the interpreter's oral renditions are recorded in written reports, implying that they are no longer transient in nature, but become replicable discourses. This may be viewed as a process of "narrative recontextualization" and "re-entextualization" (Blommaert and Slembrouck 2000, 18). The implications of these ambivalences can be observed particularly when dealing with vulnerable groups such as children (Keselman et al. 2010) or rape victims (Maryns 2013).

11.3.1.3 Cultural aspects

Within the asylum setting, there is – both cooperative and antagonistic – cultural engagement. All parties involved have a distinct (conscious or unconscious) sense of culture and particular assumptions, attributions, biases, and opinions about their own and the culture of others. The various social and cultural backgrounds of the parties involved are a part of both professional and personal life, and they lead to varied interpretations of behaviours and occurrences. This variety of interpretations may also occur in everyday exchanges, yet it becomes more prominent in an asylum interview. Similarly to all legal interpreting settings, it is characterised by "contextual constraints" (Jacobsen 2009, 158) (i.e., the ad-hoc, institutionalised nature of the speech event), involving (one or more) professionals with a certain amount of power, and a non-professional – usually the second-language speaker – with a small amount of power or no power at all (cf. Englund Dimitrova 1997; Jacobsen 2010; Roy 1999). Naturally, these and other contextual constraints have an impact on the way meanings are negotiated within the interaction. As a result, the interpreter's personality (self-image, values, attitudes, etc.) is evident and central in this meaning negotiation, as is the personality of the other (more or less "powerful") participants.

Because these aspects have an impact on the interpretation process, they must be recognised by all participants, and an understanding of the intricate make-up of this "communicative pas de trois" (Wadensjö 1998), as well as "reflexive knowledge" – broad abilities of reflection and basic knowledge to question assumptions, self-awareness and reflection – should be part and parcel of interpreter training.

The cultural relativity of certain concepts is one feature directly tied to language use of culture-bound terms (Kälin 1986, 233–235). Different concepts of the self or family, different concepts of logic or "common sense" (including concepts from the domains of magic, voodoo, or animistic religions), different values or perceptions of time and space, may all be sources of misunderstanding. Despite the fact that many asylum authorities are trained in these areas, reports and research show that culturally particular notions might be difficult to grasp. Some interpreters, particularly those who have lived in the Western world, may be unaware of or lost sensitivity towards such elements. In addition to the concepts utilised by the applicants, technical (e.g., political or legal) terminology used by the officials may be difficult to transfer into the applicants' language due to a lack of corresponding expressions or a different (legal, social, etc.) system. Maryns and Blommaert (2002, 13) have described such linguistic and cultural inequalities using the notion of "pretextuality" and "pretextual gaps."

Finally, interpreters are obliged to comprehend the type and breadth of relationships amongst asylum participants. As a result, they can better "handle ethical, emotional, procedural, and linguistic demands" (Tipton and Furmanek 2016, 88). Tipton and Furmanek (2016) explore often seen traits and emphasise the potential fragility of the three primary participants' – asylum applicant's, interpreter's, and officer's – "macro intercultures." Although these three pairings do not carry any unique privilege, they are examined because of the disparities in social solidarity and distance they imply.

11.3.1.4 Psychological aspects

Another element of asylum hearings is that they are frequently emotional. Applicants recount stories of sometimes unimaginable atrocities, they must report on harrowing facts, and all other interactants must find a means to cope with such narratives. In particular, some candidates are classified as belonging to "vulnerable" groups. UNHCR guidelines call for specific sensitivity and special interview techniques for these groups, which include children and unaccompanied minors (ECRE 2019, 29–30; Tipton and Furmanek 2016, 100), traumatised or mentally ill individuals, victims of torture, rape, or any other form of violence. LGBT people have lately been identified as a vulnerable category. The role of the interpreter in such fragile settings has been said to be crucial for the successful implementation of specific interviewing techniques, which must be part of interpreter training. However, this role is often not properly fulfilled.[9]

When dealing in emotionally charged situations, the interpreters' empathy and emotional stability are very important. Empathy should not be regarded as a threat to neutrality, since it may be a strong aspect in rapport and trust building, as well as sense making for the interpreter. Interpreters may first connect with other participants' negative feelings, and generate anger, despair, or worry (Splevins et al. 2010).

Furthermore, interpreters are also presented with and need to render descriptions of harrowing events and may be influenced depending on their personal participation and identification with the asylum seeker's challenges. For instance, when an asylum seeker's case history of torture is being extracted, the interpreter may find it difficult to have to listen to and repeat stories of pain and crimes. The danger of *vicarious trauma* is greatest for those who work with victims who have been directly traumatised. These factors may have a significant impact on the effectiveness of such interviews, which are likely to fail if interpreters are unable to execute specified interview rules and strategies. Additional training in developing resilience and personal coping techniques for both officials and interpreters is highly needed (cf. Wedam 2017).

11.3.2 Macro-ideological research: Institutional and macro-social level

Interpreting in asylum interviews has been further conceptualised in connection to the macro-ideological systems that directly or indirectly condition the interpreting process. Inghilleri (2003, 2005, 2012) has made significant research contributions in this area, discussing the ways in which the interpreting habitus is consistently attuned to reproducing target culture standards and ideologies. Her sociological study on understanding asylum settings investigates the level of the social institution and the restrictions it imposes on the individuals who act within it. She demonstrates how, on the institutional and macro-social levels, understanding interpreting as a discourse process in society elevates concerns like role, authority, and ideology.

Blommaert (2001, 2009) and Maryns (2006, 2013) conceptualised linguistic resource disparity in asylum contact, emphasising on how linguistic minority speakers are severely restrained in utilising their multilingual resources in the monolingual institutional environment. The multilingual repertoires of asylum seekers have been proven to contradict the monolingual language ideology that is still powerful in the institutional realm in the context of language usage and interpreter allocation in the asylum process.[9] Ongoing research on language shifting in interpreted asylum encounter (Angermeyer 2013, Hlavac 2010) demonstrates how mobility and displacement difficulties affect the process of defining the "dominant language" of the minority speaker. The variety of socio-discursive parameters at work in asylum interaction confirms the need for more leeway in negotiating language, including the possibility of "stand-by interpreting" (cf. Angermeyer 2013, Cooke 1996) as a means of integrating the benefits of direct and interpreter-mediated communication with authorities.

11.3.3 Repercussions on training

We have seen a continuum of conflicting views on the role and function of interpreters among scholars, the legal system and the persons involved in such settings. This has various consequences for their training, which we will explore now.

11.3.3.1 Accountability and ethical reflection

Interpreters have begun to exhibit an interest in ethical issues discussed above (Baker and Maier 2011). They increasingly acknowledge that they are crucial to a variety of (human) rights movements in today's world – from those that fight for minority rights to those that oppose global injustices – and have begun to emphasise the necessity for training to include a "deep awareness of professional ethics" (Bromberg and Jesionowski 2010).

The rising emphasis on *accountability* should be considered while creating interpreter training syllabuses, which often only promote the ethos of neutrality. More responsibility has resulted in increased visibility, and therefore increased pressure on the profession as a whole to demonstrate that it is aware of its influence over society as a whole.

In order to address the issue of accountability, trainers are called upon to directly and explicitly engage with the previously discussed issues and build them into the curriculum. They should provide student interpreters with conceptual tools to reflect on numerous topics and circumstances that they may face in their professional lives and find ethically challenging, without forcing them to rely unthinkingly on codes of behaviour. At the same time, they should also alert trainees to the ethical consequences of behaviour that they may see as ordinary or unproblematic, and hence do not perceive as morally demanding.

Decisions made while interpreting in asylum settings can have a significant impact on the quality of life of those who rely on the interpreter to mediate between host country officials and vulnerable migrants. Reflecting critically on ethical behaviour entails questioning one's own principles, becoming more aware of them, and acting on them. It is ultimately a question of *personal* integrity, not skill in following a prescribed set of rules. The classroom should therefore be a space of experimentation and reflection in which students are made to feel free to rehearse any issue and be allowed to take responsibility for the decisions they make.

11.3.3.2 A new classroom

Educators should establish a collection of pedagogical tools that may be used to create an environment in which students can make situated ethical judgments, practice the consequences of such actions, and learn from their experiences.

Firstly, debating such problems in the safe context of the classroom allows students to freely rehearse all sides of an argument and consider its ethical consequences from many angles. Bell (2010), for instance, mentions controversial issues that are not restricted to questions of war and physical violence:

> If you're pro-life, do you interpret for an abortion clinic? If you're pro-choice, do you interpret for a crisis pregnancy center? And it doesn't stop there. Legal interpreters who are against the death penalty may have to

interpret judgments they don't agree with, and feminist translators are asked to localize for adult entertainment.

(Bell 2010, 41)

Another task may be to write a critical essay on a certain topic, such as non-professional work or the exclusion of content considered insulting to the target culture. Using topics based on actual, real-life case studies and introducing interactive projects in the classroom will show students the importance of ethics and the freeing effect of being able to reflect on the influence of their behavior on others. Students who research the relevant literature on ethics and interpreting for their essay will discover that it has long been thought that interpreters are mainly responsible to their clients. However, according to Boéri and de Manuel Jerez (2011), they also have an ethical obligation to the larger society and to mankind. As a result, the overriding question can be to what degree interpreter education should teach trainees to respond to society's needs, rather than 'only' acting as professionals – and whether it is indeed possible to separate the two aspects.

A third activity might take the form of *role play* – a pedagogical tool designed to prepare students for situations in which they have to make decisions very quickly.[10] A relevant example comes from Kadrić's (2014, 2017) work, which shows how asylum interpreting involves the human being as a whole – with both the interpreter's body and mind as well as social and communicative needs. She uses methods taken from Boal's theatre pedagogy and applies them to interpreter education. This concrete example (or "scenario") is the starting point of the role-playing exercise. The group alternates between reflecting on the scenario and trying out different actions. The goal of this didactic approach is to identify habitual behaviours, analyse and deconstruct societal structures of power, and promote independent interpreting work – trying out new possibilities helps adjust and alter discourses and demonstrates that for every decision there is an alternative.

Further, Tipton's (2011) study challenges trainers and trainees by reimagining the classroom as a battle zone and fostering learning between civilian interpreters and military troops for whom they are employed. This is simple to replicate in an asylum situation. According to the author, the learning experience is a horizontal interaction in which both sides have a lot to teach the other about a foreign culture and its expectations. When they are mutually involved in a context of conflict and flux, neither develops a body of knowledge; instead, they build a greater awareness of how to "stay" in that shared circumstance.

Finally, considering the classroom as an open arena for ethical thought may complicate the issue of evaluation. By which criteria can educators evaluate students' performances? One solution may be to design grading standards that focus on the quality of thinking and contemplation – rather than the ultimate judgment made.

11.4 Conclusions

Both research and practice reveal that the interactants in asylum procedures frequently have a limited understanding of the interpreter's job and varied expectations that drive their behaviour in relation to the interpreter. While some countries and international organisations attempt to set out the duty of the interpreter in codes and guidelines, such theoretical recommendations are not always followed in reality, and may enforce a mechanical or rule-bound ethics on interpreters.

This chapter has shown the dynamic nature of the interpreters' performance dimensions. In order to deliver a "good" interpretation, interpreters should be able to apply the appropriate techniques to maintain a professional distance and manage stress, but above all they are required to be acutely aware of professional ethics and what constitutes their role of the interpreter.

Hence, ethics should form part and parcel of asylum interpreter training. This is to some extent reality but what is still lacking in many curricula. We should ensure that the concept of shared responsibility in asylum procedure truly extends to the recruitment and, above all, education of all asylum interpreters. In order for students to embrace this responsibility and develop an awareness of their impact on society, the classroom should be configured as an open space for reflection and experimentation. Different types of activity that may be incorporated in the asylum interpreting curriculum in order to provide students with an opportunity to reflect on ethical questions (related, for instance, to advocacy or the degree of cultural explanation).

Attention to education, recruitment policies, regulation (where appropriate) and raising awareness of professional consciousness and solidarity seems to be key for the path ahead. All the more, the inclusion of all key players in this process appears to be critical. In particular, authorities – from immigration officers at ports of entry, to immigration appellate authorities, from immigration lawyers to the police in any initial interviewing of illegal immigrants – are also called upon to undergo training on interpreters' role boundaries and neutrality and interpreter-user cooperation.

Without doubt, there is a significant role for systematic empirical research in this field. Specific themes that are likely to become more significant in the future include: teamwork building, the difficulties of interpreting for vulnerable groups, the increased use of remote interpreting (see Chapter 12) for asylum settings, and the development of a tailored set of guidelines that would help interpreters adapt to the requirements of the asylum settings.

Notes

1 Applicants may purposefully hide information and fail to reveal all necessary details because they do not trust the interpreter. If interpreters are primarily associated with the host country, there may be two sides to the coin: some interpreters are viewed as more '*neutral*' by applicants (because they are not associated with their home countries), which may make them more inclined to provide complete information; while other

interpreters are said to *lack the necessary language and cultural skills* to fully grasp the true meaning and context of the applicants' utterances.

2 *Impartiality* is defined in terms of the interpreter's social position and function, whereas *neutrality* in terms of the discursive construction of realities in a specific act of communication (see Prunč 2012, 424).

3 See publications on Austria (Pöllabauer 2004, Kolb and Pöchhacker 2008), Belgium (Blommaert 2001, Maryns 2006), Canada (Barsky 1994), Italy (Merlini 2009, Jacquemet 2011), the UK (Inghilleri 2003, 2005, 2012, Tipton 2008), Sweden (Keselman et al. 2010), and Spain (Gómez Díez 2010).

4 For instance, in the UK – except for situations covered by the Police and Criminal Evidence Act 1984 – no regular provision is made at any of the immigration procedure stages for an electronic recording of the interview (Colin and Morris 1996). In Italy, although Art. 14 of Legislative Decree 25/2008 (2008) states that the asylum interview is "is videotaped by audiovisual means and transcribed in Italian with the aid of automatic voice recognition systems," very few interviews are currently videotaped (personal communication).

5 Interpreters who are seen as 'cultural mediators' are given the most leeway. For example, Barsky (1994, 1996) advocates for interpreters to serve as "intercultural actors."

6 This is also true for politeness markers. A lack of (both verbal and nonverbal) politeness methods may have a detrimental impact on the evaluation of an applicant's claim. The same applies to hedges: excessive hedging is connected with a "powerless" style and may make speakers look less confidence in what they say (see, Berk-Seligson 2002; Hale 2004).

7 This is being referred to as LADO (language analysis in the determination of origins) and would normally be carried out by phoneticians, who analyse the asylum seeker's accent. However, Eades (2010: 236) claims that "this assessment is not always done by trained linguists" and "sociolinguists have given evidence in appeals against decisions made on the basis of LADO reports."

8 For instance, interpreters at times start side sequences which go beyond a normal repair, leading to the child's voice being "either excluded from interaction of guided" (Keselman et al. 2010, 89).

9 A damning case study of the consequences of these anomalous frames for interpreting human behavior for the denial of justice to an asylum seeker is presented in Blommaert (2009). who demonstrates that the sociolinguistic repertoires of asylum seekers are "indicative of time, not just space" and that they "index full histories of people and of places." As a result, for many asylum seekers, expecting an examination of their speech to give a reasonable manner of separating their place of birth from the rest of their personal history is impractical.

10 See, for instance, Bahadır (2010); Cho and Roger (2010); Niemants (2013); Rudvin and Tomassini (2011).

References

Anderson, R. Bruce W. 1976/2002. "Perspectives on the Role of Interpreter." In *The Interpreting Studies Reader*, edited by Franz Pöchhacker, and Miriam Shlesinger, 208–217. London/New York: Routledge.

Angermeyer, Philipp. 2013. "Multilingual Speakers and Language Choice in the Legal Sphere." *Applied Linguistics Review* 4 (1): 105–126.

Bahadır, Şebnem. 2010. "The Task of the Interpreter in the Struggle of the Other for Empowerment: Mythical Utopia or Sine Qua Non of Professionalism?" *Translation and Interpreting Studies* 5 (1): 124–139.

Baker, Mona. 2009. "Resisting State Terror: Theorizing Communities of Activist Translators and Interpreters." In *Globalization, Political Violence and Translation*, edited by Esperanza Bielsa, 222–242. Basingstoke: Palgrave Macmillan.

Baker, Mona, and Carol Maier. 2011. "Ethics in Interpreter and Translator Training: Critical Perspectives." *The Interpreter and Translator Trainer* 5 (1): 1–14.

Barsky, Robert F. 1994. *Constructing a Productive Other. Discourse Theory and the Convention Refugee Hearing.* Amsterdam/Philadelphia: John Benjamins.

Barsky, Robert F. 1996. "The Interpreter as Intercultural Agent in Convention Refugee Hearings." *The Translator* 2 (1): 45–63.

Bell, Terena. 2010. "Personal Ethics and Language Services." *Multilingual* 21 (8): 41–43.

Berk-Seligson, Susan. 2002. *The Bilingual Courtroom: Court Interpreters in the Judicial Process.* Chicago: University of Chicago Press.

Blommaert, Jan. 2001. "Investigating Narrative Inequality: African Asylum Seekers' Stories in Belgium." *Discourse & Society* 12 (4): 413–449.

Blommaert, Jan. 2009. "Language, Asylum and the National Order." *Current Anthropology* 50 (4): 415–441.

Blommaert, Jan, and Stef Slembrouck. 2000. "Data Formulation as Text and Context: The (Aesth)Etics of Analysing Asylum Seekers' Narratives." *Working Papers on Language, Power and Identity, Vol. 2.* http://bank.rug.ac.be/lpi

Boéri, Julie, and Jesús De Manuel Jerez. 2011. "From Training Skilled Conference Interpreters to Educating Reflective Citizens: A Case Study of the Marius Action Research Project." *The Interpreter and Translator Trainer* 5 (1): 41–64

Bögner, Diana, Chris Brewin, and Jane Herlihy. 2010. "Refugees' Experiences of Home Office Interviews: A Qualitative Study on the Disclosure of Sensitive Personal Information." *Journal of Ethnic and Migration Studies* 36 (3): 519–535.

Bromberg, Jinny, and Irina Jesionowski. 2010. "Trends in Court Interpreter Training." *Multilingual* 21 (4): 35–39.

Chesterman, Andrew. 1997. "Ethics of Translation." In *Translation as Intercultural Communication: Selected Papers from the EST Congress, Prague 1995*, edited by Mary Snell-Hornby, Zuzuana Jettmarová, and Klaus Kaindl, 147–160. Amsterdam/Philadelphia, PA: John Benjamins.

Chesterman, Andrew. 2001. "Proposal for a Hieronymic Oath." *Translator: Studies in Intercultural Communication* 7 (2): 139–154.

Cho, Jinhyun, and Peter Roger. 2010. "Improving Interpreting Performance Through Theatrical Training." *The Interpreter and Translator Trainer* 4 (2): 151–171.

Colin, Joan, and Ruth Morris. 1996. *Interpreters and the Legal Process.* Winchester: Waterside Press.

Cokely, Dennis. 2000. "Exploring Ethics: A Case for Revising the Code of Ethics." *Journal of Interpretation* (2000): 25–57.

Cooke, Michael. 1996. "A Different Story: Narrative versus Question and Answer in Aboriginal Evidence." *Forensic Linguistics* 3: 273–288.

Donk, Ute. 2000. "Dolmetscher als Hilfspolizisten – eine ermittlungstaktische Notwendigkeit [Interpreters as Auxiliary Police Officers]?" *Polizei & Wissenschaft* 2: 26–38.

Eades, Diana. 2010. *Sociolinguistics and the Legal Process.* Bristol: Multilingual Matters.

Englund Dimitrova, Birgitta. 1997. "Degree of Interpreter Responsibility in the Interaction Process in Community Interpreting." In *The Critical Link: Interpreters in The Community*, edited by Silvana E. Carr, Roda P. Roberts, Aideen Dufour, and Dini Steyn, 147–164. London: John Benjamins.

European Council on Refugees and Exiles (ECRE). 2019. *Upholding Legal Rights for Unaccompanied Children: Fostering Quality Legal Assistance in the Asylum Procedure. Module 5: Ensuring a Child-Friendly Approach to Unaccompanied Children in Asylum Procedures: Practical Dimensions.* www.ecre.org/wp-content/uploads/2019/07/4.26.-Module-5_Ensuring-a-child-friendly-approach.pdf.

Gómez Díez, Isabel. 2010. "The Role of the Interpreter in Constructing Asylum Seeker's Credibility." *Sociolinguistic Studies* 4 (2): 333–370.

Hale, Sandra. 2004. "The Discourse of Court Interpreting: Discourse Practices of the Law, the Witness and the Interpreter." *Interpreting* 8 (1): 105–112.

Hale, Sandra. 2007. *Community Interpreting*. Basingstoke: Palgrave Macmillan.

Hebenstreit, Gernot, Alexandra Marics, and Jim Hlavac. 2017. "Professional Ethics and Professional Conduct." In *Handbook for Interpreters in Asylum Procedures*, edited by UNHCR Austria, 70–84. Vienna: UNHCR Austria.

Hlavac, Jim. 2010. "Shifts in the Language of Interpretation with Bi- or Multi-lingual Clients: Circumstances and Implications for Interpreters." *Interpreting* 12 (2): 186–213.

Inghilleri, Moira. 2003. "Habitus, Field and Discourse: Interpreting as a Socially Situated Activity." *Target* 15 (2): 243–268.

Inghilleri, Moira. 2005. "Mediating Zones of Uncertainty Interpreter Agency, the Interpreting Habitus and Political Asylum Adjudication." *The Translator* 11 (1): 69–85.

Inghilleri, Moira. 2012. *Interpreting Justice. Ethics, Politics and Language*. London/New York: Routledge.

Jacobsen, Bente. 2009. "The Community Interpreter: A Question of Role." *Hermes* 42: 155–166.

Jacobsen, Bente. 2010. "Interactional Pragmatics and Court Interpreting: An Analysis of Face." In *Doing Justice to Court Interpreting*, edited by Miriam Shlesinger, and Franz Pöchhacker, 193–222. Amsterdam/Philadelphia, PA: John Benjamins.

Jacquemet, Marco. 2011. "Crosstalk 2.0: Asylum and Communicative Breakdowns." *Text & Talk – An Interdisciplinary Journal of Language, Discourse & Communication Studies* 31 (4): 475–497.

Kadrić, Mira. 2014. "Giving Interpreters a Voice: Interpreting Studies Meets Theatre Studies." *The Interpreter and Translator Trainer* 8 (3): 452–468.

Kadrić, Mira. 2017. "Make It Different! Teaching Interpreting with Theatre Techniques." In *Teaching Dialogue Interpreting. Research-Based Proposals for Higher Education*, edited by Letizia Cirillo, and Natacha Niemants, 275–292. Amsterdam/Philadelphia: John Benjamins.

Kälin, Walter. 1986. "Troubled Communication: Cross-Cultural Misunderstandings in the Asylum-Hearing." *International Migration Review* 20 (2): 230–241.

Keselman, Olga, Ann-Christin Cederborg, and Per Linell. 2010. " 'That is Not Necessary for You to Know!' Negotiation of Participation Status of Unaccompanied Children in Interpreter-Mediated Asylum Hearings." *Interpreting* 12 (1): 83–104.

Kolb, Waltraud, and Franz Pöchhacker. 2008. "Interpreting in Asylum Appeal Hearings: Roles and Norms Revisited." In *Interpreting in Legal Settings*, edited by Debra Russell, and Sandra Hale, 26–50. Washington, DC: Gallaudet University Press.

Laster, Kathy, and Veronica Taylor. 1994. *Interpreters and the Legal System*. Sydney: The Federation Press.

Legislative Decree 25/2008. 2008. *Implementation of Directive 2005/85/EC On Minimum Standards on Procedures in Member States for Granting and Withdrawing Refugee Status*. www.normattiva.it/uri-res/N2Ls?urn:nir:stato:decreto.legislativo:2008;25.

Maryns, Katrijn. 2006. *The Asylum Speaker*. Manchester: St. Jerome.

Maryns Katrijn. 2013. "Disclosure and (Re)Performance of Gender-Based Evidence in an Interpreter-Mediated Asylum Interview." *Journal of Sociolinguistics* 17 (5): 661–686.

Maryns, Katrijn, and Jan Blommaert. 2001. "Stylistic and Thematic Shifting as a Narrative Resource: Assessing Asylum Seekers' Repertoires." *Multilingua* 20 (1): 61–84.

Maryns, Katrijn, and Jan Blommaert. 2002. "Pretextuality and Pretextual Gaps: On De/Refining Linguistic Inequality." *Pragmatics* 12 (1): 11–30.

Merlini, Raffaela. 2009. "Seeking Asylum and Seeking Identity in a Mediated Encounter: The Projection of Selves through Discursive Practices." *Interpreting* 11 (1): 57–92.

Mikkelson, Holly. 1998. "Towards A Redefinition of the Role of the Court Interpreter." *Interpreting* 3 (1): 21–45.

Niemants, Natacha. 2013. "From Role-Playing to Role-Taking: Interpreter's Role(s) in Healthcare." In *Interpreting in a Changing Landscape*, edited by Christina Schäffner, Krzysztof Kredens, and Yvonne Fowler, 305–319. Amsterdam/Philadelphia, PA: John Benjamins.

Niska, Helge. 1995. "Just Interpreting: Role Conflicts and Discourse Types in Court Interpreting." In *Translation and the Law. American Translators Association Scholarly Monograph Series*, vol. 8, edited by Marshall Morris, 293–316. Amsterdam/Philadelphia, PA: John Benjamins.

Pöchhacker, Franz. 2016. *Introducing Interpreting Studies*. London: Taylor & Francis.

Pöchhacker, Franz, and Waltraud Kolb. 2009. "Interpreting for the Record: A Case Study of Asylum Review Hearings." In *The Critical Link 5. Quality in interpreting – A shared responsibility*, edited by Sandra B. Hale, Uldis Ozolins, and Ludmila Stern, 119–134. Amsterdam/Philadelphia, PA: John Benjamins.

Pöllabauer, Sonja. 2004. "Interpreting in Asylum Hearings: Issues of Role, Responsibility and Power." *Interpreting* 6 (2): 143–180.

Pöllabauer, Sonja. 2015a. "Interpreting in Asylum Proceedings." In *The Routledge Handbook of Interpreting*, edited by Holly Mikkelson, and Renée Jourdenais, 202–216. London/New York: Routledge.

Pöllabauer, Sonja. 2015b. "Role." In *The Routledge Handbook of Interpreting*, edited by Holly Mikkelson, and Renée Jourdenais, 355–360. London/New York: Routledge.

Prunč, Erich. 2008. "Zur Konstruktion von Translationskulturen." In *Translationskultur*, edited by Larisa Schippel, 19–41. Berlin: Frank und Timme.

Prunč, Erich. 2012. *Entwicklungslinien der Translationswissenschaft. Von den Asymmetrien der Sprachen zu den Asymmetrien der Macht*. Berlin: Frank und Timme.

Rudvin, Mette, and Elena Tomassini. 2011. *Interpreting in the Community and Workplace: A Practical Teaching Guide*. Basingstoke: Palgrave Macmillan.

Roy, Cynthia B. 1999. *Interpreting as a Discourse Process*. Oxford: Oxford University Press.

Setton, Robin, and Andrew Dawrant. 2016. *Conference Interpreting: A Trainer's Guide*. Amsterdam/Philadelphia, PA: John Benjamins.

Smallwood, James. 1995. "Dilemmas, Moral." In *International Encyclopedia of Ethics*, edited by John K. Roth, 228–229. London: Taylor & Francis.

Splevins, Katie, Keren Cohen, Jake Bowley, and Stephen Joseph. 2010. "Theories of Posttraumatic Growth: Cross-Cultural Perspectives." *Journal of Loss and Trauma* 15 (3): 259–277.

Tate, Granville, and Graham H. Turner. 1997/2002. "The Code and the Culture: Sign Language Interpreting – in Search of the New Breed's Ethics." In *The Interpreting Studies Reader*, edited by Franz Pöchhacker, and Miriam Shlesinger, 372–383. London/New York: Routledge.

Tipton, Rebecca. 2008. "Reflexivity and the Social Construction of Identity in Interpreter-Mediated Asylum Interviews." *The Translator* 14 (1): 1–19.

Tipton, Rebecca. 2011. "Relationships of Learning between Military Personnel and Interpreters in Situations of Violent Conflict." *The Interpreter and Translator Trainer* 15 (1): 15–40.

Tipton, Rebecca, and Olgierda Furmanek. 2016. *Dialogue Interpreting. A Guide to Interpreting in Public Services and the Community*. London/New York: Routledge.

Turner, Graham H. 2001. *Facilitating Real Interpreting: Towards Identifying Good Practice in Sign Language Interpreted Communication*. Paper presented at Addressing Communication Disadvantage Conference, Preston, United Kingdom, 1 January.

UNHCR Austria, ed. 2017. *Handbook for Interpreters in Asylum Procedures*. Vienna: UNHCR Austria.

UNHCR, ed. 1995. *Training Module RLD4 – Interviewing Applicants for Refugee Status*. www.unhcr.org/publications/legal/3ae6bd670/training-module-rld4-interviewing-applicants-refugee-status.html.

UNHCR, ed. 2005. *Self-Study Module 1: An Introduction to International Protection. Protecting Persons of Concern to UNHCR*. www.refworld.org/docid/4214cb4f2.html.

UNHCR, ed. 2009. *Self-Study Module 3: Interpreting in a Refugee Context*. www.refworld.org/docid/49b6314d2.html

UNHCR, ed. 2010. *Improving Asylum Procedures: Comparative Analysis and Recommendations for Law and Practice. Key Findings and Recommendations*. www.unhcr.org/protection/operations/4ba9d99d9/improving-asylum-procedures-comparative-analysis-recommendations-law-practice.html

United Nations, ed. 1951/1967. *Convention Relating to the Status of Refugees and Protocol Relating to the Status of Refugees*. www.unhcr.org/4ec262df9.html.

Wadensjö, Cecilia. 1998. *Interpreting as Interaction*. London: Longman.

Wedam, Uta. 2017. "The Interpreter's Emotional Experience." In *Handbook for Interpreters in Asylum Procedures*, edited by UNHCR Austria, 187–194. Vienna: UNHCR Austria.

12

TECHNOLOGY AFFORDANCES IN TRAINING INTERPRETERS FOR ASYLUM SEEKERS AND REFUGEES

Mariachiara Russo and Nicoletta Spinolo

The promotion of social and legal inclusion of asylum seekers and refugees can be greatly enhanced by providing specific training to those called upon to facilitate smooth communication between them and the relevant authorities to overcome linguistic-cultural barriers (i.e., interpreters in the field) also called humanitarian interpreters. These particularly sensitive settings are often deprived of properly trained language professionals, which jeopardises the asylum seekers' and refugees' rights to access public services and fair treatment in their dealings with the relevant authorities. The lack of trained language professionals is mainly due to a shortage of specific training on humanitarian interpreting and the language pairs required for interactions with refugees applying for international protection. Building on our expertise gained through one particular blended course with untrained interpreters working for refugee status determination bodies in Italy, this chapter illustrates the design of a conceptual and pedagogical solution based on innovative educational approaches and digital technologies for synchronous and asynchronous teaching and learning. This solution may apply to all language-pairs to meet humanitarian interpreters' challenges and needs.

12.1 Introduction

Over the centuries, interpreters have played the role of "critical link"[1] to overcome language and cultural barriers between individuals of different nationalities in times of both peace and war. The 21st century, however, has witnessed the emergence of unprecedented demands for interpreter mediation in a new, highly sensitive setting, the humanitarian setting. With the implementation of the International Humanitarian Law for the protection of victims of wars and armed conflicts – including the First Geneva Convention of 1864, the four Geneva Conventions of 1949 and the Additional Protocols of 1977, as well as the 1951 UN Refugee Convention, interpreters

DOI: 10.4324/9781003230359-15

have been increasingly called upon to work in conflict and non-conflict scenarios where migrants, forcibly displaced people, and refugees have escaped persecution, poverty, natural disasters and life-threatening risks. At the 2016 "First Symposium on Interpreter Training and Humanitarian Interpreting,"[2] Marc Orlando voiced concern about the level of preparation of interpreters working in these settings. Admittedly, this is a particularly challenging field where interpreting techniques do not suffice unless they are accompanied by intercultural and interactional skills and psychological and physical stamina.

To tackle the issue of interpreter preparation for humanitarian settings, the University of Geneva pioneered training initiatives by setting up in 2010 the *InZone* Centre for Interpreting in Conflict Zones[3] led by Barbara Moser-Mercer, and by providing short courses for humanitarian field interpreters[4] led by Lucía Ruiz Rosendo. Recently, two other academic initiatives have come to the fore (Moser-Mercer et al. 2021): the diploma courses opened by the Yarmouk University in Jordan and the University of Nairobi in Kenya. Finally, a university online asynchronous course for interpreters working with refugees is now offered by the University of Glasgow within the framework of the only European project on this topic. This Erasmus+ Inter4Ref project provides interdisciplinary resources and materials for humanitarian interpreters. Other organisations and institutions offer guidelines to humanitarian interpreters in the field, such as *Translators Without Borders' Field Guide to Humanitarian Interpreting and Cultural Mediation,*[5] the *UNHCR: Self-study module* (2009) and *The Handbook for Interpreters in Asylum Procedures* (2017). However, apart from these few training opportunities, it is generally acknowledged that interpreters working in humanitarian settings are usually non-professional bi/multilinguals who, therefore, lack both technical and deontological preparation. This lack of training may jeopardise the goal of interpreter-mediated encounters involving refugees and asylum seekers as these non-professional interpreters risk violating basic deontological principles and may engage in side conversations with refugees without involving the public officer or omit important information due to inadequate translation skills (Pöllabauer 2004). Providing adequate training is, therefore, key to professionalism, as an interpreter is not so much someone who knows languages, but someone who behaves as an interpreter, as Uvarov wrote (1981, as quoted by Straniero Sergio 1999), who is aware of their role and limits, is able to set boundaries with the other interlocutors and is prepared to learn (as also stressed in the UNHCR module 2009).

In the current chapter, we will present the design of a training course for interpreters working with refugees and asylum seekers in the Italian context where no such courses officially exist. In Italy, humanitarian interpreters are regularly required for two different types of services (González Rodríguez and Radicioni 2021). The first type is provided to asylum seekers and concerns material, legal, health, and language assistance. The second type is provided to international protection holders and concerns social integration activities and employment counselling. We will focus on the first type of service, capitalising on the experience gained in training interpreters for asylum seekers in a pilot course organised by our

Department of Interpreting and Translation of the University of Bologna at Forlì Campus and on new technological affordances, some of which were also developed within our department.

12.2 Italy, a Southern gateway to the EU

Italy has traditionally been a home country of economic migrants who, from the turn of the XIX century on, have had to leave their homes to find better livelihood opportunities either in the Northern part of the country or abroad. Yet, for several decades now, Italy has witnessed a reversal of the trend and has become a country of destination for migrants due to economic and, more recently, humanitarian reasons.

Refugees reaching Italy follow the Mediterranean route and land on its southern shores, with Lampedusa in Sicily becoming a symbolic point of arrival. The suffering of these refugees fleeing from conflicts, persecution, and natural disaster in their homelands starts even before venturing to cross the Mediterranean Sea as often they have walked hundreds of miles before arriving in Libya, where they are put in inhuman detention centres and submitted to the most degrading and atrocious conditions, or even outright criminal treatment.[6]

The Mediterranean route is hazardous. Refugees are the prey of ruthless human traffickers who embark on overcrowded fortune boats. These often sink and cause the death of its occupiers. Another deadly threat comes from Libyan coastal guards – equipped by Italy within the framework of the 2018 agreement – who push them back at gunpoint. Since 2014, when the IOM started monitoring "missing migrants," 23,150 human beings have lost their lives in the Mediterranean Sea: they are today's *desaparecidos* as they are defined by human rights associations, a new human tragedy.

Despite being aware of the deadly risks, many refugees take to the sea every day. According to UNHCR data, waves of refugees crossing the Mediterranean Sea reached a peak in 2016 (181,436 migrants), then after the Libyan-Italian agreements in 2018 ("Security Degree") there was a sharp reduction (23,370 in 2018 and 11,471 in 2019), but recently, numbers of successful landings have risen again (67,477 in 2021), and also that of victims, according to the UNHCR operational portal.[7] In descending order, the top countries of origin are: Tunisia, Egypt, Bangladesh, Iran, and Ivory Coast (ranking first in the Sub-Saharan Africa).

In compliance with the Dublin Regulation adopted in 2013,[8] migrants have to be identified in the country of entry. So, for a decade now, Italy has been struggling to meet the challenge of managing the multilingual inflow of economic migrants and refugees in its Rescue, First Assistance and Identification hotspots close to landing areas – which over the years has ranged between approximately 11,000 to over 180,000 a year. Most migrants and refugees only transit through the country, but many decide to stay and apply for international protection. If they do not meet the requirements to enter Italy, they are sent to Permanence Centres for Repatriation (CPR, *Centri di permanenza per il rimpatrio*, which are administrative *detention* centres), but if eligible for Refugee Status Determination (RSD) procedures, they enter the Italian 2-tier reception system: the First level reception centres (CPA, *Centri di prima accoglienza* for further identification and beginning of asylum application procedures) and the Second level reception and integration centers (SAI, *Sistema di accoglienza e integrazione*).[9] At each level, some sort of language assistance to enable communication between local authorities/staff and refugees is provided. This is usually carried out by unqualified interpreters in vehicular languages, as most African or Asian languages are not covered.

Interpreters' services are also required by the many NGOs active in this humanitarian setting and, most importantly, by the first-degree authorities responsible for Refugee Status Determination (RSD) called *Commissione territoriale per i richiedenti protezione internazionale* (Territorial Commission for international protection applicants, from now on TC), which have been the target setting for our training course.

12.3 Mapping local needs

As Moser-Mercer et al. (2021) rightfully stress, any humanitarian interpreter training ought to be designed within a country to cater for the needs of that particular country. In our case, Italy is a frontline country on the EU southern "border" that has to face a "by now permanent" refugee emergency situation. Its institutional and societal structures, however, are not always up to the daunting task of smooth refugee identification, protection and integration. One crucial stage of refugee protection and integration is the interpreter-mediated interview with the TC. There are 44 such TCs in Italy and one of them is located in the Prefecture of Forlì.

In 2017, we approached the TC to get to know their language assistance policy and the characteristics of the interpreting service provided. We learnt that it relied on external agencies providing 50 (mainly untrained) interpreters in 20 different languages (mainly African languages and French and English as vehicular languages). As there are no interpreter training courses between Italian and the required African and Asian languages, anyone speaking one of these rare languages was recruited with a perfunctory selection procedure. This means that the TC had very little control over interpreting quality (accuracy and faithfulness) and was bound to be faced with unprofessional behaviour, such as questioning the reason why certain questions were being asked or the occurrence of other behaviour slowing down or disrupting the interview process, as reported by one of its members and in the literature (see Pöllabauer 2004). In collaboration with the Faculté de Traduction et d'Interprétation (FTI) of the University of Geneva, our Department decided to offer a free-of-charge pilot course in humanitarian interpreting to their pool of interpreters: 12 participated representing 8 different nationalities and 15 different languages (González Rodríguez and Radicioni 2021, Russo et al. forthcoming). It was the first course of this kind to be organised in Italy. It ran from June 30 to October 27, 2017, in a blended format: i) a two-day, face-to-face session

(June 30 and July 1) to introduce theoretical and methodological topics, to get to know all participants and develop the teamwork spirit of a Community of Practice, ii) 6 online training activities with one-to-one tutorial via the virtual platform EVITA made available by FTI, iii) a one-day, face-to-face session for course evaluation (October 27). The EVITA platform also featured a forum enabling discussions and collaborative work.

A pre-course and a post-course short test on IT>IT and FR/EN>IT consecutive interpretation was administered for all the participants during the two face-to-face sessions to check their initial and final competence. The course main content and key features were the following (Russo et al. forthcoming):

- Awareness of the role: A bilingual person is not necessarily an interpreter, but someone who behaves as an interpreter (encourage reflection on what this implies and how this impacts professional performance)
- Cultural issues (encourage a reflection on aspects given for granted – like for instance that there may be also intra-cultural differences between a Nigerian who migrated to Italy 20 years ago and a young Nigerian newcomer, due to societal changes – or that not all cultural differences are relevant)
- Conversational dynamics (draw attention to turn-taking, hesitations and pauses, communicative strategies and to verbal and non-verbal communication)
- Professional ethics (focus on the principles of neutrality, confidentiality and faithfulness, but also on the issue of advocacy *vs*. empathy, on preparation before an assignment, and on how to brief the "clients" [i.e., both the interviewer and interviewee] about the interpreter's communicative needs and role, including the need to add clarifications or requests for specifications)
- Basic skills in consecutive interpreting
- Basic knowledge of the legislation and the procedures on international protection and migration laws
- Better comprehension and production skills in Italian (especially colloquial and specialised registers)
- Terminology and how to prepare glossaries

As already mentioned, in the first introductory face-to-face session the more theoretical and methodological topics were presented and discussed. In a two-way exchange, we invited the TC interpreters to share their working experiences and difficulties, and to express their learning needs and expectations. The resulting picture revealed few aspects concerning hard skills – language deficiencies-, but several soft aspects – psychological and interactional (Russo et al. forthcoming):

- Finding words: this highlighted the need for acquiring greater fluency and linguistic competence
- Asylum seekers' illiteracy: this feature was particularly challenging because it caused problems of understanding and also the need to simplify the language of interviewers and of written documents

- Listening to sad stories: this caused a heavy emotional load and could cause vicarious trauma (when not reviving personal painful experiences)
- Gender-based refusal or even hostility: for instance, a male interviewee's hostility towards a female interpreter could cause lack of collaboration; a different type of problem could arise when a homophobic interpreter and an LGBTQ+ interviewee have to interact
- Asylum seeker's doubts on his/her date of birth: this behaviour could challenge the interpreter's credibility, therefore, sometimes some additions on the part of the interpreter to explain different cultural traditions would be necessary, but not necessarily allowed
- Lack of collaboration from members of the Commission: this attitude tended to intimidate the interpreter and affected his/her performance; it was felt that in order to work efficiently and help the interviewee feel at ease and speak freely it is very important to favor an empathic climate
- Interviewers raising their voices and treating asylum seekers as in police interrogations: this made interpreters feel deeply ill-at-ease *vs* the interviewee.

Unlike conference interpreters, humanitarian interpreters usually do not work in pairs or in teams and those working for the TC in Forlì made no exception. Therefore, the very fact of being together to discuss and share working experiences, fears and dilemmas helped them to identify traits of the profession that were typical and common to all those performing that role, and, therefore, they were not just personal issues. Furthermore, the pilot course was an opportunity to get to know other interpreters' strategies and jointly try to find the best possible practices to tackle them. The need to discuss and share experiences was also described in other targeted training settings, such as that for professional interpreters working in UN field missions (Ruiz Rosendo et al. 2021).

12.4 Targeted course design

12.4.1 Taking stock

Designing a course drawing on the results of a pilot course enables trainers to take stock of trainees' experience and focus on what needs to be emphasised or added. Trainees revealed the following personal difficulties:

- Understanding and speaking Italian. This was a somehow striking comment as one would expect a proficient level of passive and active competence in Italian from foreign humanitarian interpreters working with Italian institutional personnel in a sensitive setting, where word form and substance have such a heavy weight and also specialised (legal) language is used. In a new training course particular emphasis has to be laid on Italian listening/reading and comprehension activities, including activities with Italian legal and institutional terminology.

- Self-evaluation. Untrained interpreters are not used to record and evaluate their working performances and in a sensitive setting such as a TC this would not be allowed. But self and peer evaluation based on a content, language and delivery assessment grid is a pivotal exercise that needs practice to favor skill acquisition.
- Active listening and memorisation. This is another preliminary exercise to interpreting that untrained interpreters have never practiced. As noticed, it requires a certain effort (for more details see Chapter 17).
- Note-taking. This is a new skill that needs to be developed as consecutive interpreting is explicitly required by the TC contract.
- Use of the platform. The difficulties were mostly related to poor or unstable connections, and scant familiarity with IT devices. Admittedly, in the pre-Covid 19 era, the use of remote teaching and interpreting platforms was not very common and course trainees were understandably uncomfortable having to rely on them. The interpreting market has now drastically changed with most assignments being performed remotely. However, in Italian legal settings (including humanitarian ones) video-based and telephone-based interpreting are not yet fully-fledged modalities and on-site interpreting is still the standard procedure. Nevertheless, interpreters who have been properly trained and live, for instance, in Forlì could be asked to interpret remotely for refugees landed in Lampedusa. Therefore, training them remotely and teaching them how to use remote interpreting platforms has become a prerequisite. Our Department has acquired a considerable expertise in this field having coordinated the Erasmus Plus project *SHIFT in Orality: Training the Interpreters of the Future and of Today*[10] (Russo 2018, Amato et al. 2018), and as shown later in the chapter. This is definitely an aspect of training that technological affordances can only improve.

In their opinion, the pilot course achieved the objective of improving their competence in understanding and speaking Italian, note-taking technique and knowledge of international protection legislation and terminology. Trainees' difficulties with the platform revealed their lack of familiarity with online training tools, but today the use of technology for remote communication has become a standard modality and, therefore, would be far less problematic. Finally, concerning recommendations for future editions they indicated more face-to-face training and further training.

12.4.2 New content design with more IT support

The trainees' requests stimulate some considerations. The request for more face-to-face training can probably be justified by the need for more human interaction (both one-to-one and collective) and rapport building opportunities. However, this could also be connected to the characteristics of the platform used for the pilot course that allowed only written one-to-one feedback on task completions. As we will see, the new learning platforms also allow video-based oral interactions that can favour more dynamic and efficient feedbacks and exchanges. The request for more training highlights the urgent need for a protracted and targeted training focusing on refugees' and asylum seekers' protection.

The new course could envisage a very interactive first introductory session on methodological and theoretical topics to foster human contact and collective team-work spirit and at least 12 activities with one-to-one feedback covering the following hard and soft skills.

Hard skills

- Active listening and memorisation (IT>IT, EN/FR>IT, IT>EN/FR)
- Lexical and register flexibility (IT comprehension and production)
- Terminology and how to prepare glossaries
- Background documentation on national and international legislation concerning refugees, asylum, international protection and subsidiary protection
- Command of international protection procedures in TCs
- Basic dialogue interpreting skills (sight translation, *chuchotage* and note-taking)
- Basic interpreting skills between IT and trainees' native languages
- Remote dialogue interpreting

Soft skills

- Awareness of code of ethics and deontological principles
- Awareness of interpreter relaying and coordination roles (Wadensjö ([1993] 2002)
- Empowerment and briefing (with the parties)
- Awareness of communication dynamics and specific TC communicative patterns
- Awareness of the relevant cultural differences
- Empathy and interpersonal relationship
- Self and peer evaluation

Finally, other course features could include: group discussions and sharing of learning and working experiences; role-plays of realistic situations; role-plays with ethical and deontological dilemmas and other critical issues. This format will be implemented and enhanced thanks to new IT affordances as the next section will illustrate.

12.5 Technological setup for a fully online course

12.5.1 Rationale

As explained above, a target group of students for a course on humanitarian interpreting would necessarily be a heterogeneous one, with participants covering different language combinations and also characterised by different ages, educational backgrounds, work experience, work-life balance (Bergunde and Pöllabauer 2019; González Rodríguez and Radicioni 2021). On the other hand, for the course to develop smoothly and effectively, it is very important to build a sense of community and belonging in the class by engaging participants and stimulating their commitment to class activities and self-training practice.

It is therefore of paramount importance to design a solution that, while being flexible enough to accommodate participants' needs in terms of class hours and flexibility, will "promote interaction, participation and communication in the online learning environment" (Robinson and Hullinger 2008, 7).

Remote teaching seems to be a challenge in humanitarian interpreting training; González Rodríguez and Radicioni (2021) and Russo et al. (forthcoming) report results of student evaluation questionnaires after the Forlì course and highlight that most students expressed a preference for face-to-face, synchronous learning as compared to the online mode. As a matter of fact, as illustrated above, when asked to offer suggestions on how to improve further editions of the course, they mainly asked for more face-to-face training and also for further training. While totally understandable and legitimate, these two requests may also be seen to clash with one another if applied to a group of learners who are not full-time students enrolled in an intensive "Monday-to-Friday" course, where extra face-to-face training would entail a less flexible as well as more intensive class schedule.

Furthermore, a face-to-face course undoubtedly offers advantages in terms of effectiveness of training and student engagement, but it can only address a reduced pool of participants who live in the area where the course is delivered; on the other hand, a fully online course can address a larger pool of participants located all over the country.

For these reasons, we venture this proposal for a fully online course by proposing different technologies and learning environments aimed at allowing students' synchronous and asynchronous learning, focusing as much as possible on free and open resources, not with the aim of being exhaustive in presenting all possibilities, but rather by focusing on what we found effective based on our experience both related to the course described above and as interpreter educators.

12.5.2 Asynchronous activities: Learning management system

A first decision will have to be made on the learning management system (LMS) to be used. An example of a well-known flexible, free and open-source option is Moodle.[11] Although it is not the only available option,[12] it seems to be particularly suitable for this kind of course with small groups, a high degree of interaction and a combination of synchronous and asynchronous activities.

A Moodle course can be set up to be the virtual place where all the information on the course, course materials and activities are collected. Another advantage of the Moodle platform is the wide variety of resources it offers trainers, thus making it possible to really tailor-cut the course to their selected training activities.

In the case of this course – and considering that different participants may have different IT skills – we select and propose a list of "essentials" that we believe the Moodle course should have, although they can then be tailored to the course needs.

In the first place, the *Forum tool* on Moodle can be used to set up permanent billboards for anyone to post notices and information on the course. For instance, different forums can be set up for announcements, schedule changes, important deadlines, and participants' introduction. It may also be advisable to set up a forum for troubleshooting, where quick technical problems can be notified and dealt with quickly.

Furthermore, the *Assignment activity* can be employed to present students with an assignment by uploading different kinds of written, audio and video materials. The activity allows students to upload their assignments in different formats, including audio and video recordings which, considering the kind of course being taught, will probably constitute the greatest part of student work; the *Grading tool* in Moodle allows the trainer to offer feedback in writing or via audio or video recordings, thus speeding up the grading and revision process.

Moodle also includes a *Workshop activity*, through which students can grade other students' assignments (which can be audio/video, or written, such as portfolios, glossaries, etc.) in a peer-to-peer assessment practice led by the instructor, who can also share an assessment sheet for the students to use.

Finally, Moodle can work as a repository to upload and organise materials used during synchronous lessons as well as further materials for consultation or self-study by using the *Resources feature* to share links, documents, folders, etc.

Figure 12.1 is a (double) screenshot of Moodle's list of activities and resources; the "essentials" suggested here are circled. However, as it can be noted, many

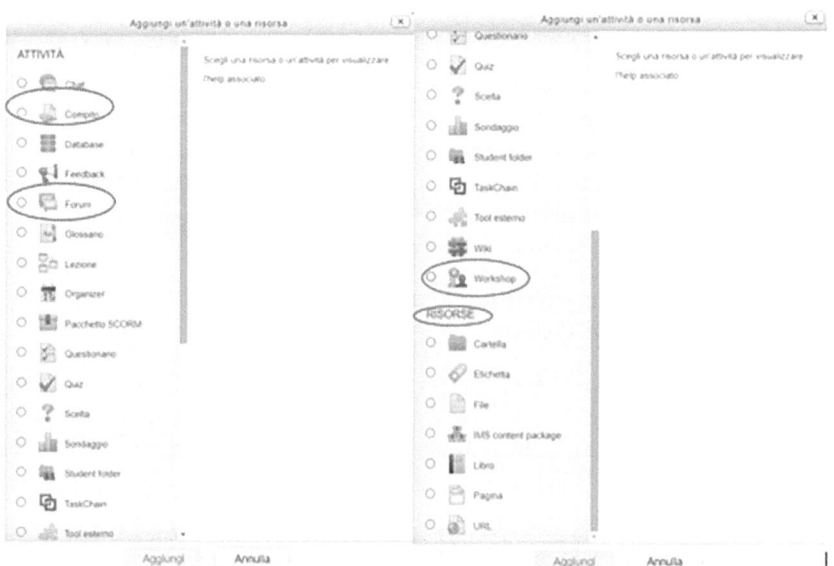

FIGURE 12.1   List of Moodle's activities and resources

other options can be available and used by trainers depending on their teaching style and course contents, as well as on the group's proficiency with technology.

12.5.3 Synchronous activities

For synchronous activities, a variety of tools and platforms can be used. The choice of platform may vary depending on each Higher Education Institution's practices and guidelines. However, and especially for interpreting practice, some specific platforms could be employed.

For plenary lessons, any videoconferencing platform suitable for teaching (i.e., allowing for screen and sound sharing and for interaction with participants) can be used.

It might be advisable to also encourage students to use videoconferencing platforms to meet among themselves as a whole class or in groups not only to practice, but also to exchange opinions and get to know each other outside class activities.

Since the student group will be a heterogeneous and multi-language one, intensive peer-to-peer practice and assessment will be required, and participants will have to be paired up with partners with the same language combination. For peer-to-peer practice, different platforms and tools can be used besides or in combination with regular videoconferencing tools.

For peer-to-peer practice, for example, the InTrain[13] (Carioli and Spinolo 2019) platform can be used. It is a free and open-source platform developed at the Department of Interpreting and Translation of the University of Bologna at Forlì which can be used by anyone with no need to subscribe or download.

InTrain was conceived and designed as a web-based training system for Remote Simultaneous Interpreting (RSI). However, it can also be used more creatively to practice other interpreting modes, since RSI is likely not to be the focus of a course in humanitarian interpreting. The platform has three different user profiles: Interpreter, Speaker and Supervisor, where the interpreter is the student practicing interpreting, the supervisor is the trainer or the peer assessing the student, and the speaker is the person delivering a speech or, alternatively, a video played by the supervisor. In the case of humanitarian interpreting, it can be used to practice *chuchotage*; the supervisor can listen to the original video and to the interpreter at the same time and record the interpreter's performance for self-assessment.

The same platform (Figure 12.2) can also be used for practicing dialogue interpreting in groups of three as, in the briefing mode, it allows all participants (interpreter, supervisor, speaker) to speak and to hear everyone in the session, which can also be recorded and downloaded for posterior assessment either by the trainer or by peers.

Another platform, shown in Figure 12.3, that seems particularly suitable for the trainer to work with groups of students is ReBooth[14] (Carioli and Spinolo 2020). It is a free and open-source platform that was also developed at the Department of Interpreting and Translation of the University of Bologna as a follow-up and further development of InTrain. ReBooth is free and open source, too, but, differently from InTrain, it

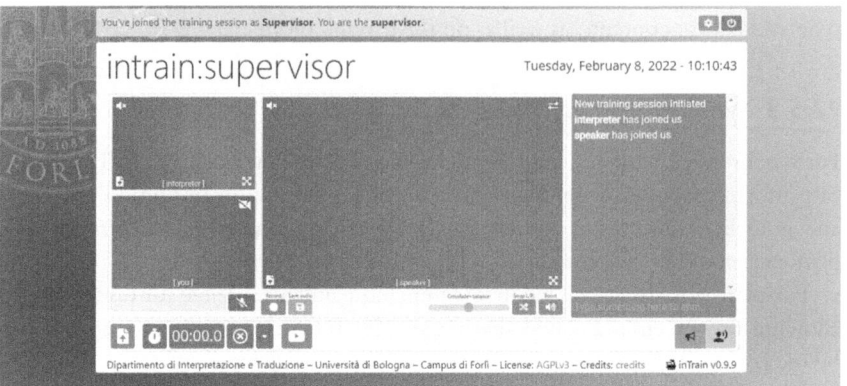

FIGURE 12.2 InTrain: Supervisor view

FIGURE 12.3 ReBooth, trainer's view

requires having an account to access it. This is because, differently from InTrain, ReBooth needs to be hosted on a server, and therefore accesses need to be controlled. It can, however, be freely downloaded from GitHub and installed on any other institution's server.

ReBooth allows a trainer to remotely deliver practice sessions of simultaneous and consecutive interpreting while recording the performance of various students at the same time. An average ReBooth class can host 8–10 students (the exact number depends on the teacher's connection and hardware). In the case of humanitarian interpreting, again, it can be useful to practice *chuchotage* with multiple students at the same time as well as consecutive interpreting.

Finally, a simple, yet useful, free and open tool for practicing sight translation is the DIT Scroller[15] (Carioli and Negretti 2008). It was developed in 2008, also within the Department of Interpreting and Translation of the University of

FIGURE 12.4   DIT Scroller

Bologna, to support trainers and students when practicing sight translation. It is freely available and can be used by anyone in its online version; it is a text scroller that allows the user to paste any text to be sight translated in the text box, determine the size of the text to be visualised and the speed of scrolling and then play it for him/herself (self-practice) or for students (Figure 12.4).

The set of IT tools suggested will ensure an effective and dynamic interpreter training in the interpreting techniques required in humanitarian settings – sight translation, *chuchotage*, and note-taking – and in the more theoretical aspects of interpreter education. It will also enable trainers and trainees to take advantage of IT resources to engage in intense and fruitful interaction.

12.6 Conclusions

Italy is a frontline, outer border country receiving large flows of desperate individuals seeking international protection every day. Bureaucracy and linguistic-cultural barriers hamper swift procedures to grant the satisfaction of this basic human right. From our perspective as interpreter educators and researchers, designing tailored training initiatives exploiting the most inclusive technological affordances is a necessity. Italian institutions and NGOs working with refugees and asylum seekers have specific needs that must be catered for. It must be noted, however, that institutions both at national and European levels pay very little attention to the quality of the interpreting services provided and the need to support upskilling and adequate qualification of interpreters. In the light of the shortcomings of present Dublin Regulations, the Commission proposed a New Pact on Migration and Asylum[16] to better share responsibility among member states and speed up asylum procedures, and return when applicable, based on the following rationale:

> Migration is a complex issue, with many facets that need to be weighed together. The safety of people who seek international protection or a better life, the concerns of countries at the EU's external borders, which worry that migratory pressures will exceed their capacities, and which need solidarity

from others. Or the concerns of other EU Member States, which are concerned that, if procedures are not respected at the external borders, their own national systems for asylum, integration or return will not be able to cope in the event of large flows.[17]

The legislative train schedule "to promote our European way of life" to final approval and implementation is still underway at the moment of writing. In this comprehensive and forward-looking document no mentioned is made of guaranteeing professional language assistance, as if linguistic and cultural mediation would not be part of a successful Pact implementation and refugee integration in European societies.

In the light of the importance of training to grant qualified language assistance, the aim of this chapter was to suggest an interpreter education proposal capitalising on today's technological affordances. It first provided an overview of Italy's current situation concerning needs and requirements for humanitarian interpreting services, and then, building on the experience of a blended course for humanitarian interpreters offered at our department, it provided suggestions for the use of technological tools in order to deliver a fully online course. While a blended course has the obvious advantage of fostering discussion, networking and a sense of belonging among participants, a fully online course would grant accessibility to a wider range of suitable participants over the country and allow more flexibility in managing synchronous and asynchronous activities. We hope that this by no means exhaustive overview of available IT training tools could be a useful source of inspiration for institutions involved in humanitarian interpreter education.

Acknowledgement

The authors wish to acknowledge the invaluable contribution to the training of interpreters of Gabriele Carioli and Daniele Negretti, IT technicians of our Department.

Notes

1 To recall the seminal "critical link" conference series https://criticallink.org.
2 www.monash.edu/arts/languages-literatures-cultures-linguistics/news-and-events/articles/2016/symposium-on-humanitarian-interpreting-and-interpreter-training.
3 www.unige.ch/inzone/
4 www.unige.ch/formcont/cours/field-interpreters
5 https://translatorswithoutborders.org/resource/field-guide-to-humanitarian-interpreting-and-cultural-mediation/
6 www.amnesty.org/en/location/middle-east-and-north-africa/libya/.
7 https://data2.unhcr.org/en/situations/mediterranean/location/5205.
8 https://ec.europa.eu/home-affairs/policies/migration-and-asylum/common-european-asylum-system/country-responsible-asylum-application-dublin-regulation_it.
9 For a detailed account of the Italian refugee protection system see Arcella in this volume and www.openpolis.it/parole/come-funziona-laccoglienza-dei-migranti-in-italia/ (last accessed 5 February 2022)

10 Project details and all resources developed are available at www.shiftinorality.eu/ (last accessed 5th Feb 2022)
11 https://moodle.org/; credits: https://docs.moodle.org/dev/Credits.
12 A list of open-source LMSs is provided here:

https://en.wikipedia.org/wiki/List_of_learning_management_systems

13 https://intrain.ditlab.it/
14 https://rebooth.ditlab.it/
15 www.ditlab.it/scroll/
16 www.europarl.europa.eu/legislative-train/theme-promoting-our-european-way-of-life/file-a-new-pact-on-migration-and-asylum
17 https://ec.europa.eu/info/strategy/priorities-2019-2024/promoting-our-european-way-life/new-pact-migration-and-asylum_en

References

Amato, Amalia A., Nicoletta Spinolo, and María Jesús González Rodríguez. eds. 2018. *Handbook of Remote Interpreting*. http://amsacta.unibo.it/5955/1/HANDBOOK_SHIFT.pdf

Bergunde, Annika, and Sonja Pöllabauer. 2019. "Curricular Design and Implementation of a Training Course for Interpreters in an Asylum Context." *Translation and Interpreting* 11 (1): 1–21.

Carioli, Gabriele, and Daniele Negretti. 2008. *DIT Scroller*. [software]. www.ditlab.it/scroll/

Carioli, Gabriele, and Nicoletta Spinolo. 2019. *InTrain*. [software]. https://intrain.ditlab.it/credits

Carioli, Gabriele, and Nicoletta Spinolo. 2020. *ReBooth*. [software]. https://rebooth.ditlab.it/credits.

González Rodríguez, Maria Jesús, and Maura Radicioni. 2021. "Interpretazione Umanitaria." In *Interpretare da e verso l'italiano. Didattica e innovazione per la formazione dell'interprete*, edited by Mariachiara Russo, 373–394. Bologna: Bononia University Press.

Moser-Mercer, Barbara, Somia Qudah, Mona N. A. Malkawi, Jayne Mutiga, and Mohammed Al-Batineh. 2021. "Beyond Aid: Sustainable Responses to Meeting Language Communication Needs in Humanitarian Contexts." *Interpreting and Society* 1 (1): 5–27.

Pöllabauer, Sonja. 2004. "Interpreting in Asylum Hearings: Issues of Role, Responsibility and Power." *Interpreting* 6 (2): 143–180.

Robinson, Chin C., and Hallett Hullinger. 2008. "New Benchmarks in Higher Education: Student Engagement in Online Learning." *Journal of Education for Business* 84 (2): 101–109. https://doi.org/10.3200/JOEB.84.2.101-109.

Ruiz Rosendo, Lucía, Alma Barghout, and Conor H. Martin. 2021. "Interpreting on UN Field Missions: A Training Programme." *The Interpreter and Translator Trainer* 15 (4): 450–467. https://doi.org/10.1080/1750399X.2021.1903736

Russo, Mariachiara. 2018. "Settings and Subject Areas Requiring Remote Interpreting." In *Handbook of Remote Interpreting*, edited by Amalia Amato, Nicoletta Spinolo, and Maria J. González Rodríguez, 47–52, http://amsacta.unibo.it/5955/1/HANDBOOK_SHIFT.pdf

Russo, Mariachiara, María Jesús González Rodríguez, Manuela Motta, and Maura Radicioni. forthcoming. "Humanitarian Interpreting: A Pilot Training Course in Italy." In *Comunicación interlingüística e intercultural en contextos de asilo y refugio/Cross-linguistic and Cross-cultural Communication for Asylum Seekers and Refugees*, edited by Francisco Vigier-Moreno. Granada: Comares.

Straniero Sergio, Francesco. 1999. "Verso una sociolinguistica interazionale dell'interpretazione." In *Interpretazione simultanea e consecutiva. Problemi teorici e metodologie didattiche*, edited by Caterina Falbo, Mariachiara Russo, and Francesco Straniero Sergio, 103–139. Milano: Hoepli.

UNHCR. 2009. *Self-Study Module 3: Interpreting in a Refugee Context.* www.refworld.org/docid/49b6314d2.html

UNHCR Austria, ed. 2017. *Handbook for Interpreters in Asylum Procedures.* Vienna: UNHCR Austria. www.unhcr.org/dach/wp-content/uploads/sites/27/2017/09/AUT_Handbook-Asylum-Interpreting_en.pdf

Uvarov, Valentin. 1981. "Paradoksy rolevogo povedenija u~astnikov situacii perevoda." *Tetradi Perevodcika* 18: 13–16.

Wadensjö, Cecilia. [1993] 2002. "The Double Role of Dialogue Interpreting." In *The Interpreting Studies Reader,* edited by Franz Pöchhacker, and Miriam Shlesinger, 354–370. London: Routledge.

PART IV

Crosscutting implications of interpreter training in conflict and post-conflict scenarios

13

INTERPRETING TRAUMA

Service providers' and interpreters' perspectives

Simo K. Määttä

This chapter analyses service provider's and interpreters' views on dialogue interpreting through two datasets. The first dataset is extracted from data collected in a large European project whose goal was to improve counselling methods for refugee women who have experienced gender-based violence (GBV). The second dataset consists of selected passages of interpreting diaries, most of which are related to trauma experienced by the (migrant) client.[1] By combining the perspectives of the service provider and the interpreter, the chapter aims to offer novel insights into the multiple facets of the phenomena that emerge when the interpreter is faced with the client's trauma. Another goal is to reflect on the heuristic potential of the two different data collection methods and propose new directions for future work on the intersections of trauma and public service or community interpreting. In addition, the chapter proposes a method to train interpreters to cope with trauma through problem solving exercises combined with expert knowledge of the mechanisms of vicarious traumatisation, as well as concrete tools to fight it.

13.1 Interpreting trauma

Analyses of the emotional and psychological issues in public service interpreting include Wessling's and Shaw's (2014) study focusing on sign language interpreting and Valero Garcés' (2015) scrutiny of the issue from the viewpoint of interpreting in spoken languages. These studies have dealt with various topics, such as psychological stress in general, burnout, and vicarious traumatisation.

The ability to process and tolerate stress is regarded as one of the most important qualities of a professional interpreter in all modes and types of interpreting (Moser-Mercer 1985; Gile 1995). In addition to haste and the exigence of accuracy, the simultaneous and consecutive processing of two languages is a stress factor in and of itself. In community or public service interpreting, including legal interpreting, stress

DOI: 10.4324/9781003230359-17

caused by emotional strain is particularly salient because the interpreter-mediated encounters often involve some of the most difficult experiences in a person's life, such as mental health issues, armed conflict, and various forms of violence and abuse. Such experiences can potentially trigger trauma, defined broadly as "an emotional response to a terrible event" (American Psychological Association 2021).

Interpreting related to traumatic experiences causes intense stress and may lead to burnout and/or vicarious traumatisation (Shlesinger 2007; Bontempo and Malcolm 2011). The risk of vicarious traumatisation, or the transfer of trauma symptoms from the person being helped to the helper, is particularly high among interpreters of war crime courts and conciliation committees (Wiegand 2000; Ndongo-Keller 2015). Some analyses (e.g., Westermeyer 1990) indicate that the risk is greater when the interpreter and their clients belong to the same ethnic group.

In addition, contradictory expectations toward the interpreter increase the psychological load of interpreting and the risk of burnout (Pöchhacker 2000; Angelelli 2004; Morris 2011). Another risk factor is constant exposure to ethical stress, or a mismatch between one's professional role and values (see Hubscher-Davidson 2020) when the interpreter feels that the client is not treated fairly by the authorities or when the client's position is particularly vulnerable. Asylum interviews are a typical example of such encounters, characterised by multiple layers of vulnerability (Määttä et al. 2021).

13.2 Data and methods

The first dataset analysed in this chapter was collected by the European Institute for Crime Prevention and Control (HEUNI) within the project titled "Co-creating a Counselling Method for Refugee Women GBV Victims," funded by the EU's Equality and Citizenship Program (Lilja 2019; Lilja et al. 2020). Seven NGOs, providing counselling for migrant and refugee women in six EU member states, participated in the project, and its aim was to improve the quality of counselling by exchanging information about challenges and best practices produced through self-reflection. To this end, social workers, psychotherapists, and lawyers working for the NGOs wrote weekly journal entries consisting of approximately seven to ten sentences from March 2018 to March 2019. To facilitate comparisons between the entries, the 28 counsellors wrote their diaries in English rather than in their first language. They were asked to reflect on the challenges in the counselling situation, its impact on the client, and the lessons learned. The data amounts to 579 entries (242,637 words), most of them related to trauma, and trust between the service provider and the client emerges as an important challenge (see Lehti et al. 2021). The author of this chapter was granted access to the data by HEUNI.

Interpreting between the various European languages used by the counsellors and the several languages used by the clients is often mentioned in these journals even though the instructions given to the counsellors did not specifically address this topic. The scope of the phenomenon was assessed through a text search with key search stems related to interpreting, namely *interpret, translate, mediate*,[2] yielding

322 occurrences in 199 paragraphs (37,520 words). These data were classified into 14 themes, and the 13 paragraphs containing the theme "interpreter's emotions and affect" form the dataset analysed in this chapter.

The second dataset consists of the 75 journal entries from my own interpreting diaries, written in the early 2010s, when I worked as a freelancer public service interpreter in the greater Helsinki area. The handwritten journal entries were transformed into a typewritten form (10,706 words) and anonymised. The journal depicts interpreter-mediated encounters in which the interpreter and the migrant(s) communicate in English, French, or Spanish, whereas the interpreter and the service provider(s) communicate in Finnish. Most clients are originally from sub-Saharan Africa, and English or French is not the client's first language; the interpreter's first language is Finnish.

The interpreting diaries were originally produced to map sociolinguistic issues related to language ideologies, namely "cultural conceptions of the nature, form and purpose of language" (Gal and Woolard 1995: 130). The encounters represent a wide variety of public service interpreting situations, and in almost all of them, the client has a refugee background and gives an account of trauma. However, the interpreter's reactions in relation to trauma or his emotions are depicted only in 16 entries, and these were chosen for analysis in this chapter. The examples have been translated from Finnish into English by the author, and the unorthodox nature of this auto-ethnographic data collection method is discussed in the concluding remarks.

The analysis of the examples is essentially a content analysis of the salient phenomena from the perspective of the interpreter's emotional involvement. Recurrent themes are synthesised in the concluding remarks. To ensure the privacy of the persons involved in both datasets, no names, dates, places, or other details enabling identification are given, and some words have been altered and passages removed for the same purpose. In addition, since the analysis focuses on the contents rather than the forms, typos and erroneous punctuation have been corrected in the examples. In the first dataset, idiosyncratic usage has been standardised because it may reveal the native language of the writer.

13.3 Counsellors' diaries

The interpreter's affective burden is explicitly mentioned in a few journal entries. In the following excerpt, the interpreter appears to be a volunteer working for the same organisation as the counsellor:

> (1) For the last few weeks, our biggest concern was a . . . woman who has been raped by her husband. She is having emotional breakdowns, eating and sleeping problems, nightmares, and is experiencing huge pressure from family members living in other European countries. . . . Each time, I try to give her support and empower her. But what makes the situation even harder is the language barrier and the fact that she is illiterate . . . so she is completely

dependent on someone else's help. This burden falls especially on our interpreter and volunteer who speaks . . . language.

The example suggests that the interpreter's role is somewhat ambiguous, including not only interpreting but also accompanying the client and talking with her outside the interpreter-mediated encounters, in addition to performing other tasks as a volunteer. This picture reflects the fact that many NGOs lack the financial resources to employ professional interpreters. From the viewpoint of professional interpreting scholarship, the interpreter's emotional burden intersects with this role ambiguity.

Another case of role ambiguity is presented in example (2), where the interpreter's identity has been divulged to the client's relatives in another country.

(2) As our team and interpreters are regularly working with her on integration, somehow (probably through . . . community), her family from . . . got the phone number of one of our interpreters, and the husband's brother called him. It was quite an unpleasant call, he said.

When the client's situation was assessed after this phone call, the interpreter's situation was pivotal in suggesting a solution to the difficult situation, and he did much more than just interpreting:

(3) I talked to her about the possibility to report all this harassment and talking to the police, which would be good also in case her husband tries to cross the border and take the kids. The client was afraid and really unwilling to do it. But as our client, interpreter and I talked, at one point the interpreter suggested to call her husband's brother (from whom he received a call earlier) and try to resolve this situation in a calm way . . . to honestly and openly put all the cards on the table and talk about our client's wishes and intentions, and to warn them what we would do if they kept on with threats. She accepted this suggestion.

In this case as well, the interpreter's duties include other tasks in addition to interpreting, and his contacts with the community imply that he comes from the same ethnic group as the client. In his active role in the resolution of the conflict, this membership may intersect with his being concerned for his personal safety. While most codes of conducts of public service interpreters emphasise the interpreter's impartiality and many provide specific role definitions (Hale 2007, 101–136), these examples do not qualify the problems related to the interpreter's extended role as jeopardising their status as interpreters, which probably reflects a lack of knowledge of the existence of interpreters' ethical codes and the rationale behind them. As a result, the interpreting takes place in a borderline zone between non-professional interpreting, language brokering, and cultural mediation.

In most other data excerpts, the interpreters' emotional strain intersects with their gender and availability. Typically, female interpreters are not always available although they are almost invariably preferred. In (4), the discomfort related to the interpreter's gender is aggravated by the fact that the interpreter is a family member, which also implies that he is probably a non-professional interpreter.

> (4) Once more I had difficulty in counselling with a male interpreter from the same family. The client seemed hesitant to talk and the interpreter seemed stressed about translating while knowing the person's history. The whole situation was even harder because we had to talk about women's examinations. The most frustrating part was that there was no other interpreter available, and it was important to inform her about medical examinations.

In the following example, regarding the preparation for an asylum interview, the presence of a male interpreter is at first motivated by the availability issue as well. However, after the first encounter, the client says that she prefers the same male interpreter. This may be due to the difficulty of recounting the same traumatic experiences in the presence of a new person every time:

> (5) The only mediator available the first time was a man, actually not in line with the standard of an interview with a woman suspected to be a victim of trafficking. The first meeting was very difficult, she was extremely shy, speaking with difficulty and not looking at me at all. During the second counselling session, she had a bit more confidence and she preferred the male mediator instead of the woman we provided for the second time. Nevertheless, she felt a bit embarrassed talking about the violence suffered in the presence of a man. I also regretted the fact that, although he was a good interpreter, he was shocked and sorry because of her story and made many comments on it.

This excerpt introduces another typical feature of non-professional interpreting: the interpreter reacts to the client's sad story as a fellow human being and cannot control his emotions. The exact nature of the comments made by the interpreter is not explicit, although the fact that "he was shocked and sorry" suggest that the interpreter expressed perturbation and empathy.

In another entry, the interpreter's emotional reaction is such that the meeting cannot continue:

> (6) We had to interrupt because the interpreter was emotionally overwhelmed. That woman was indeed heavily abused and traumatized. She was also labour- and sex-trafficked before being sold to a man. She had difficulty in talking about her experience.

While the interpreter's gender is not specified, it is safe to assume that she was probably a woman, because in most cases the interpreter's gender is specified only when it is a problem – when the interpreter is a man. The following excerpt constitutes an exception to this rule:

> (7) I have met the . . . several times at the reception centre (a safe location) and in presence of a mediator of the same sex whom I consider really empathic and with expertise.

There is also one entry in which a male interpreter is praised for his appropriate rapport with the clients, but in this case, he is qualified as possessing *exceptional* qualities.

> (8) Also, on this occasion was present the . . . mediator, a very sensitive guy and perfectly able to make people feel comfortable, especially women. He probably has an extraordinary talent and sensitivity.

Thus, both experience and empathy are presented as guarantees of quality interpreting. However, as the previous examples have shown, quality is jeopardised when the interpreter expresses their emotions overtly. This becomes clear in the following excerpt, exemplifying a phenomenon found in several journal entries: many counsellors prefer to use a lingua franca, usually English, even when the client is not fully proficient in that language:

> (9) I always try, when they can, to speak English or French, not to bring any translator if not needed, to help them feel more secure to share sensitive information. Even with a very good translator who doesn't become emotionally involved with the client, the clients always have the sense that a third person is hearing what they are saying. And it is more intense when the translator comes from the same ethnicity/community. . . . Refugees of the same ethnicity know each other.

Many examples above are related to non-professional or semi-professional interpreting because of the cost and/or availability of professionals. However, community membership and the lack of psychological preparation may also constitute an obstacle to using non-professional interpreters:

> (10) We have some difficulty finding professional interpreters and ones that will be able to provide an hour every week for a psychotherapy session. There are many beneficiaries we could use but they are either too involved with the community or are not psychologically ready to hear and translate the information they will hear.

In light of the issues exemplified by these excerpts, it is somewhat surprising that the provision of training and counselling for interpreters is mentioned in only one out of all the entries dealing with interpreting:

(11) We need to investigate more whether the translators are willing to be involved in a therapeutic situation and maybe inform them and train them more about the consequences of their actions.

13.4 Interpreting diaries

While the gender of the interpreter is a major issue in the dataset analysed in the previous section, the second dataset contains only one entry related to this theme. However, in many entries, the male interpreter translates accounts of sexual violence and torture experienced by a male client:

(12) [Drawing of the sitting order: three social workers facing the client and the interpreter]

The client seems content, he smiles. . . . Social worker asks what he expects from migrant social work (many misunderstandings occurred previously), the client tells his story (in a confusing manner): political activity, arrest, torture, rape, threat of execution, escape, torture of his new-born baby [details of torture], torture of the baby's mother [details]. . . . Nobody knows what to say. Everybody tries to say something. [Male social worker] is crying. Finally, they say that it was good that he told this, that they are shocked, etc. I almost lose my own voice when interpreting the account of torturing the baby. [Social worker] is looking at me when talking to the client, which is bothering.

Problems: emotion, incoherent story . . . the client's piercing look especially after he has mentioned that his wife thinks that he is gay after the rape . . . the client's general mental condition, preventing him from expressing himself, making himself understood.

Instead of giving a detailed description of the emotions, the entry explains the reasons why the situation was so overwhelming emotionally: a particularly chilling story of sexual violence and torture, the client's psychological state, and the fact that the service providers are caught by surprise in this situation, where the goal was to talk about something completely different. It is impossible to know whether factors such as the interpreter's gender, ethnic origin, or the fact that the interpreter and the client had met before in other interpreter-mediated encounters had had an impact on this course of events.

Another challenging encounter contains an explicit description of the interpreter's coping mechanisms:

(13) The most difficult thing was once again to control my emotions. When he started to cry, I did not have a problem, but when the crying went on, I had to gulp a couple of times. I resorted to taking notes and constantly took notes this time. And at times I would look out of the window or at the baby.

> And I did not watch [the client] and the caseworker while interpreting, like I did at the beginning of the encounter. I interpreted in a particularly precise manner, although I had a hard time when he was describing his feelings.

Here, the interpreter uses a common technique among interpreters when facing a distressing encounter: he concentrates on the technical side of the interpretation, which allows him to control his emotions. Importantly, the distancing technique also implies avoiding eye contact, thus preventing a mirror reaction to the client's crying (see Tymoczko 2012, 96–97).

Another coping mechanism used by the interpreter is resorting to the distancing techniques (and contextual knowledge) he has learned when supporting a friend whose situation is similar to that of the client:

> (14) Suicide attempt with medication overdose, a long history of depression in the background, a previous suicide attempt in [country]. . . . The strange thing about this situation is that it resembles [friend's name] situation – it was easy to interpret and take an appropriate distance.

In the next example, emotional stress intersects with the interpreter's role. The excerpt depicts an asylum interview related to an asylum application originally classified as unfounded, therefore justifying an expedited process:

> (15) [The client] shows marks of torture and hitting on his body, tells that he has spent two weeks in a prison without light. He bursts out crying when asked about the problem in [home country]: his parents were burned alive, which is why he left the country. At this point, it is difficult to interpret, impossible to make out what he says. I manage to keep a straight face, only after his emotional account full of tears, my own eyes become wet as well, which I try to hide as best as I can. . . . Many details related e.g. to torture are left out from the interview record. . . . However, some information about the concrete problems is included in the record, which according to the legal counsel contributes to the transfer of his file to the Immigration Service. Otherwise, he would have probably been sent back to [country] where he came from. After the interview, the lawyer thanks me for having noticed the mistakes on the record – according to her, it is not the interpreter's duty to point them out. Yes, she should have noticed them, but she did not even look at the record! Noticeable: haste, trauma experience, difficulty of interpreting when the client was crying.

Experienced interpreters readily notice when the asylum or police interview is not conducted in due form, and such a situation may cause ethical stress: the interpreter's professional role prevents them from intervening even when they feel that the client is not treated fairly. In the Finnish system, the agent conducting the interview types the interview record as well, and at the end of the interview the record is printed out for oral translation and verification. Again, the interpreter is not supposed to point out errors unless they notice that their interpretation has not been transcribed correctly, and many interpreters use this caveat to call attention to other errors as well. In this excerpt, the lawyer's remark suggests that the interpreter mentions omissions he thinks should have been written down, instead of merely correcting the transcription of his interpretation. In other words, the interpreter's behaviour is unprofessional, but the interpreter also blames the counsel's lack of professionalism. Importantly, the passage also depicts the difficulty of accurately interpreting an emotional delivery combined with sobbing. The interpreter's reaction to the client's crying is described as a classical mirror reaction of empathy. While the reaction does not appear to jeopardise the quality of the interpretation, the interpreter is careful not to show his wet eyes to the other participants.

The journal also contains several passages where the interpreter reflects on his own actions and wonders whether he has done wrong when adopting a particular interpreting strategy, sometimes in contravention of the code of ethics. For example, in a screening interview preceding the asylum interview with two non-accompanied minors, the interpreter ponders whether his tone of voice was correct in the interview:

(16) There is also talk about fingerprints. I am not sure whether they under-stand this word.[3] At one point, I tell the agents . . . that I try to speak as sim-ply as possible because the clients' French proficiency is clearly low. They say it's a good idea. At some point, the boy also says that their French proficiency is very low. There is talk about their mother tongue. Afterwards, I wonder whether I should have used a harder and stronger tone of voice when the agents repeatedly say that it is no good to continue lying because it will just make their situation worse.

According to the code of conduct of Finnish legal interpreters, the interpreter should also reproduce the tone of voice of the primary speaker as faithfully as pos-sible (SKTL 2016, §6). However, using a harsh tone and raising one's voice could break down the communication in fragile situations such as this one, in which French is used as the language of communication between the interpreter and two children who barely know the language.

Mixed feelings about the clients are described in entries depicting the aftermath of the encounter, where the interpreter and the client typically leave the premises at the same time. Such examples reflect a strikingly different conception of the interpreter's role when compared to the excerpts discussed in the previous section:

(17) The client walks with me again until we reach the [name of building], I have to talk with him again. He is a nice guy, but these situations always make me feel a bit uncomfortable.

13.5 Concluding remarks

The datasets analysed in this chapter are quite different: one consists of journals written by counsellors who assist GBV victims and often have to use interpreters to establish communication with their clients, whereas the other is produced by an interpreter. Naturally, interpreting is the central theme in the interpreter's diaries. At the same time, it is interesting that interpreting would receive so many mentions in the counsellors' diaries as one of the main challenges on which they were instructed to write. In, addition, while neither of the datasets was explicitly produced to map the role of emotions and affect, they are pervasive in both, which bears witness to the meaningfulness of these phenomena in public service and community interpreting.

In the counsellors' diaries, non-professional interpreting, sometimes provided by family members, is a common feature. Many interpreters have other functions inside the organisation, and from the perspective of professional interpreting, the boundaries of their role as an interpreter are ambiguous. However, these boundaries are discussed only when the interpreter's emotional involvement becomes an issue. In such cases, the interpreter does typically not work for the organisation and has not received special training to deal with the psychological burden. Very often, the interpreter in these cases is a man, which is problematic because the topics evolve around GBV and female medical issues. In addition, in most cases, the interpreter seems to come from the same ethnic group as the client.

The interpreter's diaries are written by a professional interpreter who does not belong to the same ethnic group as the clients. This dataset provides more detailed information about the factors that trigger an emotional involvement – in some cases, the emotional reaction seems to be a prototypical response activated by the mirroring mechanisms of the mind. Contrary to the counsellors' journals, these journals also inform us about the interpreter's coping mechanisms and his reflections about his own and the service providers' role. In addition to an analysis of emotional involvement, these journals depict issues such as ethical stress, contact with the client outside the interpreter-mediated encounter, and actions that may lead to a communication breakdown with the client.

A triad composed of the two primary speakers (service provider and client) and the interpreter as a liaison between these two is the normative setting for dialogue interpreting. However, the interpreter has to be sensitive and build rapport with both primary speakers in order to make communication possible. This ability is particularly important in situations where a lack of trust constitutes a barrier to the creation of a connection between the parties. It is not easy to theorise the thin line that divides sensitivity and rapport that is impartial and appropriate from emotional involvement that is undesirable, and more research is needed in this area. Ideally, this line of research could involve the perspectives of all participants: interpreters, service providers, and clients. To gain more information about the interpreters' strategies, resources, and solutions, the diary method could be developed further by instructing the writers to reflect specifically on the challenges related to the expression, interpreting, and control of emotions, their coping mechanisms, the perceived roles and responsibilities of other participants, and their feelings during and after the encounter. In addition, a collective reflection and supervision session before and after the encounter, involving at least the interpreter and the service provider, would be beneficial (for examples, see Costa 2010; del Pozo Triviño and Toledano Buendía 2016).

Strategies needed in interpreter-mediated encounters with people who are experiencing or have experienced trauma should be an inherent part of interpreter training as well. A useful method consists in combining theoretical knowledge about psychological trauma and vicarious traumatisation, problem-solving in small groups, and professional advice of tools to prevent vicarious traumatisation.

Such a workshop was organised at the annual Finnish symposium on translation and interpreting studies at the University of Turku in April 2018 (Määttä et al. 2019). The workshop started with a 30-minute presentation by a professional psychotherapist specialised in trauma and supervision, with the goal of understanding the different factors that may cause psychological stress especially in interpreter-mediated encounters. Subsequently, the participants were divided into small groups, and each group discussed three particularly stressful and potentially traumatising scenarios based on real-life interpreter-mediated encounters. The groups were instructed to talk about the general feelings triggered by each scenario, discuss and list the specific stress factors present in the situation from the interpreter's viewpoint, analyse the potential expectations of other participants towards the interpreter, and list the physical and psychological reactions the interpreter may have in such a situation and how to cope with them. In the debriefing session, each scenario was discussed together with all participants of the workshop, with a specific emphasis on the best practices and strategies to fight vicarious traumatisation. The workshop concluded with a short lecture in which the trauma therapist synthetised the discussion and presented concrete, research and practice-based tools to fight vicarious trauma.

The problem-solving method based on real-life scenarios can also be used in classroom settings or in ad hoc training for example in conflict zones. To ensure the efficiency of the method, it is important that the trainers represent both interpreting and psychotherapeutic expertise. In addition, the method is more successful when the participants also include interpreter trainers, persons recruiting interpreters, and persons who need interpreters in their daily work.

To conclude this chapter, it is necessary to say a few words about the data. As mentioned above, I was not involved in the collection and the organisation of the data consisting of the counsellors' diaries. These data are unique in that they offer a wide variety of perspectives on various issues related to interpreting in counselling sessions. Contrarily, the dataset consisting of my own interpreting diaries, does not consist of "real" data in the sense that the journals were written by me and depict events in which I participated as an interpreter several years ago. I am fully aware of the problems related to impartiality and neutrality in this approach.

However, I should acknowledge that the first dataset is my production as well: my classification and delimitation, as well as my methods of analysis and the ideologies guiding this process, have altered these data – rather than being given, they *became data* because of my actions and interpretations (see Brinkmann 2014, 724). For example, my experience as an interpreter and my scholarly curiosity about the affective dimension of language and the relationship between language and power certainly had an impact on my approach to these data.

When processing the second dataset in retrospect, having not worked as an interpreter for several years, I realise that I may not have written the diaries just to gather evidence of language ideologies but for therapeutic purposes as well. I never received psychological counselling or supervision when working as an interpreter, although accounts of trauma were a constant feature of this work. Writing can be a tool to help us heal from trauma and vicarious traumatisation, and perhaps all community and public service interpreters should keep a diary or do creative writing related to their experiences (see Costa 2017). And perhaps these diaries could be used as data by scholars of interpreting and other fields to shed light on the mechanisms by which interpreters of different profiles navigate between adversities in their own life and the traumatic accounts they hear, feel, and interpret in their work.

Notes

1   From the viewpoint of the dialogue interpreter, both the service provider and their client, typically a migrant, are clients. Consistent with the typical usage among public service interpreters in Finland, the term client in this chapter refers to the migrant who needs interpretation because of their insufficient or nonexistent proficiency in the language in which the (public) service is provided.
2   In some countries, community and public service interpreters are referred to as (cultural) mediators. In certain cases, the boundaries between cultural and linguistic mediation are not clear-cut.
3   The French compound *empreintes digitales* is composed of two "learned" words that are markedly less frequent in everyday language than the English words *finger* and *print*.

References

American Psychological Association 2021. *Trauma*. www.apa.org/topics/trauma
Angelelli, Claudia V. 2004. *Revisiting the Interpreter's Role*. Amsterdam: John Benjamins.
Brinkmann, Svend. 2014. "Doing without Data." *Qualitative Inquiry* 20 (6): 720–725.
Bontempo, Karen, and Jemina Napier. 2011. "Evaluating Emotional Stability as a Predictor of Interpreter Competence and Aptitude for Interpreting." *Interpreting* 13 (1): 85–105.
Costa, Beverley. 2010. "Mother Tongue or Non-native Language? Learning from Conversations with Bilingual/Multilingual Therapists about Working with Clients Who Do Not Share Their Native Language." *Journal of Ethnicities and Inequalities in Health and Social Care* 3 (1): 15-24.
Costa, Beverley, ed. 2017. *In More Words. First International Anthology of Interpreters' Stories*. Reading: Mothertongue.

del Pozo Triviño, Maribel, and Carmen Toledano Buendía. 2016. "Training Interpreters to Work with Foreign Gender Violence Victims in Police and Court Settings." *Language and Law – Linguagem e direito* 3 (2). http://aleph20.letras.up.pt/index.php/LLLD/article/download/1760/1605.

Gal, Susan, and Kathryn A. Woolard. 1995. "Constructing Languages and Publics: Authority and Representation." *Pragmatics* 5 (2): 129–138.

Gile, Daniel. 1995. *Basic Concepts and Models for Interpreter and Translator Training*. Amsterdam: John Benjamins.

Hale, Sandra B. 2007. *Community Interpreting*. New York: Palgrave MacMillan.

Hubscher-Davidson, Séverine. 2020. "Ethical Stress in Translation and Interpreting." In *The Routledge Handbook of Translation and Ethics*, edited by Nike K. Pokorn, and Kaisa Koskinen, 415–430. New York: Routledge.

Lehti, Lotta, Simo Määttä, and Minna Viuhko. 2021. "Guiding Refugee Women Who Have Experienced Violence: Representation of Trust in Counsellors' Journals." *Journal of Refugee Studies*. https://academic.oup.com/jrs/advance-article/doi/10.1093/jrs/feab100/6375743

Lilja, Inka, ed. 2019. *Handbook on Counselling Asylum Seeking and Refugee Women Victims of Gender-based Violence. Helping Her to Reclaim Her Story*. Helsinki: HEUNI.

Lilja, Inka, Elina Kervinen, Anni Lietonen, Natalia Ollus, Minna Viuhko, and Anniina Jokinen. 2020. *Unseen victims. Why Refugee Women Victims of Gender-Based Violence Do Not Receive Assistance in the EU*. Helsinki: HEUNI.

Määttä, Simo, Eeva Puumala, and Riitta Ylikomi. 2021. "Linguistic, Psychological and Epistemic Vulnerability in Asylum Procedures: An Interdisciplinary Approach." *Discourse Studies* 23 (1): 46–66.

Määttä, Simo, Riitta Ylikomi, and Eeva Puumala. 2019. "Asioimis- ja oikeustulkkauksen psyykkinen hinta: sijaistraumatisoitumisen ehkäisy kuormittavissa tulkkaustilanteissa." [The Psychological Price of Community and Legal Interpreting – Prevention of Vicarious Traumatization in Psychologically Stressful Interpreting Situations]. *MikaEL* 12: 195-209.

Morris, Ruth. 2011. "Images of the Court Interpreter: Professional Identity, Role Definition and Self-image." In *Profession, Identity and Status: Translators and Interpreters as an Occupational Group: Part II: Questions of Role and Identity*, edited by Rakefet Sela-Sheffy, and Miriam Shlesinger, 20-40. Amsterdam: John Benjamins.

Moser-Mercer, Barbara. 1985. "Screening Potential Interpreters." *Meta* 30 (1): 97-100.

Ndongo-Keller, Justine 2015. "Vicarious Trauma and Stress Management." In *The Routledge Handbook of Interpreting*, edited by Holly Mikkelson, and Renée Jourdenais, 337-351. New York: Routledge.

Pöchhacker, Franz. 2000. "The Community Interpreter's Task: Self-Perception and Provider Views." In *The Critical Link 2: Interpreters in the Community*, edited by Roda P. Roberts, Silvana E. Carr, Diana Abraham, and Aideen Dufour, 49–65. Amsterdam: John Benjamins.

Shlesinger, Yael. 2007. "Vicarious Traumatization among Interpreters Who Work with Torture Survivors and their Therapists." In *Interpreting Studies and Beyond: A Tribute to Miriam Shlesinger*, edited by Franz Pöchhacker, Arnt Lykke Jakobsen, and Inger M. Mees, 153-172. Frederiksberg: Samfundslitteratur.

SKTL = Suomen kääntäjien ja tulkkien liitto [Finnish Association for Translators and Interpreters]. 2016. *Oikeustulkin etiikka* [Legal Interpreters' Ethics]. www.sktl.fi/@Bin/952493/Oikeustulk.16.pdf.

Tymoczko, Maria. 2012. "The Neuroscience of Translation." *Target* 24 (1): 83–102.

Valero Garcés, Carmen. 2015. "The Impact of Emotional and Psychological Factors on Public Service Interpreters: Preliminary Studies." *Translation & Interpreting* 7 (3): 90-102.

Wessling, Dawn M., and Sherry Shaw. 2014. "Persistent Emotional Extremes and Video Relay Service Interpreters." *Journal of Interpretation* 23 (1): article 6. https://digitalcommons.unf.edu/joi/vol23/iss1/6.

Westermeyer, Joseph 1990. "Working with an Interpreter in Psychiatric Treatment." *Journal of Nervous and Mental Disease* 178: 745-749.

Wiegand, Chriss 2000. "Role of the Interpreter in the Healing of a Nation: An Emotional View." In *The Critical Link 2: Interpreters in the Community*, edited by Roda P. Roberts, Silvana E. Carr, Diana Abraham, and Aideen Dufour, 207-218. Amsterdam: John Benjamins.

14

THE PSYCHOLOGICAL IMPLICATIONS OF INTERPRETING IN CONFLICT ZONES

Elements for potential mental-health and self-care training for interpreters

Eleonora Bernardi

Due to the highly emotional and primarily negative nature of the interpreted message, interpreters in healthcare, police, court and humanitarian settings experience increased occupational stress and emotional/psychological strain that can lead to permanent conditions such as burnout, compassion fatigue and vicarious traumatisation. This is even more true of interpreting in conflict zones, where PTSD has long been documented among soldiers. Little attention has been paid, however, to the specifics of interpreter traumatisation in this highly particular setting and no attempt has yet been made to identify key elements of possible "trauma training." To fill this gap, interpreters who worked in Croatia and Bosnia–Herzegovina during the 1990s were interviewed in this study to explore the specific features of their traumatic experience, considering the specific context-related, job-related and content-related trauma factors. This analysis was then combined with existing trauma guidelines for community interpreting, to identify elements of possible trauma training and adapt them to this psychologically very particular setting, where the provision of any kind of training is itself a challenge.

14.1 Introduction

Interpreting has long been considered an emotionally uninvolved activity but its psychological implications have recently been the subject of research in the fields of sign-language, community, court, and humanitarian interpreting. Although not all interpreters experience psychological problems, research has shown that interpreters, who do not merely listen and translate, but channel traumatic content often using direct speech and the first-person singular, are asked to empathise and thereby identify with speakers, potentially increasing "the interpreter's risk of experiencing vicarious trauma" (Bontempo and Malcolm 2012, 111). Lacking both the training and support services of other professionals, interpreters may, therefore, experience

DOI: 10.4324/9781003230359-18

trauma even more than carers or therapists (Raval 1996, 36). Burnout, compassion fatigue, secondary traumatic stress disorder and vicarious traumatisation are some of the terms used to describe the different but overlapping consequences of empathic engagement with traumatic events or content, which will, generically, be termed "traumatisation" here. This traumatisation can generate symptoms such as intrusive thoughts, isolation, depression, phobias, anger, and sleep disorders, which can eventually modify a person's ego resources, identity, and world view. While the research and training on traumatisation are in their infancy in community/humanitarian interpreting, interpreters in conflict zones and their service users seem to be completely unaware of the interpreters' need for psychological support (Todorova and Rosendo 2021, 286), even in low-intensity conflicts (Snellman 2014, 66–67). Although Post-Traumatic Stress Disorder (PTSD) and emotional trauma are recognised in subjects who witness the atrocities of war and genocide, the issue has rarely been approached in Interpreting in Conflict Zones (henceforth ICZ), with few exceptions (Ruiz Rosendo and Persaud 2016; Barea Muñoz 2021), and no attempt has been made to conceive appropriate trauma training. This study attempts to fill this gap by analysing the specific features of trauma among interpreters working in conflict zones – described here as context-, job-, and content-related factors – that emerged from the interviews carried out with interpreters working in Croatia and Bosnia–Herzegovina during the 1990s. Although subjective, these first-hand experiences of interpreters help us identify common features of their traumatic experience, which can then be used to propose key elements for trauma training, also adapting existing training for other professions/dialogue interpreting settings.

14.2 Method

The data were obtained from a broader doctoral project investigating the role, position, and practice of interpreting during the war in former Yugoslavia through an analysis of archive material and semi-structured interviews with former military personnel and interpreters.[1] Next to fourteen military representatives, a total of twelve interpreters working in either Croatia or Bosnia-Herzegovina were interviewed (two for ECMM, six for UNPROFOR/UNHCR, one for local government, one for foreign media and two for IFOR/SFOR national contingents). Three interpreters preferred to answer in written form for security reasons, while nine took part in oral interviews. Interestingly, trauma was not present in the original 24-question list, but this topic emerged spontaneously in eight out of the nine oral interviews. When asked about the difficulties of their job, the interpreters often ranked emotional and psychological strain first and stressed the need they had felt, at the time, for psychological and trauma training rather than terminological training. The interviews were, therefore, analysed trying to identify elements relating to their emotional response to the conflict and the coping strategies they adopted, fully aware that more than 20 years have passed, and that no differential analysis was carried out by a professional therapist at the time.

14.3 Specific features of trauma in conflict zones

War is the epitome of trauma, the wounds of which are not always visible. This is an issue that first started to be considered more than a century ago when PTSD was labelled as "shell-shock." Unfortunately, despite its alarming consequences,[2] little has changed in military settings, where a frank discussion on the mental health of soldiers is still hampered by ideal masculinity representations and stigmatisation, with only a few courageous exceptions (Finkel 2013; Doucette 2015). Interpreters in conflict zones seem to be at risk of not only the PTSD often experienced by soldiers, haunted by what they have seen and their inability to help the local population, but also of traumatisation resulting from the content of what they are called on to translate. Among the interpreters interviewed, those who admitted psychological discomfort or consequences were all active between 1991 and 1995, and in one case trauma was the reason for quitting the job: "It was getting to be a bit too much, you know, I was having, you know, psychologically it was getting quite . . . I was just exhausted" (Interpreter 02, personal communication, 12 November 2020). Even those who were not personally affected, or who refused to admit that they had been affected, have someone else's PTSD story to tell:

> During the war, my husband's cousin worked for UNPROFOR and do you know how that ended? She went crazy. She lost her mind [and] I also remember a young interpreter, very nice, cute, she was also good, but she was fired within 24 hours because when she found herself before troops from the other side she just blanked, she was paralysed, she couldn't speak.
>
> *(Interpreter 10, personal communication, 02 February 2021)*

For one of the interpreters, the breakdown occurred years later, triggered by a seemingly innocuous experience:

> I went for psychotherapy 19 years after the war. It was because during one job. . . . I broke down and I started crying and I had an episode – I couldn't stop for about two hours. Fortunately, I was interpreting . . . training for psychologists, who were dealing with victims of trauma and this lady . . . she noticed something was going on with me, so she approached me and asked me if I had had experience of war or of any traumatic events and she suggested I seek psychological support.
>
> *(Interpreter 08, personal communication, 11 January 2021)*

ICZ, therefore, involves the risk of both PTSD and content traumatisation, like that occurring in medical, police, refugee, and court interpreting, in a harmful mix of specific features that will now be described, analysing them in the three categories of context-, job-, and content-related trauma factors.

14.3.1 Context-related factors

Unlike their colleagues in police or healthcare interpreting, what seems to emerge from the interviews is the tendency for interpreters in conflict zones to experience trauma not just professionally, but also privately – living in besieged cities, fearing for their own lives and those of their families and friends, and despairing over failed attempts to achieve peace. There is little doubt in the literature as to the psychological impact of war on the civilian populations in Croatia and Bosnia-Herzegovina (White 2002). The population of Sarajevo[3] was particularly affected by trauma and depressive mania during the war years, with suicidal tendencies extremely high among children during the siege, and it makes sense to extend such issues to interpreters as well. Available literature has shown that, as members of societies at war, interpreters did not just translate the conflict, they also experienced it, and could also be victims of violence, ethnic cleansing or genocide. Being embedded in the sociopsychological setting of war (M. Baker 2010), especially when it runs along religious/ethnic or political lines, it seems that interpreters were particularly traumatised when working for the "other" side, to such an extent that they often tried to disguise their ethnic identity or accent. Stahuljak (1999) sustains that interpreters were traumatised twice in the conflict, by what she calls the "violence of neutrality," that is the impossibility of giving their own testimony because they were bound by interpreters' neutrality, but also by the lack of recognition for their work, which in post-Yugoslavian societies has been either forgotten or heavily criticised as this Croatian interpreter explains: "We all have some sort of wound, some smaller, some bigger . . . that we are forgotten, that in fact, no one knows how we lived, what we did, how it was, and if interpreters are remembered, they are remembered as those who worked for the UN and made a lot of money [my translation]" (Interpreter 02, personal communication, 12 November 2020).

14.3.2 Job-related factors

The working conditions in ICZ have been described as increasing stress and trauma. While the pay is generally good, the job is extremely challenging (long hours, night shifts, constant duty, travelling in hostile areas and adverse weather conditions), dangerous (landmines, gunfire, kidnapping and lack of protective equipment) and insecure, with contracts sometimes renewed monthly. Moreover, interpreters do not, usually, have social security, pension schemes, or the same healthcare provisions of troops (C. Baker 2012a; Fitchett 2019, 199), despite working in the line of fire, and when wounded they often rely on the charity of troops to access healthcare (C. Baker 2012b), where available.

Operating as freelancers within a military structure, interpreters generally have no civil supervisor they can turn to when they have to discuss problems or issues, like sexual harassment in the workplace (Interpreter 02, personal communication, 12 November 2020), which was reported as a trauma factor by two of the interpreters interviewed. For those living in repressive regimes and/or conflict situations, just simple knowledge can be dangerous and disturbing in itself, and, in some areas, interpreters are targeted because of their collaboration with foreign forces, and they cannot count on the protection of their employers or obtain a visa to get out of the country, as the recent evacuation of Kabul has shown. Even when no actual violence is involved, distrust or animosity towards foreign forces is usually extended to interpreters, both females, who are criticised for their "sleeping with the enemy," and males, who can be verbally abused for not taking up arms (Military 01, private communication, 19 October 2021). This results in episodes of envy and the ghettoisation from their community, family, and friends: "You are really in a very lonely kind of position. Lonely is perhaps too strong a word, but you are in a world of your own with this group of people that you're working with, a lot of people that you meet don't understand what you're doing" (Interpreter 02, personal communication, November 12, 2020).

This sense of estrangement and isolation, augmented by the fear of being considered weak or unprofessional when raising mental health issues, and the imperative of confidentiality, has led interpreters to deal with trauma alone since they are treated with suspicion by their own community and foreign military personnel. This perception can turn into betrayal when the military fail to protect them, or abandon them or their loved ones to their fate:

> I never refused any job, any task . . . [that] involved very high risk for my life. I even joined them on foot patrols, and it happened that several times we walked through a minefield and so basically . . . this was an additional reason why I felt so betrayed when they handed over my family to the Serbs who killed them.
>
> *(Interpreter 01, personal communication, November 19, 2020)*

14.3.3 Content-related factors

In all settings, content-related trauma is usually what leads to discomfort, long-term psychological strain and/or vicarious traumatisation,[4] and war, unfortunately, offers some of the most traumatic content. Interpreters working for foreign military forces are exposed to the most gruesome scenarios of human suffering: they may be validating requests for medical evacuations, supervise body counts and exchange, examine scenes of shelling or explosions or interview victims of war crimes, as this interpreter, operating in Bosnia-Hercegovina, remembers: "One day we went to a concentration camp . . . just a day after it was won back by the Bosnian army and [I was] with this woman, who was a protection officer. She was taking notes and I was sent to 'look there is a brain on the wall'!" (Interpreter 08, personal communication, 11 January 2021).

Being the only point of contact with the local population, locally recruited civilian interpreters are sometimes the first and only recipients of horrifying stories, which can be also their own stories, as many have gone through some form of refugee or violent experience, but which can affect them, even when they regard the "other," as one Croatian interpreter recounts:

> I remember once in western Slavonia we went to the occupied territory, and we were driving, and we saw people that . . . the Serbian people, population, local population, civilians and they did not . . . they did not have shoes, they were barefooted, and so I felt for them.
>
> *(Interpreter 07, personal communication, January 12, 2021)*

Many of the people in need of interpreting were refugees, women and children who had often been victims of sexual violence, which is even more difficult for women interpreters to convey (most interpreters were women), as gender has been proven to play a role in further aligning the interpreter with the client's experiences (Shakespeare 2012):

> I did the interview with . . . the first woman prisoner of war. She was a woman with two children, one was six years the other was six months, and they were all, all three of them were violated and that wasn't, that wasn't easy to translate not only because of the knowledge of . . . and you know learning what actually happened to them, but also because of . . . you know, seeing them and even though I was very young and not really knowing anything at 21, but I could see that the child, the six-year-old girl, was, you know, disturbed and wasn't OK and it was, it was a difficult moment to witness.
>
> *(Interpreter 08, personal communication, January 11, 2021)*

This seems to confirm the enormous traumatic potential of interpreting violent language underlined by interpreters at the International Criminal Tribunal for the Former Yugoslavia (ICTY)[5] and other international tribunals (Elias-Bursać 2015; Ndongo-Keller 2015), whose clients frequently recurred to violent outbursts, slurs or distorted evident truths as this ICTY interpreter confirms: "You feel depressed because you feel you have been misused as a tool of violence and you have helped create violence and aggression, and this is actually the opposite of the nature of what we do" (McCloskey and Dobričić 2018).

14.4 Elements of training for conflict zones interpreters

Although scholars and practitioners (Spahić-Šagolj n.d.) have called for specific training or pre-deployment psychological counselling for interpreters in conflict zones (Cappelli 2014), as far as we know, no trauma modules have been developed in recent training initiatives, nor included in the training modules proposed, like, for example, Mahasneh and Obeidat's (Mahasneh and Obeidat 2018). This is not surprising, as even in community interpreting, "trauma training is an add-on at best, a few minutes tacked onto the last part of the program" (Bancroft et al. 2015, 86), which seems to focus more on what skills interpreters should have to help others, rather than to help themselves. We will therefore try here to use the analysis of interpreters' traumatic experience and combine it with training programmes/guidelines available for therapists (Figley 2002), mental health workers in conflict zones (White 2002) and community interpreters (Bancroft et al. 2015; Crezee et al. 2015), to propose a number of elements for an adaptable "trauma curriculum" for ICZ, which will follow the common triangular structure of prevention, self-care and support strategies. While ICZ shares some trauma elements with other interpreting settings, some will be unique to it (see Chapter 1), especially training delivery, which may be heavily influenced by lack of time, internet resources, secured connections, interpreters' lack of concentration and military operations (Moser-Mercer et al. 2013). Training modules should, therefore, be conceived as short, adaptable content, available both on- and offline to be downloaded easily in no-bandwidth environments. Training should also include follow-up/supervision (Hetherington 2012) either in presence/remote sessions or through secured phone/mail connections. That said, as reactions to trauma vary greatly, so do strategies to cope with it, which is why any training should offer a wide range of options interpreters can choose from.

14.4.1 Prevention

The first element in trauma support training is prevention which means providing interpreters with a theoretical framework that can help them make sense of what is happening to them, as they are often not even aware that PTSD or vicarious traumatisation exist. Since being forewarned means being forearmed, interpreters should be informed that frequently interpreting distressing material can affect people more than they might realise, so they need to be trained to recognise traumatisation. They should be encouraged not to wait or to minimise symptoms, numbing their feelings with alcohol or tobacco, but to seek help immediately, and to express their emotional reactions, without fear of being considered "emotionally vulnerable and receiving fewer interpreting assignments as a result" (Crezee et al. 2015, 75). Prevention could be done through on-site or online sessions or with printed or virtual material, which could also include awareness maps, like the one proposed by Crezee et al. (2015, 81) for self-evaluation of symptoms.

Secondly, interpreters should be trained, maybe using mock sessions (Cappelli 2014), on how to work with victims of war and traumatised individuals, following the literature available for therapists or relief workers, as communication structure changes when one has gone through extreme shock or trauma as this ECMM observer points out:

> Interviewing combatants can be very frustrating for both the interviewer and the interviewee because in many cases there's very little to learn. Soldiers may want to cooperate, but they don't remember the details of the experience they have gone through. All due to the anxiety and tension, which stimulates the defence mechanism called "survival stress reaction" or "fear-induced stress." During this defensive process, the combatant's body

concentrates on vital aspects, disregarding periphery details, which lead to something similar to an amnesia, restricting those stressful moments. . . . [My interpreter], Milan had a special way of getting through with the interviews.

(Gonçalves 2020, 393–394)

Thirdly, if emotional preparation is essential (Bancroft et al. 2015), it is often not feasible in ICZ, as little or no information is provided before an assignment and the context is highly unpredictable. Interpreters can, nevertheless, be trained to keep their distance (i.e., "therapeutic distance") or to maintain some emotional detachment from the traumatic content and to set boundaries by clarifying their role and tasks, breaking off interviews when the traumatic content becomes unmanageable and refusing to perform tasks that are not strictly related to interpreting. Although they might at first feel guilty about refusing to help a traumatised person, by getting something to eat, for example, situations that shift the emotional burden from the professional act of translation to the private sphere have serious consequences on the mental health of interpreters. They should be made aware of this and offered models, such as the *Say-no Model* (Bancroft et al. 2016, 69–72) that they can use to decline a request but offering valid reasons and alternatives, without compromising their professional role and rights, and most importantly their mental wellbeing. Emotional distance from the content could also be established by shifting from first- to third-person singular (Bancroft and Bot, as quoted in Crezee et al. 2015, 79) and by carefully managing positioning and physical proximity (Bancroft et al. 2015, 89). Barea Muñoz also mentions, as a coping mechanism, the act of focusing exclusively on the form "without personally (mentally) attributing any content to the words being uttered" (2021, 204), that may be achieved by visualising the actual form of the words in their heads.

Finally, the collaboration of their employers – that is, military institutions and representatives – is paramount not just for training, but also for resolving some of the job-related trauma factors, to ensure protection, healthcare, social security, and reasonable working hours and to make them feel part of the team, to avoid isolation and estrangement.

14.4.2 Self-care

Self-care is any coping strategy that the individual implements to protect and improve mental, physical and emotional wellbeing. Self-care is essential in traumatic settings and interpreters who do not implement self-care strategies are described as being "at increased risk for developing symptoms of emotional exhaustion" (Schwenke 2012, 26), especially since they are themselves victims of the conflict. Self-care encompasses coping strategies divided into short-term or event-related strategies and long-term strategies (also called wellness plans) addressing all areas of life (Bancroft et al. 2015). Examples are provided below of both types of strategies that interpreters can be trained to develop, and most importantly write down, as specific, measurable objectives.

Short-term self-care helps interpreters keep a distance from the traumatic content using techniques such as objects (for example a stone or an elastic band) that they take to potentially traumatic assignments to touch or snap to return to themselves and detach from distressing content during or after the session. Rituals, like uttering a sentence or repeating a gesture, can have a similar role and help them set a clear boundary around the encounter and the interpreter's persona. Another set of short-term coping strategies are self-calming drills, to use a military term, or exercises, which can include breathing and grounding[6] exercises, and the visualisation of safe, peaceful places, scenes or pieces of music. There is also a whole set of cognitive techniques that interpreters can be taught to block or avoid negative thoughts, such as self-instruction and self-distraction (Aguilera Ávila 2015, 289).

While strategies that are implemented before, during and after an assignment help interpreters address its immediate stressful or traumatic effects, general wellness strategies or plans protect them over the long term, especially since psychological consequences can last for several years after the actual traumatic event. They usually prescribe adequate sleep, exercise, a healthy diet and relaxation to counter the effects of adrenaline, psycho-physiological stimulation and high stress hormone cortisol levels that make people temporarily forget to eat and sleep. Scholars also suggest social activities that provide hope and optimism (McCann and Pearlman 1990, 146), regular vacation and leave (Bancroft et al. 2015, 97), contact with nature, and creative expression, but unfortunately interpreters in conflict zones, clearly, cannot access many of these self-care *escamotages*: it's hard to sleep in a city that is being bombed and where food is scarce, let alone take vacations, or engaging in yoga or painting classes, with interpreters fending for their lives. Interpreters can, nevertheless, be helped to build their own feasible self-care plan and establish a routine of sleep, eating and exercising at home or, if they live on a base, at the military canteen or gym. Self-reflection/exploration, constructive thinking, reading, listening to music, having a pet, meditation, prayer, and voluntary work are also (sometimes) possible even in conflict zones, while mindfulness, a contemplative Buddhist practice for personal wellness, showed great potential in reducing stress and increasing resilience to stressors (Bernay 2012). Employers could also help here, by offering interpreters vacations or leave in less dangerous neighbouring areas, or in the troops' countries, as it was sometimes done with interpreters during the war in Bosnia–Herzegovina and Croatia (Military 10, 08, and 15, personal communications, 2021).

14.4.3 Support

A third important pillar to prevent or offset traumatisation is professional, peer, and personal support. Professional counselling, therapy and/or psychotherapy is fundamental to establish a differential analysis of symptoms and appropriate support, but it may be difficult in conflict zones. While the military, in theory, does have professional counsellors for this purpose, the actual use of their services is unclear and seems to be limited in practice, as well as being highly stigmatised for soldiers, let alone interpreters. In the most perfect of worlds, interpreters could access military psychological support, but a more feasible and realistic option could be to establish a protocol of briefing/debriefing to discuss and seek help with co-workers and principals. When interpreters have centralised management, as in NATO bases, this could take the form of sessions with their supervisor or periodical collective exercises like the ones proposed in the UNHCR *Handbook for Interpreters in Asylum Procedures* (2017, 193), while in less regulated contexts it could simply mean talking with colleagues, a system that was suggested by one of the Croatian ECMM interpreters interviewed:

> We had a kind of improvised psychological support . . . in that whenever somebody came from a field mission, we had a rule that, even if it was midnight, somebody had to be there at the headquarters to wait for them and to debrief them. The debriefing was really nothing else than listening to them talking very agitatedly for an hour about everything that happened because people kind of need to share. It was very intense emotions involved quite a bit of the time and they needed to share that, and they just need somebody who understands, who has been in a similar situation to listen to them. And that really, that's such a simple thing, but it's an enormous help. That's how we manage not to.
>
> *(Interpreter 02, personal communication, 11 December 2020)*

Peer support is especially important for interpreters in conflict zones, who are usually not socialised as interpreters and are rarely part of a wider community of professionals to turn for help or advice. Finally, the support of family/partners to help interpreters maintain a sound private life separate from their work is also recommended, although complicated by confidentiality and the estrangement interpreters experience. It might, therefore, be hard to share openly with friends and family, especially unless specific protocols are agreed upon with employers that allow interpreters to partially disclose the information that is necessary to get emotional support from their family and partners.

14.5 Conclusion

In this brief contribution, an attempt has been made to highlight how trauma dominates the daily experience of interpreters in conflict zones and how they need to be trained to be better able to cope with the added context-, job- and content-related trauma factors. Using this categorisation of interpreters' trauma experience and existing modules from other professions/interpreting settings, some basic elements have been put forward for trauma training in conflict zones, following a triangular structure based on prevention, self-care and support. This contribution is, of course, just a first, tentative approach to a vastly under-researched topic that requires further research and feedback from interpreters, military, humanitarian organisations and mental health professionals. The collaboration of therapists is essential to help interpreters counter trauma repercussions and develop what is called 'vicarious post-traumatic growth' (Splevins et al. 2010) or 'compassion satisfaction', which is a positive and empowering take-home approach from the traumatic experience that comes from helping others through one's work, perfectly described by one of the interpreters interviewed as follows:

> When you interpret for a victim of violence . . . you really feel that you are necessary in this situation, that you are providing not only a service, but that you're also lending your voice . . . and I think that it is somehow the fact that you're doing something really meaningful and important that somehow protects you from the trauma.
>
> *(Interpreter 06, personal communication, 2 September 2021)*

Notes

1   On the use of interviews in research into languages and war, see C. Baker (2019).
2   According to Doucette (2015, 170), US, UK and Canada have been losing veterans at an alarming rate. In the Canadian Armed Forces, for example, between 2002 and 2012, there were more victims of suicide than those killed during operations in Afghanistan.
3   Ismet Cerić, late professor from the Neuropsychiatry Department in Sarajevo (as quoted in Pirjevec 2014, 366).
4   The profound, potentially disruptive and painful psychological effects, that can affect those who help traumatized persons and that can persist for months or years after work with traumatized persons (McCann and Pearlman 1990, 131–132).
5   See the short movie *In flow of words* (Bots 2021) on the topic.
6   Grounding, also known as earthing, is a technique that helps connecting with the earth to control and/or fight anxiety.

References

Aguilera Ávila, Laura. 2015. "Estrategias de prevención y autoayuda para intérpretes que trabajan en contextos de violencia de género." In *Interpretación en contextos de violencia de género*, edited by Carmen Toledano Buendía, and Maribel del Pozo Triviño. http://sosvics.eintegra.es/Documentacion/Interpretar_en_contextos_de_violencia_de_genero.pdf.

Baker, Catherine. 2012a. "Prosperity without Security: The Precarity of Interpreters in Postsocialist, Postconflict Bosnia-Herzegovina." *Slavic Review* 71 (4): 849–872.

Baker, Catherine. 2012b. "When Bosnia was a Commonwealth Country: British Forces and their Interpreters in Republika Srpska, 1995–2007." In *Languages and the Military*, edited by Hilary Footitt, Michael Kelly, and Catherine Baker, 100–114. London: Palgrave Macmillan UK.

Baker, Catherine. 2019. "Interviewing for Research on Languages and War." In *The Palgrave Handbook of Languages and Conflict*, edited by Michael Kelly, Hilary Footitt, and Myriam Salama-Carr, 157–179. Cham: Springer International.

Baker, Mona. 2010. "Interpreters and Translators in the War Zone." *The Translator* 16 (2): 197–122.

Bancroft, Marjory A., Katharine Allen, Carola E. Green, and Louis M. Feuerle. 2015. *Breaking Silence – Interpreting for Victims Services. A Training Manual*. Washington, DC: Ayuda.

Bancroft, Marjory A., Sofia Garcia Beyaert, Katharine Allen, Giovanna Carreiro-Contreras, and Denis Socarras-Estrada. 2016. *The Medical Interpreter – A Foundation Textbook for Medical Interpreting*. n.p.: Culture & Language.

Barea Muñoz, Manuel. 2021. "Psychological Aspects of Interpreting Violence: A Narrative from the Israeli-Palestinian Conflict." In *Interpreting Conflict. A Comparative Framework*, edited by Marija Todorova, and Lucía Ruiz Rosendo, 195–212. London: Palgrave Macmillan.

Bernay, Ross. 2012. *Mindfulness and the Beginning Teacher*. PhD diss., AUT University.

Bontempo, Karen, and Karen Malcolm. 2012. "An Ounce of Prevention is Worth a Pound of Cure." In *In Our Hands. Educating Healthcare Interpreters*, edited by Laurie Swabey, and Karen Malcolm, 105–130. Washington, DC: Gallaudet.

Bots, Eliane Esther. 2021. *In Flow of Words*. Directed by Eliane Esther Bots. The Netherlands: Near/By Films.

Cappelli, Paolo. 2014. "Wartime Interpreting. Exploring the Experiences of Interpreters and Translators." In *(Re)Visiting Ethics and Ideology in Situations of Conflict*, edited by Carmen Valero-Garcés, 15–24. Madrid: Universidad de Alcalá.

Crezee, Ineke, David Atkinson, Robyn Pask, Patrick Au, and Sai Wong. 2015. "Teaching Interpreters About Self-Care." *International Journal of Interpreter Education* 7 (1): 74–83.

Doucette, Fred. 2015. *Better off Dead: Post-Traumatic Stress Disorder and the Canadian Armed Forces*. Halifax, NS: Nimbus.

Elias-Bursać, Ellen. 2015. *Translating Evidence and Interpreting Testimony at a War Crimes Tribunal*. London: Palgrave Macmillan.

Figley, Charles R. 2002. *Treating Compassion Fatigue*. New York: Brunner/Routledge.

Finkel, David. 2013. *Thank You for Your Service*. New York: Sarah Crichton.

Fitchett, Linda. 2019. "Interpreting in Peace and Conflict: Origins, Developing Practices, and Ethics." In *The Palgrave Handbook of Languages and Conflict*, edited by Michael Kelly, Hilary Footitt, and Myiriam Salama-Carr, 183–204. London: Palgrave Macmillan.

Gonçalves, Paulo. 2020. *Bosnia 95: Peacekeeping in a War Zone*. Great Britain: Amazon.

Hetherington, Ali. 2012. "Supervision and the Interpreting Profession: Support and Accountability through Reflective Practice." *International Journal of Interpreter Education* 4 (1): 46–57.

Mahasneh, Anjad A., and Mohammed M. Obeidat. 2018. "Conflict Zones: A Training Model for Interpreters." *The Interpreters' Newsletter* 23: 63–81.

McCann, Lisa, and Laurie A. Pearlman. 1990. "Vicarious Traumatization: A Framework for Understanding the Psychological Effects of Working with Victims." *Journal of Traumatic Stress* 3 (1): 131–149.

McCloskey, Peter, and Jelena Dobričić. 2018. "Resolution 808: Inside the Yugoslavia Tribunal." In *Resolution 800 Conference*, Forlì, November 20.

Moser-Mercer, Barbara, Carmen Delgado Luchner, and Leila Kherbiche. 2013. "Blended Learning in Complex Environments: Reaching Learners in the Field." In *Sixth Conference of MIT's Learning International Networks Consortium (LINC)* 7, Cambridge, MA, June 16–19.

Ndongo-Keller. 2015. "Vicarious Trauma and Stress management." In *The Routledge Handbook of Interpreting*, edited by Holly Mikkelson, and Renée Jourdenais, 337–351. New York: Routledge.

Pirjevec, Joze. 2014. *Le guerre jugoslave: 1991–1999*. Torino: Einaudi.

Raval, Hitesh. 1996. "A Systemic Perspective on Working with Interpreters." *Clinical Child Psychology and Psychiatry* 1 (1): 29–43.

Ruiz Rosendo, Lucía, and Clementina Persaud. 2016. "Interpreters and Interpreting in Conflict Zones and Scenarios: A Historical Perspective." *Linguistica Antverpiensia* 15: 1–35.

Schwenke, Tomina J. 2012. *The Relationships between Perfectionism, Stress, Coping Resources, and Burnout among Sign Language Interpreters.* PhD diss., Georgia State University.

Shakespeare, Claire. 2012. *Community Interpreters Speaking for Themselves: The Psychological Impact of Working in Mental Health Settings.* Ph.D. diss., University of Hertfordshire.

Snellman, Pekka. 2014. "The Agency of Military Interpreters in Finnish Crisis Management Operations." MA diss., University of Tampere.

Spahić-Šagolj, Edina. n.d. "Prevodilac u ratnoj zoni" [Translator in a War Zone]. In *Udruženje Prevodilaca u Bosni i Hercegovini,* http://upbh.ba/v4/wp-content/uploads/2018/09/Edina-Spahic-Sagolj_Prevodilac-u-ratnoj-zoni.pdf.

Splevins, Katie A., Keren Cohen, Stephen Joseph, Craig Murray, and Jake Bowley. 2010. "Vicarious Posttraumatic Growth among Interpreters." *Qualitative Health Research* 20 (12): 1705–1716.

Stahuljak, Zrinka. 1999. "The Violence of Neutrality-Translators in and of the War [Croatia, 1991–1992]." *College Literature* 26 (1): 34–51.

Todorova, Marija, and Lucía Ruiz Rosendo. eds. 2021. *Interpreting Conflict. A Comparative Framework.* London: Palgrave Macmillan.

UNHCR Austria. 2017. *Handbook for Interpreters in Asylum Procedures.* Vienna: UNHCR Austria.

White, Geoffrey D. 2002. "Trauma Treatment Training for Bosnian and Croatian Mental Health Workers." In *Treating Compassion Fatigue,* edited by Charles R. Figley, 171–179. New York: Brunner/Routledge.

15

ENHANCING SHORT-TERM MEMORY FOR CONFLICT ZONE INTERPRETERS

Anjad A. Mahasneh

According to the conflict zones training model suggested by Mahasneh and Obeidat (2018), interpreting in conflict zones requires both non-linguistic competencies and linguistic skills. Necessary linguistic skills include interpretation skills involving memory skills, and note-taking skills, among others. Memory skills comprise good working memory. However, psychological studies of human memory distinguish between short-term memory (STM) and long-term memory (LTM). STM refers to retaining information for a short period of time without creating the neural mechanisms for later recall. Although it is crucial for interpretation, memory training has been disregarded by interpreting scholars for quite some time. The present descriptive study aims to identify the importance of short-term memory in interpretation in conflict zones and examine existing exercises to enhance short-term memory. For an interpreter to develop a better perception of the source language and its message, their working memory has to be effectively trained. To this end, several exercises suggested by some scholars are studied such as shadowing, listening, and segmentation, among others. Understanding the role of short-term memory in interpreting in conflict zones and the efficacy of short-term memory training may aid in improving the performance of conflict zone interpreters.

15.1 Interpreting

Interpretation is the form of translation that demands individuals to perform high cognitive tasks and requires skills of rapid understanding of the auditory material in the source language to reproduce it in the target language, either simultaneously or within the shortest time possible, as in consecutive or sight interpretation. Unlike translators, interpreters do not have the liberty of time to consult dictionaries. An interpreter is a multitasker who listens to, understands, analyses, and processes

DOI: 10.4324/9781003230359-19

information (or takes notes while listening and processing information) and appropriately articulates the speech in another language.

There are different types and modes of interpreting, including *Conflict zone/ Disaster interpreting*, which, according to the National Language Service Corps website, "supports individuals affected by conflict, disaster or other emergency situations. These may include humanitarian and military interpreting, depending on the context."

Hence, there is an increasing academic and professional interest related to interpreters in conflict zones and an urgent need to improve their performance for various reasons. These include the turmoil sweeping through different areas worldwide, including Yemen, Syria, and Iraq, among others, the scarcity of studies and dearth of research about interpreting in conflict zones (Baker 2006, 2010; Palmer and Fontan 2007; Moser-Mercer et al. 2014), the lack of professional training and education for field interpreters, the insufficiency of existent models for conflict interpreters, the urgent need to deliver humanitarian aid to people in conflict zones, and the different challenges and risks faced by the field interpreters (Mahasneh and Obeidat 2018).

A conflict zone interpreter (henceforth, CZI), like any other interpreter, should acquire certain linguistic and non-linguistic skills. Mahasneh and Obeidat suggested a CZI training model, which highlights both. The linguistic competencies include interpretation competence. It covers memory skills and note-taking, among other things (2018, 76). Thus, interpretation is a demanding process in which memory functioning is at the highest level. Furthermore, memory is a crucial component in the interpretation process.

After discussing the psychological effects of interpretation on interpreters working in conflict zones and the importance of having mental health and self-care training for CZIs (Chapter 13, Chapter 14), this chapter will shed light on the importance of enhancing memory for CZIs to improve the quality of their work.

15.2 Interpreting in conflict zones definitions, overview, skills, and training

Each domain, where the act of interpretation is undertaken, has its own treatment and deliberations to be considered by the interpreter to deliver an intact message and fulfil the needs of the domain accurately. For example, in the legal domain, the interpreter has to be cautious of every keyword that might flip the course of the legal affairs if incorrectly interpreted. The medical field is another sensitive domain, where caution should be taken while accounting for medicines, diseases, symptoms, and patients. War and conflict zones are also highly caution-demanding domains as translation and interpretation affect the safety and lives of people. For example, military and humanitarian interpretation is of great service in the field (Tesseur 2019; Mahasneh and Obeidat 2018; Baker 2010).

According to Ruiz Rosendo and Persaud (2016), interpreting in conflict zones cannot be simplistically analysed because relations between the parties involved in conflict tend to be complicated and "interpreters may potentially play an important role in intelligence work performed before and during a given conflict" (3). Baker (2010) describes interpreters working in war zones as crucial chroniclers of war even if they are invisible actors in such a setting as they provide narrations of chronicles of events defining a war.

Interpreters hired to work within the settings of conflict zones are usually not subjected to special training and might be selected because they possess the knowledge and basic command of two languages. They may have little to no experience of working in conflict zone conditions. This causes many problems owing to the sensitive circumstances of the conflict zones and might even threaten people's lives (Baker 2010; Mahasneh and Obeidat 2018; Tesseur 2019). For this reason, CZIs not only have to be linguistically competent in both languages they work with, but also must be aware and understand the context and terminology of conflict zones. According to Mahasneh and Obeidat (2018), an interpreter will benefit from acquiring strategic sub-competence, psycho-physiological components, and instrumental sub-competence. The nature of conflict zone interpretation requires interpreters to have the ability to perform under difficult conditions and circumstances. Therefore, they need to be self-confident, have decision-making ability, and be able to work under pressure.

CZIs are trusted for how they interpret the utterances of others, for what they understand, and for the assurance that they are not forced to interpret another way (Baker 2010). Consequently, the interpreter carries the burden of being faithful to deliver the message as intended and avoiding manipulation that affects it. Hence, given the fact that an interpreter comes from certain ethnic, religious, and ideological background and loyalties, these factors can impact and influence the way they perform (Tesseur 2019). Hence, the role of ethics highlights the sensitive matter in the interpreter's work within the setting of war, conflict, and crisis zones. An example of the urgent importance of ethics in interpretation is the assumptions and impressions that were produced by the interpretations around the War on Terror and in the aftermath of the 9/11 attacks. Thus, as Tesseur (2019, 217) argues, "several contributions emphasise the need to bring the 'human' back into practice by looking beyond existing professional codes of ethics for translators and interpreters."

Interpreting in a conflict zone is unique in certain aspects, such as the danger and the risk interpreters can face, the ethical importance, and the cultural and psychological aspects. However, like any other type of interpreting, memory constitutes a basic element in this process. The next section illustrates the importance of memory and its types.

15.3 Memory types and skills: Special emphasis on short-term memory/working memory

Darò (2002) names two types of memory: long-term memory (LTM) and short-term memory (STM). STM temporally stores and retains information for a limited time and has limited capacity. Accordingly, the method of operation of STM and its characteristic of limited capacity and time present the concept of working memory, which describes the memory that maintains units of information when being processed. Although both STM and working memory work together interchangeably, they have some differences in function. They can be distinguished by the extent to which the information stored is manipulated. This difference can be described as follows:

> Short-term memory refers to the more passive store of information in immediate memory. Working memory refers to the more active store of information in immediate memory. . . . The simple manipulation in the backward digit span task highlights the difference between the ability to remember information in the short term and the ability to remember and manipulate that information.
>
> *(Bauernschmidt et al. 2008, 199)*

Working memory can be used for some cognitive abilities like attention. Darò (2002) mentions a part in the STM called the "attentional systems," controlled by the "central executive systems in the memory" and linked to "slave systems" like the "phonological loop system," which is linked with processing information based on speech and utterances. In this kind of slave system, the verbal information that the memory temporally processes "within the phonological store decay and thus become irretrievable after 1.5 to 2 seconds, unless they are 'refreshed' by the process of *subvocal rehearsal*" (623). The phonological loop is the system that supports the connection between language processing and working memory. The system of the phonological loop includes two key elements in this context: the *phonological store*, which temporally stores information based on speech, and the *articulatory control process*, the process in charge of the translation of visual material into codes based on speech and their maintenance in the phonological store. Then, in order to keep the phonological store maintained in the memory for a longer time, the articulatory control process refreshes such stored information (Bauernschmidt et al. 2008).

LTM represents the memory that stores the information in stable and permanent storage. This includes several subsystems. Firstly, LTM includes a declarative of explicit memory that encompasses the semantic memory in which the "individuals store their encyclopaedic knowledge about the world," and the episodic memory, which reflects the memory that retains the individual's personal experiences. In contrast, the non-declarative or implicit memory "includes motor, cognitive, perceptual habits and skills, priming, simple classical conditioning, and no associative learning." This reflects the ability to acquire languages and the way to use it and store this into the implicit memory (Bauernschmidt et al. 2008, 624).

Consequently, the two main types of interpretation (i.e., simultaneous and consecutive interpretation) employ memory abilities differently. In simultaneous interpretation, working memory and its phonological loop system are the key players in maintaining information at the time of being processed, while on the scale of LTM tasks, this kind of interpretation poorly keeps and maintains the information already translated because the interpreter is busy doing multiple tasks in a very small-time frame, and incoming information at the time of processing previous information creates interference. Therefore, enhancing and improving memory is essential for CZIs, as highlighted by the NATTI (2016) (The National Accreditation Authority for Translators and Interpreters in Australia), the standards organisation responsible for setting, promoting, and maintaining high professional standards that issue accreditation for practitioners who would like to work as interpreters in Australia. Their interpretation competencies include eight different types: language, intercultural, technological, thematic, transfer, service provision, and ethical. They also included memory skills as one element in the transfer competency. Moreover, Moser-Mercer et al. suggested a model for CZIs that includes three components, including memory support with the acquisition of note-taking skills (2014).

15.4 Enhancing memory for interpreting

A trained memory is an essential part of the process of both consecutive and simultaneous interpretation as the interpreter heavily relies on memory to retain what is heard. STM is involved in the process of interpretation and is responsible for recalling and retaining information within a short duration. Unlike LTM, which preserves information for a longer duration, STM has a heavier load in simultaneous interpreting, as it requires multi-cognitive processing when receiving, processing, and producing the interpretation of the source language into the target language. Thus, the interpreters must get their memory trained to utilise it more efficiently. In the case of consecutive interpretation, even if the workload of the memory is less than simultaneous interpreting, the interpreter has a short duration to process the utterances during the pauses of the speech and find ways to take notes briefly and more efficiently (writing every word of the speaker consumes time). Therefore, training memory expands working memory capacity and makes it more proficient in interpreting (Duong 2006; Kriston 2012; Zhang and Yu 2018; Yenkimaleki and van Heuven 2017). Zhang and Yu (2018, 162) enlist benefits of memory training to interpretation quality:

(1) memory training helps improve interpreting learning outcomes;
(2) memory coordination training contributes more to interpreting learning outcomes as compared to memory capacity training;
(3) the impact of memory training on interpreting learning outcomes exhibits different features at different stages. That is, in the primary stage of learning, memory capacity training plays a significant role. With the accumulation of more experience in interpreting learning, memory coordination training starts to play a more prominent role in enhancing the outcome of interpreting learning.

Both consecutive and simultaneous interpreting can be enhanced and improved for better performance by the interpreters. Further, the circumstances of each field of interpreting require highly trained interpreters to adequately fulfil the goals of interpretation. One initiative of providing training for CZIs is a centre for interpreting in conflict zones under the name of InZone. It has been set up to provide on-set training for interpreters working in conflict zones. InZone provides modules on skill and memory development in interpreting, professional codes of ethics, and basic skills of conflict resolution.

As previously mentioned, CZIs are expected to be aware of the conditions of conflicts and wars, confidant, trustworthy, and able to abide by the code of ethics considering the sensitivity of such a field. They are also required to be trained linguistically, as many interpreters are usually recruited without professional training to work in conflict zones. In this setting, the interpreters ought to find ways to develop their skills in interpretation and enhance their memory to achieve more accurate interpretation with less memory load to cope with the conditions of conflict zones. Many scholars have suggested several exercises and/or techniques to enhance and improve memory while interpreting; those exercises can also help interpreters in conflict zones to improve the quality of their memories, enhance their skills, and, therefore, their performance during interpreting. The following paragraphs illustrate some of those exercises and techniques.

15.5 Exercises and techniques for memory enhancement

Interpreters in general listen, understand, and interpret between two languages. This requires certain conditions and tools such as headphones, speakers, and interpreting devices. Moreover, the place where interpreting is taking place should be quiet to provide the interpreters with the right environment to reach a high level of focus and concentration to be able to use the STM to its highest capacity with the intent of offering good quality interpreting. Conflict zone interpretation takes place during wars and conflicts. These conditions provide CZIs with neither the tools and devices required for interpreting, nor with the quietness and focus which are essential for the best use of STM. Therefore, training CZIs on certain techniques and exercises for memory enhancement is crucial. It is more important than enhancing memory for interpreting outside war zones. Furthermore, this section offers the most suitable techniques of memory enhancement that fulfil the goal of conflict zone interpretation in line with its necessities.

Bauernschmidt et al. (2008) observe that the probabilistic structure of adaptive conditioned training under constrained conditions is beneficial to the enhancement of working memory capacity. They state that "using probabilistic sequences capitalises on the observation that everyday life is not random. The results of this study indicate that using probabilistic sequences may be more ecologically valid when studying working memory" (213).

Sakalli (2016) mentions the dual in-back task used in working memory training, which mainly depends on updating and refreshing the incoming information. This task is used in working memory training "where verbal auditory stimulus and spatial visual stimulus are presented at the same time and the person needs to remember the n previous auditory and visuo-spatial stimuli separately" (5). Sakallı observes that the dual n-back task achieves a high level of efficiency in improving memory capacity, interference control, and updating information.

Darò (2002) argues that in the case of simultaneous interpreting, the complex cognitive tasks, which divide attention in the case of interpretation, can be improved with task-specific practices. This represents an example of behaviour acquisition of the implicit memory's implying strategies. Also, the skill components of the interpretation process can be enhanced by specific, repeated practices. In the same line, Babcock et al. (2017) suggest that applying strategies like predicting the new information through contextual cues can help reduce the huge memory load occurring during interpreting. In the case of consecutive training, Darò (2002) suggests ways to enhance the performance of consecutive interpretation by using symbols instead of letters for the words and syntagmatic units in order to reduce the phonological interference caused by the inner articulation that happens while listening and note-taking simultaneously. The scholar also suggests another way to support the content of the consecutive interpretation episodic memory of the interpreter when they recall "the episode which marked the representation of that particular piece of information" (627).

Moreover, Zhong (2003), Duong (2006), Kriston (2012), Movahedi and Rahmatabadi (2016), and Yenkimaleki and van Heuven (2017) suggested *retelling a story in the source language* as an exercise that can enhance memory where the interpreter can reproduce a story out of the information they receive. This can be achieved through four techniques (Yenkimaleki and van Heuven 2017; Duong 2006):

- Categorisation: grouping the points that share the same properties to find a link or make a sequence simpler to recall.
- Generalisation: generally concluding or summarising from a certain message that conveys the full intended meaning.
- Comparison: distinguishing and rearranging features of things throughout, noticing the similarities and differences between them.
- Description: describing a shape, a scene, or the size of an object to make the interpretation clearer.

Further, Zhong (2003), Duong (2006), as well as Movahedi and Rahmatabadi (2016) suggested *exercises with inference* to enhance memory while interpreting: "The method is provided in order to prevent information loss in the STM, since the environment and other information present in the storage may reduce the information encoded" (Duong 2006, 41). This can be done by inserting noises while recording material for classroom practice to increase concentration and thus enhance STM for students (Zhong 2003).

Kriston (2012), Yenkimaleki and van Heuven (2017), Roberts (2014), and Naseri (2017) suggested the *Note-taking method*, which represents a key element of interpretation, particularly consecutive, and is considered an important strategy that reduces the pressure on the working memory. In this method, an interpreter can use symbols, abbreviations, and colourful mnemonic tools to organise cues in interpretation, to deliver the interpretation in an accurate and organised manner, achieving a lower load on the working memory. Naseri (2017) mentions three questions an interpreter should remember while note-taking: what, when, and how to note. For the "what to note" part, the main idea is the one that requires the interpreter to pay attention, note important and relevant ideas, and draw links between them to rebuild the overall meaning, which helps them construct the interpretation and deliver the intended message: "The link markers are transition signals, conjunctions, and subordinators that indicate consequences, causes, and effects" (10). In the case of note-taking, since it is hard and time-consuming to write words, it is preferable to use symbols or abbreviations that are considered economical and time-saving. In the "when to note" stage, it is important to start taking notes as soon as the speaker begins the speech, as any delay can lead to loss of information.

Zhong (2003), Duong (2006), Roberts (2014), Kriston (2012), Yenkimaleki and van Heuven (2017), Movahedi and Rahmatabadi (2016), and Language Connections LLC (henceforth LLC) suggested **Mnemonics to memory**, which "aims at remembering something that seems difficult in a form that you remember much easier" (Kriston, 2012, 83). Thus, the interpreter should use positive, strong mental images, stories, familiarity, humour, etc., as tools to make recalling things much easier (Kriston 2012; Yenkimaleki and van Heuven 2017). According to Duong (2006, 40–41), there are five techniques to enhance the STM by using Mnemonics:

- Acronyms: Formed by using each letter from the group of words to form a new word;
- Sentences/Acrostics: Like acronyms, the first letters of each word are used to make a sentence in the easiest way to remember;
- Rhymes and songs: Rhythm, repetition, melody, and rhyme can all aid memory, that is, help STM users to be familiar with what has been said before;
- Method of Loci: In order to remember speeches with unrelated items, this technique is applied to combine the use of organisation, visual memory, and association. After receiving information, STM users create a vivid visual memory of the 'path' and the objects along it, then visualise it when interpreting;
- Chunking: This is a technique generally used when remembering numbers; based on the idea that STM is limited in the number of things that can be contained.

Zhong (2003), Duong (2006), Kriston (2012), Movahedi and Rahmatabadi (2016), Roberts (2014), Naseri (2017), and LLC (n.d.) suggested *shadowing*, while Roberts (2014) suggested *shadowing, shadowing with a twist, and free shadowing with a twist*. Shadowing, mostly used in simultaneous interpreting, in general, involves repeating what a speaker says, word for word, in the same language. For shadowing in general, tapes and videotapes can help interpreters practice simultaneous interpreting to develop their STM. In addition, multi-tasking is another way to practice shadowing that enhances the memory under the pressure of doing other tasks while interpreting (Roberts 2014; Duong 2006; Naseri 2017). Although the shadowing with a twist technique is used in consecutive interpreting, meaning that in addition to repeating what a speaker says word for word in the same language, this repetition comes after the utterance, after a short pause which makes the interpreter more focused on the memory. Free shadowing with a twist should be done after practising shadowing with a twist, in which longer utterances are repeated. This exercise trains the acoustic memory and the memory of meaning (Roberts 2014; Movahedi and Rahmatabadi 2016). In this type, a freer paraphrasing can be used in rendering the longer utterances, yet, in legal and court interpretation, it is highly unacceptable for the sensitive nature of this domain (Roberts 2014). This is also unacceptable and risky in the case of conflict zone interpretation since any manipulation of words can be dangerous. Roberts (2014), Naseri (2017), and LLC (n.d.) suggested *segmentation*: "This technique involves remembering sentences in chunks, as smaller bits of information are easier to remember" (LLC, n.d.). This exercise is based on breaking a large piece of information into a limited and smaller chunk so that the interpreter can recall and process them faster and more efficiently (Roberts, 2014). This technique is also conceptualised as Chunking, "used when remembering numbers; based on the idea that short-term memory is limited in the number of things that can be contained" (Duong 2006, 41).

Duong (2006), Roberts (2014), Naseri (2017), and LLC (n.d.) suggested **visualisation** or creating mental images for the material the trainee is listening to so they can describe it later (Naseri 2017). Since most people depend on visual learning, using visualisation helps recall information by creating mental images. Speeches that include unrelated items can require the use of the visualisation technique in which "STM users create a vivid visual memory of the 'path' and objects along it, then visualize it when interpreting" (Duong 2006, 41).

Roberts (2014) and Naseri (2017) suggested *attentive listening for key elements* as a method for improving memory, while Duong (2006) and Movahedi and Rahmatabadi (2016) suggested *comprehensive and intensive listening*. In all of them, the trainees listen to audio material and repeat it exactly or listen to descriptive or narrative material and then answer questions. This technique relies on acoustic memory that helps and trains interpreters to recall the largest number of details possible. Comprehensive and intensive listening aims at listening and recalling specific details and information and repeating these details exactly: "The purpose of this approach is to encourage the quick response to the received information and the accuracy of language expression" (Duong 2006, 32).

Finally, Roberts (2014) suggested *progressively expanding the capacity to recall, recognising incoherent or ambiguous messages, and remembering messages that you disagree with or find offensive* as techniques to improve memory. In the *progressively expanding the capacity to recall* exercise, memory is improved gradually through constant training. Each time, memory is trained to recall a number of items and gradually increase this number in the following exercises. This helps expand the capacity of memory and recall.

Recognising incoherent or ambiguous messages helps recall incoherence or ambiguity in speech considered hard to remember. After listening to these kinds of speeches, the ambiguous or incoherent aspects are identified, along with the reason they are so. This can help recall and manage them during the interpretation. Ambiguity can be clarified, and incoherence can be corrected or omitted. Yet in the case of conflict zone interpretation, "ambiguity of words must be transmitted in the same way. You may intervene to ask for clarification" (Moreno Bello 2014, 70). As for *remembering messages that you disagree with or find offensive*, this can rely on "confirmation bias," which "describes a tendency to favour information that confirms a personal belief or hypothesis" (Moreno Bello 2014, 24). This means gathering or recalling information selectively can impact the interpretation. In order to recall information, the interpreter disagrees with or finds offensive, they should identify with the speakers' beliefs and put themselves in the place of the speaker. Though this technique helps the interpreter to recall such message, the interpreter should be careful of any bias, as CZI code of ethics highly restricts bias, and personal opinions and sympathies should convey the message without intervention.

In conclusion, training memory is essential for interpreters, in general, and CZIs. The exercises and techniques discussed above are very beneficial if applied; they are highly recommended for better interpretation. Figure 15.1. summarises

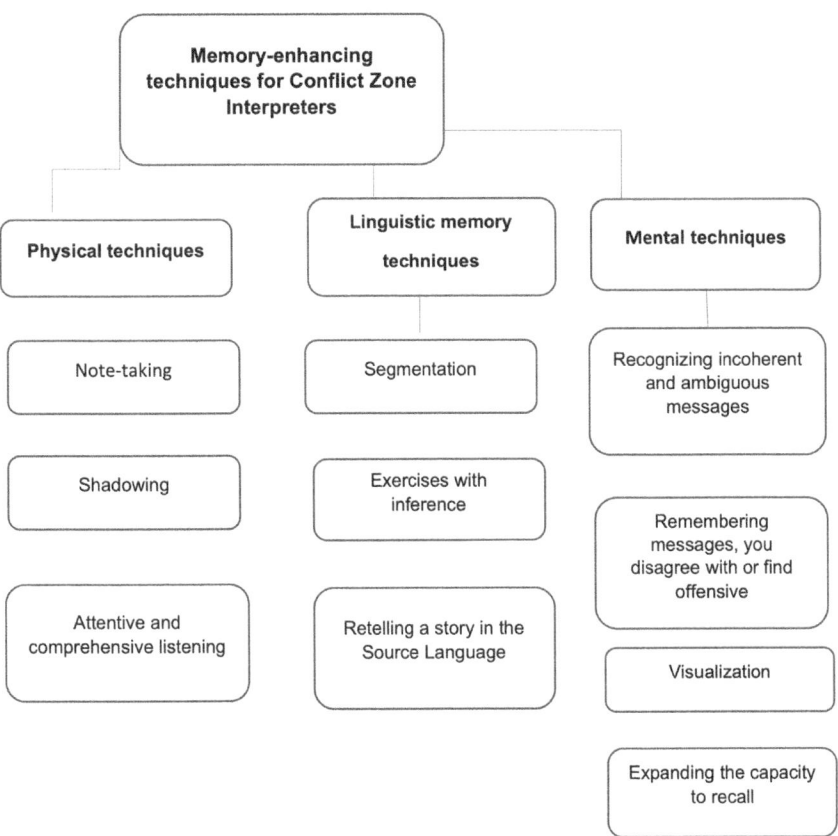

FIGURE 15.1 Memory enhancing techniques for CZIs

the techniques that go along with the nature of conflict zone interpretation and groups them under three categories: mental, physical, and linguistic.

15.6 Conclusion

The process of interpretation requires complex cognitive processing and is highly dependent on the short-term memory. Therefore, training this part of memory is crucial for producing a fast and more accurate interpretation in both simultaneous and consecutive interpretation used in conflict zone interpretation.

This chapter points out that memory training exercises and techniques help train STM as well as improve and manage interpretation processing. With STM being a key player in interpretation, memory training becomes a requirement for interpreters before starting their careers. In the case of conflict zones, where interpreters trained especially for such conditions may be difficult to find, the need to train interpreters is paramount.

This chapter is limited to the studies found by researchers in the English language; additional relevant studies in other languages may exist. More studies about memory in other languages like Arabic, its benefits, and its enhancement are needed. Furthermore, related studies concerning conflict zone interpretation training should be carried out.

References

Babcock, Laura, Mariagrazia Capizzi, Sandra Arbula, and Antonino Vallesi. 2017. "Short-Term Memory Improvement after Simultaneous Interpretation Training." *Journal of Cognitive Enhancement* 1 (3): 254–267. https://doi.org/10.1007/s41465-017-0011-x.

Baker, Mona. 2006. "Contextualization in Translator- and Interpreter-Mediated Events." *Journal of Pragmatics* 38 (3): 321–337. https://doi.org/10.1016/j.pragma.2005.04.010.

Baker, Mona. 2010. "Interpreters and Translators in the War Zone." *The Translator* 16 (2): 197–222. https://doi.org/10.1080/13556509.2010.10799469.

Bauernschmidt, A., C. M. Conway, and D. B. Pisoni. 2008. "Working Memory Training and Implicit Learning." *Research on Spoken Language Processing Progress Report* 29: 197–215.

Darò, Valeria. 2002. "Experimental Studies on Memory in Conference Interpretation." *Meta* 42 (4): 622–628. https://doi.org/10.7202/002484ar.

Duong, Tran Thuy. 2006. *How to Improve Short-Term Memory in Interpreting*. PhD diss., Hanoi University.

Kriston, Andrea. 2012. "The Importance of Memory Training in Interpretation." *PCTS Proceedings Professional Communication & Translation Studies* 5 (1): 79–86.

Language Connections LLC. n.d. "5 Memory Exercises for Medical Interpreters." *Medical Interpreter Certificate & Legal Interpreter Certificate Training*. https://interpretertrain.com/5-essential-memory-training-exercises-for-medical-interpreters/.

Mahasneh, Anjad A., and Mohammed M. Obeidat. 2018. "Conflict Zones: A Training Model for Interpreters." In *The Interpreters' Newsletter* 23: 63–81. https://doi.org/10.13137/2421-714X/22399.

Moreno Bello, Yolanda. 2014. "The War Interpreter: Needs and Challenges of Interpreting in Conflict Zones." *Situations of Conflict* 65."

Moser-Mercer, Barbara, Leïla Kherbiche, and Barbara Class. 2014. "Interpreting Conflict: Training Challenges in Humanitarian Field Interpreting." *Journal of Human Rights Practice* 6 (1): 140–158. https://doi.org/10.1093/jhuman/hut025.

Movahedi, Mahnaz, and Nessa Dashti Rahmatabadi. 2016. "The Importance of Listening and Short-Term Memory in Interpreting." *Translation Journal*, April. https://translationjournal.net/April-2016/the-importance-of-listening-and-short-term-memory-in-interpreting.html.

Naseri, Mansoor. 2017. *The Importance of Memory and Notetaking in the Process of Interpreting.* www.researchgate.net/publication/346680753_The_Importance_of_Memory_and_Notetaking_in_the_Process_of_Interpreting.

National Accreditation Authority for Translators and Interpreters NAATI. 2016. *NAATI Interpreter Certification: Knowledge, Skills and Attributes.* www.naati.com.au/media/1262/interpreter-ksa-paper-final_290216_2.pdf.

Palmer, Jerry, and Victoria Fontan. 2007. "Our Ears and Our Eyes." *Journalism* 8 (1): 5–24. https://doi.org/10.1177/1464884907072419.

Roberts, Roda P. 2014. "Enhancing Short-Term Memory for Accurate Interpreting." *The ATA Chronicle.* www.ata-chronicle.online/wp-content/uploads/4307_18_roberts.pdf.

Ruiz Rosendo, Lucía, and Clementina Persaud. 2016. "Interpreters and Interpreting in Conflict Zones and Scenarios: A Historical Perspective." *Linguistica Antverpiensia, New Series – Themes in Translation Studies* 15: 1–35. https://doi.org/10.52034/lanstts.v0i15.428.

Sakalli, Buse. 2016. *Effect of Working Memory Training on Simultaneous Interpreting Performance: Dual n-Back Task.* Thesis, Ankara University.

Tesseur, Wine. 2019. "Translating and Interpreting in Danger Zones." *Journal of War & Culture Studies* 12 (3): 215–219. https://doi.org/10.1080/17526272.2019.1644417.

Yenkimaleki, Mahmood, and Vincent J. van Heuven. 2017. "The Effect of Memory Training on Consecutive Interpreting Performance by Interpreter Trainees." *FORUM* 15 (1): 157–172. https://doi.org/10.1075/forum.15.1.09yen.

Zhang, Wei, and Dewei Yu. 2018 "Can Memory Training Help Improve Interpreting Quality? A Case Report in China." *The Interpreter and Translator Trainer* 12 (2): 152–165. https://doi.org/10.1080/1750399x.2018.1452121.

Zhong, Weihe. 2003. "Memory Training in Interpreting." *Journal of Translation Studies* 6: 45–57.

INDEX